Future of Business and Finance

The Future of Business and Finance book series features professional works aimed at defining, describing and charting the future trends in these fields. The focus is mainly on strategic directions, technological advances, challenges and solutions which may affect the way we do business tomorrow, including the future of sustainability and governance practices. Mainly written by practitioners, consultants and academic thinkers, the books are intended to spark and inform further discussions and developments.

More information about this series at http://www.springer.com/series/16360

Gurdip Kaur • Ziba Habibi Lashkari •
Arash Habibi Lashkari

Understanding Cybersecurity Management in FinTech

Challenges, Strategies, and Trends

Springer

Gurdip Kaur
Canadian Institute for Cybersecurity
(CIC), Faculty of Computer Science
University of New Brunswick
Fredericton, NB, Canada

Ziba Habibi Lashkari
Universidad Politécnica De Madrid
Escuela Técnica Superior de Ingenieros
Informáticos
Madrid, Spain

Arash Habibi Lashkari
Canadian Institute for Cybersecurity
(CIC), Faculty of Computer Science
University of New Brunswick
Fredericton, NB, Canada

ISSN 2662-2467 ISSN 2662-2475 (electronic)
Future of Business and Finance
ISBN 978-3-030-79914-4 ISBN 978-3-030-79915-1 (eBook)
https://doi.org/10.1007/978-3-030-79915-1

This Springer imprint is published by the registered company Springer Nature Switzerland AG.
The registered company address is: Gewerbestrasse 11, 6330 Cham, Switzerland

Preface

If you have ever paid for anything online, chances are you have dealt with some form of FinTech, or financial technology: the space where technological innovation and the financial services industry intersect. As a broad term, "FinTech" encompasses a wide array of technological strategies, many of which have either improved the functionality of existing financial products and services or enabled the development of novel technological solutions for the financial sector. In an era of rapid technological change, it has become imminently necessary for banks and other financial institutions to categorically rethink and revitalize their fundamental operational structures, particularly including those which fall under the categorization of fintech.

One of the most common concerns regarding rapid adoption of FinTech is rooted in the fear that such services may increase the risk of privacy and data security breaches for organizational entities as well as individual consumers. Undoubtedly, any external exploitation of those risks could have the potential to be devastating to the industry. With the rapid growth of digital platforms, the fintech industry has become more vulnerable to digital network security breaches. Simultaneously, the recent mass inundation of consumers living and working under lockdown conditions, and the corresponding decreased reliance on traditional physical financial institutions during the COVID-19 pandemic, has increased the consumer demand for access to safer, more secure, and more reliable digital financial services.

Understanding Cybersecurity Management in FinTech is the first book in the Understanding Cybersecurity Series (UCS), and explores a range of cybersecurity issues which impact banks and other financial institutions in the provision of their specific financial services. As such complex financial systems face cybersecurity challenges that include both technological and operational elements, this book proposes a FinTech Information Security Governance framework to guide corporations, board members, directors, and management personnel in the effort to secure critical data from unforeseen cyber-attacks. This book provides insight into the cybersecurity implications which stem from the unique FinTech ecosystem or environment. This includes the issues of navigating cyber threats, detecting vulnerabilities, mitigating risks, and creating proactive governance frameworks, policies, and infrastructures, with the goal of enabling the design of a comprehensive cybersecurity framework for FinTech used by banks and other financial institutions to provide services.

Fredericton, NB, Canada Gurdip Kaur
Madrid, Spain Ziba Habibi Lashkari
Fredericton, NB, Canada Arash Habibi Lashkari
May 2021

Contents

About the Authors

Gurdip Kaur is a Postdoctoral Fellow at the Canadian Institute for Cybersecurity, University of New Brunswick, Canada. She is CompTIA certified CyberSecurity Analyst (CySA+) and a gold medalist in Bachelor of Technology from Punjab Technical University, India. She completed her PhD in Computer Science and Engineering from the National Institute of Technology, India with specialization in malware analysis. She was awarded a silver medal for the project titled "Implementation and deployment of High Interaction honeypot for research purpose" by the National Defense and Research Forum (NDRF), India in 2013. Her research areas focus on cybersecurity, malware analysis, reverse engineering, vulnerability management, incident reporting, and data science.

Ziba Habibi Lashkari is an Assistant Professor of Finance in the Department of Organization Engineering, Business Administration, and Statistics, the Technical University of Madrid, Spain. She had been participating in the project of "Análisis de Modelos en Dinámica de poblaciones Estructuradas en Valoración de Derivados Financieros" financed by the Spanish Ministry of Economy. She has more than 15 years of academic and industry experience in financial management. Her research focuses on asset pricing, risk management, cybersecurity risk in digital financial and data science in fintech.

Arash Habibi Lashkari is a senior member of the IEEE, an Associate Professor at the Faculty of Computer Science, University of New Brunswick (UNB), and the Research Coordinator of the Canadian Institute for Cybersecurity (CIC). Dr. Lashkari has over 20 years of teaching experience, spanning several international universities, and has been the recipient of 15 awards at international computer security competitions—including three gold awards. In 2017, he was recognized as one of Canada's Top 150 researchers who will shape the future of Canada. In 2020, Dr. Lashkari was recognized with the University of New Brunswick's prestigious Teaching Innovation Award for his personally created teaching methodology, the Think-Que-Cussion Method. He is the author of ten published books and more than 90 academic papers on various cybersecurity-related topics. He is the founder of the Understanding Cybersecurity Series, which is an ongoing five-year research and development project, to culminate with a varied collection of online articles, published books, open-source packages, and datasets tailored for researchers and readers at all levels. The first article series of this project entitled "Understanding Canadian Cybersecurity Laws" has been recently recognized with a Gold Medal at the 2020 Canadian Online Publishing Awards, remotely held in 2021. Building on over two decades of concurrent industrial and development experience in network, software, and computer security, Dr. Lashkari's current work involves developing vulnerability detection technology to protect network systems against cyberattacks. He simultaneously supervises multiple research and development teams working on several projects related to network traffic analysis, malware analysis, Honeynet, and threat hunting.

Introduction to FinTech and Importance Objects

1

FinTech is an acronym for financial technology that associates technology with financial services (Schueffel 2016). It is also spelled as Fin-Tech or fin-tech. It describes the connection of contemporary internet-related technologies such as cloud computing, mobile internet, and big data analytics with business activities, including payments, lending, mortgage, loan, and the stock market. In simple words, FinTech is an alternative term for financial technology that refers to companies that use technology to perform financial operations.

The origin of this term can be traced back to the early 1990s when Citigroup initiated the "Financial Services Technology Consortium" project to facilitate technological cooperation efforts. FinTech was first used in 1866 and has transformed business processes into the digital era ever since. It comprises financial institutions such as traditional banks and digital payment systems, including Amazon Pay, Apple Pay, PayPal, and Samsung Pay, to name a few. These digital payment systems are called digital wallets, which allow easy payment for online services and purchases.

Although FinTech has been adopted in traditional financial operations, the rise in innovative technology and business models has had a notable impact on present-day financial industries. With the rise of digital finances, all the players in FinTech are undergoing tremendous transformations to uplift their businesses (Milian et al. 2019). Therefore, small-scale startup companies have entered the business by adopting FinTech, leaving behind the traditional financial giants who fail to cope up with the changing nature of the financial industry. The financial business transformations can be attributed to three main reasons (Gomber et al. 2017):

(a) FinTech companies offer products and services to customers that were never offered by traditional business companies. For example, use of magnetic card readers or point of sale equipment to pay by credit or with debit card to facilitate cashless transactions.
(b) FinTech companies use internet-based business models to compete with traditional companies.

G. Kaur et al., *Understanding Cybersecurity Management in FinTech*, Future of Business and Finance, https://doi.org/10.1007/978-3-030-79915-1_1

(c) FinTech companies use agile and innovative technology and applications to sell products and services to speed up transactions.

The use of web-based technologies by FinTech companies has allowed them to excel in different domains such as mobile finance, e-commerce, management, and social media (Gai et al. 2018). The development of current digital financial platforms has facilitated online payment transfer in the form of e-interac applications supported by banks. Moreover, FinTech customers also use mobile banking services to pay for online purchases and bills.

This chapter introduces financial technology and its importance in modern businesses. It presents a correlated relationship of FinTech with big data analytics, online banking, traditional banking, and its impact on the global economy. FinTech evolution and its ecosystem comprising important objects are also presented. Finally, the chapter concludes by listing some popular FinTech applications.

1.1 Introduction to Financial Technology

Financial technology refers to new processes, applications, business models, or products offered by the financial industry. According to the National Digital Research Centre, FinTech is an innovation in financial services. It broadly covers five essential areas, including the insurance industry, banking, e-commerce, lending, and personal finance management. A deep insight into the essential areas reveals that the insurance industry involves processes related to payments, financing, cross-product support, financial information, investments, and financial advisory. Banking is used in our day-to-day transactions for all types of payments. It includes private, retail, and corporate banking transactions. The third essential area covered by FinTech is e-commerce, which involves business-to-business, business-to-customer, and customer-to-customer processes. The fourth essential area is complimentary services. FinTech is incomplete without lending services. Financing firms or banks may provide these services. Finally, personal finance management is an inseparable component of FinTech that covers personal income, expenditure, assets, and investment details. Figure 1.1 presents an overview of the five essential areas covered by FinTech.

FinTech has evolved tremendously in the twenty-first century because big companies have started investing in financial technology. To begin with, global investment in financial technology in 2008 was only $930 million, which jumped to $12 billion in 2014. According to a survey conducted in 2014, 40% of the workforce in London used to work in the FinTech industry. For the past 5 years, financial technology companies grew to $23 billions of growth equity and venture capital and that number is increasing continuously. There were some important events that took place in FinTech across the globe. For example, Wharton school of the University of Pennsylvania founded its financial technology department in 2014 to connect innovators, academies, investors, and other thought leaders. A financial technology hub was opened in Sydney, Australia in 2015. In the same year, a financial

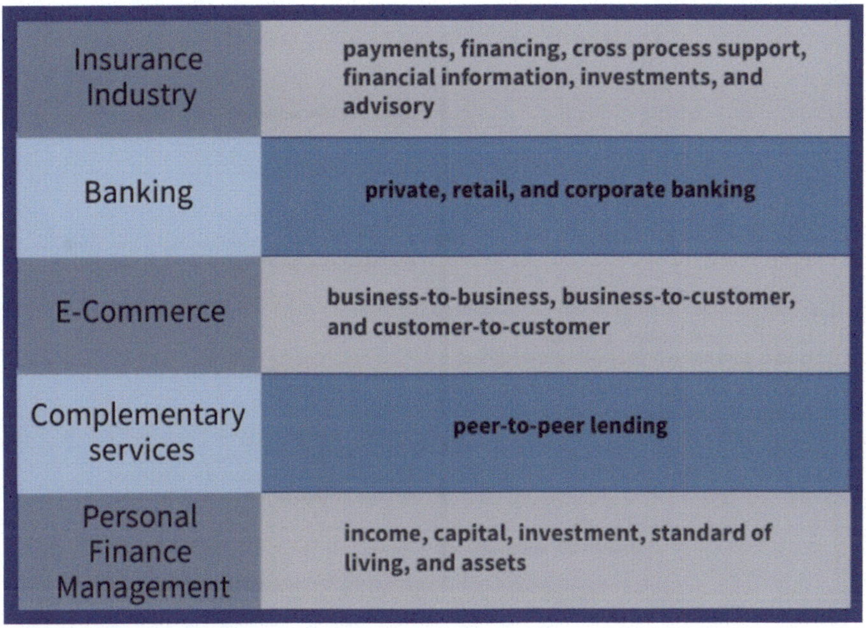

Fig. 1.1 Five essential areas covered by FinTech

technology innovation lab was inaugurated in Hong Kong. These events paved the way to enhance financial research in this sector. Figure 1.2 highlights some of the important global investment statistics related to FinTech.

Although FinTech was originally used in back-end applications in trade and financial institutions, it turned out to be an emerging service sector applied to several domains, including the financial sector and financial literacy, investment, education, cryptocurrencies, and retail banking. Its significant growth as a blend of technological innovations in commercial and personal finance can be attributed to the internet and mobile technology (Swanson 2016). The following factors contribute to the growth of FinTech:

- The development of new technologies such as artificial intelligence and cybersecurity have fueled innovation in FinTech.
- The destruction caused by the 2008 financial crisis has led investors to invest their money in FinTech.
- Economic ups and downs in the UK and Europe have slowed down funding to startup companies.

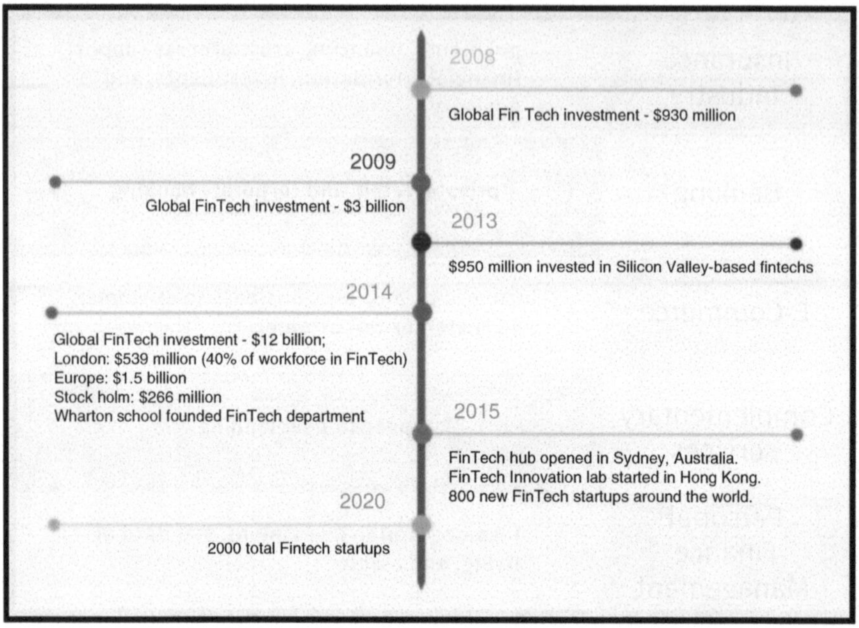

Fig. 1.2 Timeline of global FinTech investment statistics and important events

1.2 Importance of FinTech

The present state of the financial markets has no value without technology. Technology creates more value for a business strategy. It provides hassle-free data storage, retrieval, analysis, reporting, and redistribution. It is common for financial institutions to project their annual growth and long-term objectives. Technology acts as a tool to improve the visibility and operations carried out to achieve those objectives. It reduces the effort and time needed in disseminating information. Further, knowledge of the environment is important to determine the available resources needed to attain objectives.

Economic volatility and government regulations also affect businesses. Economic volatility and the ever-changing market require technology systems and platforms to adapt to changes while ensuring stability within the organization. Formulating strategies, supporting the decision-making process, and gaining risk insights require information. The data analysts can do all this by using tools to manage risks and optimize and strategy processes. Similarly, risk management is also an important component of a business that needs technology.

How technology transforms FinTech? Well, the answer to this question is very simple. FinTech has opened new opportunities for the financial world. Its importance has increased during the COVID-19 pandemic because more businesses are conducted online. People are using technology to do business online and follow social distances. Digital wallets are becoming an inseparable part of our day-to-day life. Contactless payments are used as global payment solutions nowadays. FinTech has reached out to the common people in every sector, including transportation, health care, grocery, banking, shopping, and education.

In addition to digital payments, FinTech solutions are adopted in three smart cities (London, Singapore, and Hong Kong). London has been reputed as the "FinTech capital" of the world. The number of FinTech giants in the city is valued at more than $1 billion. FinTech has the potential to transform the economy of any nation by allowing national and international business payments quickly. It allows people greater access to the global financial market. This way, FinTech is leading the financial institutions from the front.

According to a survey conducted by the World Economic Forum, innovation makes established financial services companies rethink how they traditionally handle their business. It investigated the financial services industry to see what the future holds for it. Over 100 financial industry experts were interviewed, and a series of workshops were held to discuss the issue.

To delve a bit deep into this issue, insurers and bankers used highly profitable but relatively static business models in the past. However, they did not significantly impact the financial services industry had the sales, regulatory expertise, and trust of the customers. At present, innovators disrupt businesses with high value and various products. The following are the characteristics of an innovator:

- Innovators focus on deploying certain products and services for high profit. They provide the most valuable products and services. For example, traditional banks used to charge high remittance fees but provided poor customer experience. Now, some innovators provide a user-friendly web interface and use an innovative network to ensure money transfers are cheaper, easier, and faster.
- Innovators automate and commoditize high-margin processes using technical skills. They can provide services like wealth management to new customers at a lower cost. Traditional players cannot compete with innovative people.
- Financial institutions often rely on customer data for the decision-making process. Lenders use the customer's credit score to decide whether they will lend money or not. Insurers check the driving record or medical record of the applicant before they decide to issue a policy. These interconnections can use real-time data in making financial decisions. For example, a company may conduct analyses of the social networking patterns of consumers to determine borrowers' creditworthiness. Insurance companies may use various data streams in making better pricing decisions. Some insurers may provide a gadget for their policyholders to wear to track their fitness.
- Some companies grow revenues exponentially without increasing costs. Innovators suggest the use of crowdfunding platforms to gather financial support for startup companies.

1.3 Big Data and Financial Technology

Big data refers to the large volumes of data that are growing rapidly. It encompasses large volumes of a variety of information that is processed at high speed. Big data can be alternatively presented by three characteristics, including volume, velocity, and variety of information. It contains terabytes of records, tables, files, and transactions. This data is treated as real-time data and is processed in the form of batches. It includes various data such as Relational Database Management System (RDBMS), images, videos, songs, and Extensible Markup Language (XML) files. Therefore, big data can be presented as three Vs corresponding to volume, velocity, and variety, as shown in Fig. 1.3.

Big data has created numerous opportunities for the analysis of unstructured and structured data. Structured data includes information managed by the entity in spreadsheets and relational databases. Unstructured data is unorganized information with no predetermined data like information from social media.

With its ability to process such a large volume of data, big data analysis has emerged as cutting-edge technology for businesses. Organizations use big data to gather significant and relevant insights to help their leaders make informed decisions. Various industries such as financial services, health care, marketing, and information technology use big data. Big data is instrumental in providing better information to make investment decisions in financial services. It can be integrated

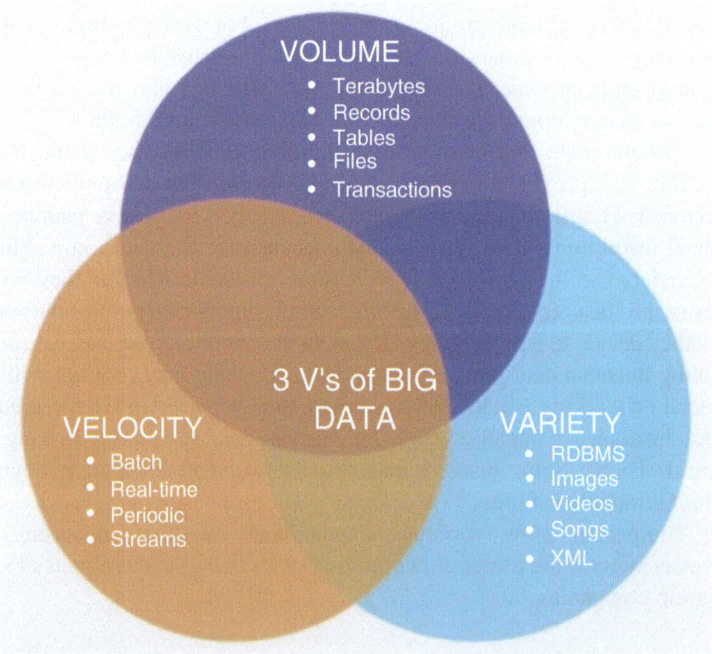

Fig. 1.3 3V's of big data

with mathematical models to maximize the profits earned from investment portfolios.

Three characteristics (volume, velocity, and variety) of big data make it a prime candidate for data processing and analysis at high speed. It is adopted by the FinTech industry to operate efficiently despite increasing customer requirements, regulatory constraints, and competition. It provides a competitive advantage for the FinTech industry.

Without any shadow of a doubt, data on FinTech is increasing very rapidly. FinTech institutions must learn to manage their surged data. Big data can help the FinTech industry in the following ways:

- A large volume of historical data can be analyzed to draft strategies and policies. This can help asset management and investment banks to make informed decisions. Similarly, retirement and insurance companies can use big data analytics to predict and manage risks.
- The velocity of big data analytics possesses the capability to automatically execute critical transactions at high frequency and speed as compared to manual processing. Automation makes it possible to reduce human errors. Automated trading provides execution of trade at the best possible prices. FinTech can use algorithms with big data to test their strategies and make informed decisions.
- Big data can help eradicate low value data. It allows FinTech to focus on the fast and efficient processing of transactions.

Despite the multifaceted advantages provided by big data, FinTech faces many challenges related to the privacy of unstructured data collection. Further, historical data analysis predicts long-term investments. There is a lack of support for short-term investments.

After understanding the pros and cons of big data in FinTech, the question that needs to be addressed is, "What are FinTech's expectations from big data?" To find an answer to this question, we need to understand the changing requirements of FinTech in the digital age. FinTech is rapidly transforming its manual processing into online systems. It comprises new directives and regulations that are burdensome and costly. FinTech managers need to be well-versed with online portals, electronic records, and databases to store vast amounts of data.

Traditional financial institutions used to outsource a few functions and maintain the rest of the infrastructure independently. However, it is possible to outsource the entire infrastructure in the FinTech era. Regulatory requirements have also become stricter. Apart from these aspects, protecting proprietary and personal information is also crucial for FinTech. The use of cloud servers for data storage is one of the critical requirements of this era as it is difficult to store such a volume of data on-site. Nevertheless, the introduction of technology has also raised concern for the security of infrastructure and privacy of data.

All these facts were treated as the critical requirements of FinTech in the digital era. For a smooth relationship between big data and FinTech, big data must support all these requirements. Big data can contribute to letting people know the current trends instantaneously. Similarly, FinTech industries can easily follow their competitors (Swanson 2016).

1.4 Impact of FinTech on Global Economy

Global FinTech statistics reveal that FinTech is growing in all possible aspects such as investments, people, competition, predictions, and outcomes. Global investments in FinTech have been continuously increasing since 2008. There are a few innovation labs established to do research on FinTech. All these facts contribute to the flourishing of FinTech. With the invention and use of new technological solutions, FinTech has contributed a significant share of the global market. Nonetheless, there is another angle to FinTech and its impact on the global economy. FinTech poses an inherent risk to the job market. According to a report published by Citigroup, it is estimated that 30% of the employees in the global financial sector are on the verge of losing their jobs to FinTech (Egan 2016).

The digital era is indeed based on online communication between various global markets. The tasks performed by employees can be completed by technology in a much more efficient and accurate way. Technology also eradicates human errors in financial transactions. In a rare turn of global events, it is not the USA and North American banks that dominate the development in FinTech. China has embraced investment in these technologies at even higher levels. Banks in Africa and Southeast Asia are aware of the potential for making lucrative profits in these markets (Reed 2016).

1.5 FinTech and Banking

Traditional financial institutions play a significant role in building the economy. These are highly regulated and have a monopoly of risk-taking and credit insurance. They are also the principal repository for customer deposits. They remained the major gateway of payment systems. The banking system suffered a major blow due to the fiscal crisis. Many customers lost their trust in banks. With the popularity of smartphones, payment systems are revised. Technological revolutions affect how consumers save, invest, store, pay, protect, and borrow money.

FinTech and banking, when combined, can do wonders. FinTech can bring down prices and reduce margins for retail banking businesses in mortgage, wealth management, retail payments, and small to medium scale enterprises. FinTech faces many challenges to grab the business of traditional banking systems and transform it into a completely new structure. Figure 1.4 illustrates the major issues faced by FinTech with respect to banking.

These challenges are briefed below:

- **Attract customers:** One of the main challenges before FinTech in banking is to attract customers. Most of the customers were bound to traditional banking in the

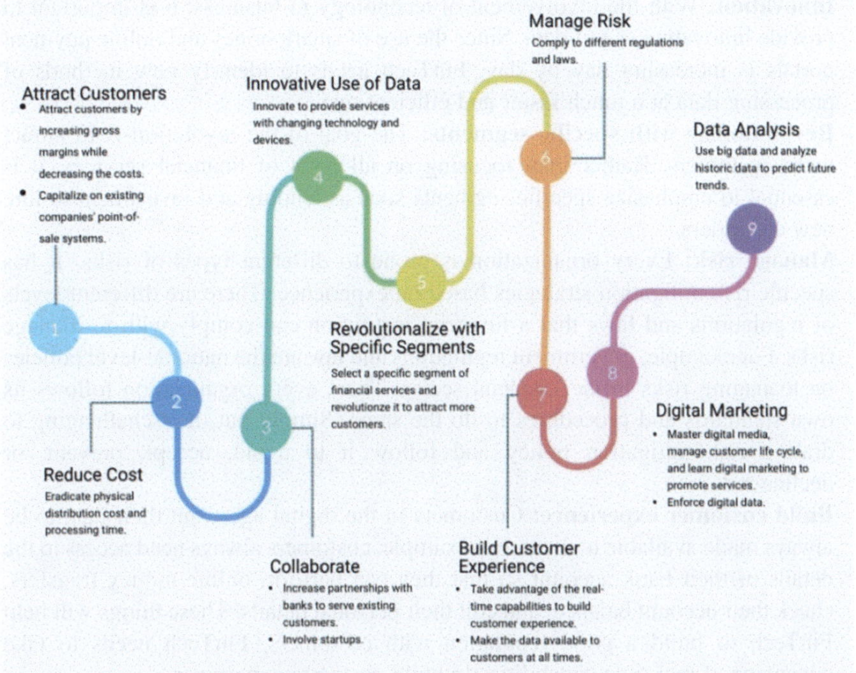

Fig. 1.4 Challenges faced by FinTech in the banking system

past. Banks had a trust relationship with their customers. This makes it very difficult for FinTech to lure those customers to innovation and technology. The measures adopted by FinTech to do so are to increase gross margins and decrease distribution costs. Since the system is turning into paperless transactions, the motivation to attract is to capitalize on existing companies' point-of-sales systems.

- **Reduce cost:** Reducing physical distribution cost and processing time for loan and lending systems. Since paperless and online lending systems are developing in the FinTech era, it is important to reduce the cost and time required to approve insurance and loan documents for customers. It will ultimately inspire customers to join FinTech.
- **Collaborate:** Making partnerships with traditional banks and involving startup companies is another challenge for FinTech. Such collaborations can build trust with customers associated with banks and are a good source of initial funding for startup companies. Startups have a big competitive advantage over traditional banking systems. They believe in using technology and online portals to provide essential financial services to customers. As evident, online systems for e-commerce transactions such as business-to-business, business-to-customer, and customer-to-customer also collaborate with technological innovations.

- **Innovation:** With the involvement of technology in business, it is important to provide innovative use of data. Since the use of smartphones and online payment portals is increasing day by day, FinTech needs to identify new methods of processing data at a much faster and efficient rate.
- **Revolutionize with specific segments:** The goal of the revolution is to attract more customers. Rather than focusing on all parts of financial services, it is essential to emphasize specific segments such as lending and investment to lure new customers.
- **Manage risk:** Every organization is prone to different types of risks. It has specific risk mitigation strategies based on experience. There are different levels of regulations and laws that a financial institution can comply with to manage risks. For example, government regulations and law are the national-level policies on managing risks in the financial sector. Then, every organization follows its own standards and procedures to do the same. Simply put, it is challenging to draft a risk mitigation policy and follow it to avoid, accept, prevent, or decline risk.
- **Build customer experience:** Customers in the digital age want their data to be always made available to them. For example, customers always need access to the details of their bank account so that they can perform online money transfers, check their account balance, and edit their personal details. These things will help FinTech to build a good reputation with customers. FinTech needs to take advantage of real-time capabilities to build customer experience.
- **Digital marketing:** With the invention of technology in finance, marketing strategies have gone online. FinTech finds it challenging to promote services in a very interactive way to customers, make use of digital media to learn customer likings, offer relevant opportunities, and learn digital marketing.
- **Data analysis:** The biggest challenge for FinTech is to collect large volumes of data, process it in lesser time, and analyze it to predict future trends. Big data is the key to FinTech to achieve all these objectives.

1.6 FinTech and Online Banking

FinTech has made brilliant strides by allowing banks to automate their processes and be more efficient in their transactions. Online banking has adopted technology and improved upon achieving its short-term and long-term objectives. This revolution is the outcome of implementing a variety of techniques to correlate statistical data and relationships between data elements. FinTech provides an interactive user interface to perform complex customer transactions that appear one click away.

Although there are many obstacles before FinTech reshaping the banking system, as discussed in the previous section. Some additional issues include data validation and security. Automated processes need to understand the constraints applied to data and then map that data to obtain fast results. This makes further investigation easier. Customer feedback to the automated processes measures the success of an accurate system.

The online banking system needs to have a competitive edge in providing reliable financial transactions. One of the currently explored solutions in FinTech and online banking is forecasting cash flow. This is estimated by analyzing historical transactions and predicting future trends based on the analyzed information. This forecast is then provided as an added value to a part of a client's profile. Smart companies utilize transaction clusters to generate cash flow projections.

Every cluster is uniquely modeled and then combined with other clusters to determine a customer's parameters. Cluster parameters include transaction type, geolocation, category, whether a transaction is outgoing or incoming, and the related counterparts. Additionally, time-based clusters can be arranged on how dissimilar they are to one another, though there are typically other connections that make more sense.

Accurate and adequate predictive analysis is especially important for small or medium enterprises. It has several advantages:

- It allows them to make well-informed decisions and frame a more concrete view of their strengths, weaknesses, and dependencies.
- It makes it easier to predict the demand for potentially profitable products.
- These enterprises will be able to provide hazardous supply chain decisions based on currency trends while remaining on top of their cash flow.

Banks must strive to keep track of macroeconomic data by allowing users to opt in to services that will track customers, vendors, location, sectors, employees, and revenue data. The initial data sample will provide the basis for more personalized content. Additionally, system data and data from any accountants or accounting software should be used to help improve the accuracy of various algorithms. This will also improve the accuracy of any outcome scenarios.

If a customer is connected directly to any other bank, it is mandatory to consult this information to ensure the complete picture. FinTech solutions that provide these types of predictive algorithms create the strong business models that the banks are looking for. Treasury as a service is a byproduct of this trend.

It also poses a potential risk for investors because the credibility of the results of these statistical algorithms is not yet proven. Additionally, when pushed to the fullest limits, it has yet to be seen what the average customer thinks about their data being so vividly displayed (Reed 2016).

1.7 FinTech Evolution

FinTech has evolved in three phases. The first phase witnessed the struggles with innovation but eventually landed up with telegraph services, a fundamental means of communication at that time. The second phase involved the invention of the internet and the world wide web. It transformed the traditional means of communication into digital platforms by supporting cashless and online financial transactions. Finally, the third phase experiences the use of techno-savvy and sophisticated technology in

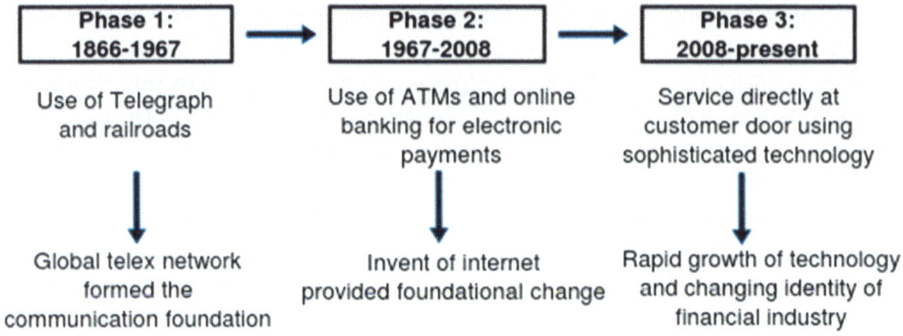

Fig. 1.5 FinTech evolution

digital wallets that support direct service for the customers. Figure 1.5 uncovers the phases of the FinTech evolution.

1.8 FinTech Ecosystem

The FinTech ecosystem comprises five key elements that contribute to innovative technology, competitive dynamics, and stimulating economics, as shown in Fig. 1.6. FinTech startups form the heart of this ecosystem, including payment, lending, wealth management, crowdfunding, capital market, and insurance companies. These companies contribute to significant innovation in the FinTech ecosystem. Financial regulators and legislature are the second components of the FinTech ecosystem. It includes government bodies that provide economic policies and development plans to stimulate innovation and global financial competitiveness in startups. The government is primarily involved in the licensing of financial services, tax relaxation, and capital requirements for startups.

Financial customers are the third component of this ecosystem. They include individuals and organizations who apply for mortgages, loans, or equity services provided by the government. The fourth component, called traditional financial institutions such as banks, insurance companies, stock markets, and capitalists, adopt the innovative technology developed by FinTech startups and collaborate with them to transform their work environment. Finally, technology developers provide digital platforms for big data analytics, cloud computing, cryptocurrency, and social media. These platforms facilitate FinTech startups to launch innovative services such as smartphone applications to pay online through digital wallets.

1.9 FinTech Applications

FinTech has a diverse range of applications that are spread in several domains. Some of the prominent applications of FinTech are presented in Fig. 1.7 and are summarized below:

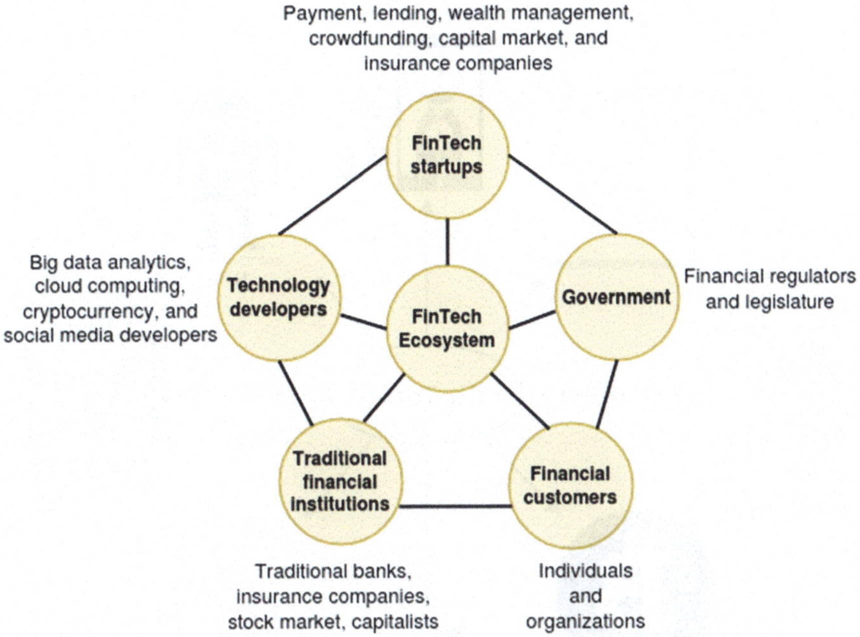

Fig. 1.6 FinTech ecosystem

- **E-commerce:** E-commerce applications related to Business-to-Business (B2B) and Business-to-Consumer (B2C) transactions involve digital wallets to pay for the delivery of goods and services.
- **Mobile banking:** Mobile banking acts as a gateway that provides support for online payments in terms of sending/receiving digital cash at a minimum transaction fee. In addition to that lending, loans, and trading are also an inseparable part of mobile banking.
- **Wealth management:** FinTech allows investors to manage their financial assets and portfolios. Could-based bot-enabled platforms are being used to advise users about managing investments.
- **Crowdfunding:** FinTech provides crowdfunding platforms to allow startup companies to cross geographical boundaries and reach out to international investors to raise funds.
- **Cryptocurrency and blockchain:** Several FinTech companies utilize virtual currency to do business. Cryptocurrencies are shaping the future of the FinTech landscape. Blockchain is also being used in many financial sectors such as forex. It facilitates faster transactions, easy verification of identities, and the use of smartphones for purchases.
- **Social media:** Traditional banks and social media influencers are using social media equally to share the latest offers and opportunities with their customers. FinTech marketing is the term given to luring customers by utilizing social media platforms such as LinkedIn, Twitter, Facebook, Instagram, etc.

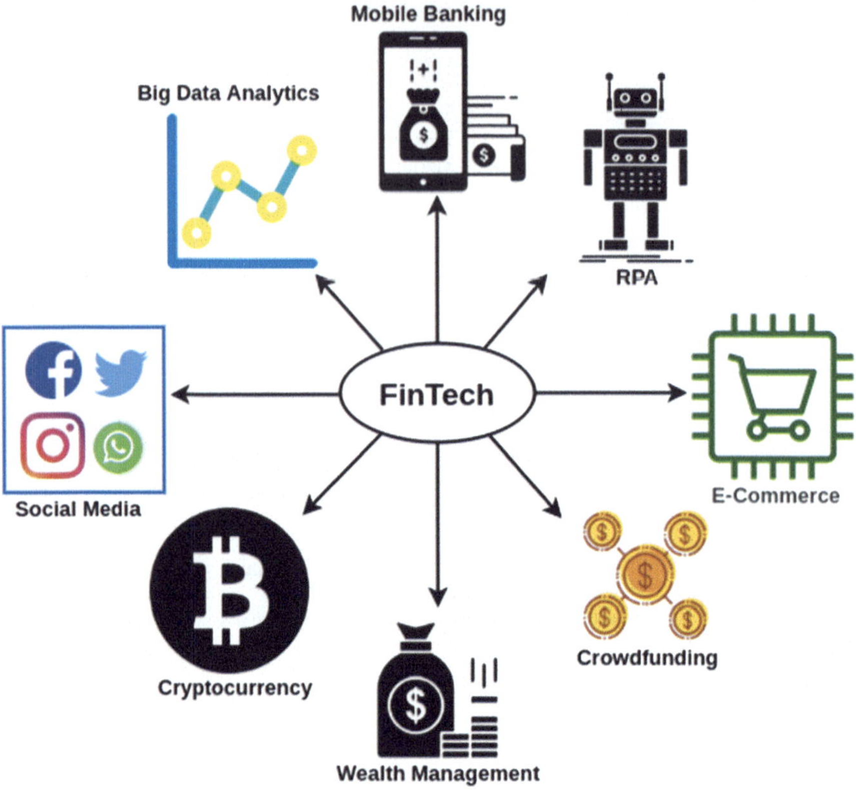

Fig. 1.7 FinTech applications

- **Big data analytics:** FinTech has added value to big data analytics by allowing companies to analyze data using big data processing techniques to enable lenders to provide credit to customers at reduced costs.
- **Robotics Process Automation (RPA):** RPA provides a virtual environment to major FinTech companies to automate certain sets of functions including automated bank account opening, fraud detection, and customer service.

1.10 Chapter Summary

This chapter provides a detailed overview of FinTech and its importance in the contemporary era. It presents a correlated relationship between FinTech and big data analysis, traditional banking, and online banking system. It analyzes the positive and negative impact of FinTech on the global economy. There are several challenges faced by FinTech to reach end users. All these challenges are discussed and correlated. FinTech has evolved in three phases over the decades and its ecosystem comprises important objects that form the basics of FinTech. Finally, some popular

FinTech applications are listed that can be explored further. Overall, the following questions are answered in this chapter:

- Why is it important for financial institutions to adopt FinTech?
- What are the challenges faced by FinTech to rebuild traditional banking systems?
- What are the pertinent financial sectors that are restructured by FinTech?
- How is FinTech affecting the global economy?
- How is big data helping FinTech to predict future trends?
- What are the essential elements of a FinTech ecosystem and how do they contribute to FinTech?

References

Egan, M. (2016). *30% of bank jobs are under threat*, CNN Money, April 4, 2016. https://money.cnn.com/2016/04/04/investing/bank-jobs-dying-automation-citigroup/.

Gai, K., Qiu, M., & Sun, X. (2018). A survey on FinTech. *Journal of Network and Computer Applications, 103*, 262–273.

Gomber, P., Koch, J.-A., & Siering, M. (2017). Digital finance and FinTech: Current research and future research directions. *Journal of Business Economics, 87*, 537–580. https://doi.org/10.1007/s11573-017-0852-x.

Milian, E. Z., de Mauro, M. S., & de Carvalho, M. M. (2019). Fintechs: A literature review and research agenda. *Electronic Commerce Research and Applications, 34*, 100833.

Reed, J. (2016). *FinTech, financial technology and modern finance in the 21ST century*. Torrazza Piemonte, TO: Printed by Amazon Italia Logistica S.r.l. isbn: 9781539587019.

Schueffel, P. (2016). Taming the beast: A scientific definition of Fintech. *Journal of Innovation Management, 4*(4), 32–54.

Swanson, S. (2016). *Fintech for beginners! Understanding and utilizing the power of financial technology*. Torrazza Piemonte, TO: Printed by Amazon Italia Logistica S.r.l. isbn: 9781539919315.

Introduction to Cybersecurity

2

Cybersecurity risk is an inherent part of cybersecurity practice. It defines the essential elements needed to secure technical infrastructure, tangible and intangible assets, technology in use, and the reputation of the organization in case of a cyberattack or data breach. It also defines the objectives of an organization to protect itself from data theft that can cause potential damage. It is important from the perspective of security professionals to compute the cybersecurity risk of an organization so that appropriate measures can be taken in advance to prevent cyber risks.

This chapter delves deep into the basic principles of cybersecurity, motivation to breach cybersecurity, the CIAAA principle, the importance of data science in cybersecurity, and a list of important data breaches. We begin with a simple definition of cybersecurity and continue toward the basic building blocks of cybersecurity throughout this chapter.

2.1 What Is Cybersecurity?

Cybersecurity refers to designing, developing, and using technologies, processes, and practices to protect organizational assets, customer data, and intellectual property from intentional or unintentional breaches by unauthorized personnel. The unauthorized personnel are also called cybercriminals. However, it is untrue that only unauthorized personnel can be involved in the violation of sensitive data. There are several examples of the involvement of authorized persons who breached the code of conduct and stole critical organization data for misuse.

Simply put, cybersecurity is the collection of technologies, processes, and practices that aim to protect an organizational asset from unauthorized access or authorized misuse. Unauthorized personnel can be classified as hackers, nation-state activists, and script kiddies, while authorized personnel who misuse their assigned privileges are called malicious insiders. We will explore all these terms in the later chapters.

G. Kaur et al., *Understanding Cybersecurity Management in FinTech*, Future of Business and Finance, https://doi.org/10.1007/978-3-030-79915-1_2

Every organization has its unique needs, assets, resources, and sensitive data. Therefore, cybersecurity planning to protect these entities is also different for every organization. However, to mitigate cyberattacks and protect sensitive data and assets, it is desired that every organization plans for a cybersecurity policy that drafts the risk appetite of the organization. The risk appetite ensures the amount of risk that the organization can accept without any negative impact on its business.

2.2 Motivation

Widespread use of computers and networks in all sectors such as communication, finance, transportation, education, military, and government, has become a source of attraction for cybercriminals to target these sectors for financial gain. Some of the important motivations behind cyberattacks are listed below:

- **Data breach:** According to the analysis of major cyberattacks between 2001 and 2013 (Vaidya 2015), the primary motivation behind launching a cyberattack is to steal sensitive data and cyber espionage.
- **Financial instability:** Cyber risk is potentially cited as the top priority for all types of organizations, especially financial systems. Cyberattacks pose a substantial risk to the financial stability of the overall financial sector (Boer and Vazquez 2017).
- **Service disruption:** Apart from financial instability, cyberattacks can disrupt business and financial markets as well. During the WannaCry ransomware outbreak in 2017, over 200,000 computers were affected in around 150 countries. It disrupted essential services including hospitals, telecommunications, railways, and automobile companies.
- **Political:** Cyberattacks are also politically motivated at times. Stuxnet is the popular example of a malware attack on Iranian nuclear plant. Cyberwarfare is the term assigned to online cyberwar between politically rival countries.

Although all industries are at risk of a cyberattack, some of the industries are the most breached. These industries include health care, food, retail, finance, and government. The health care industry is dominantly under phishing attacks during the COVID-19 pandemic to interrupt services and steal patient data. On the other hand, financial institutions are targeted to gain financial benefits, steal passwords, and face reputation loss among competitors.

2.3 The CIAAA Principle

Based on the motivation to launch cyberattacks, the ultimate objective of every organization is to ensure confidentiality (C), integrity (I), and availability (A) of data. These are the three principles that play a pivotal role in the security of every organization. However, the level of importance varies for every organization

Fig. 2.1 The CIA triad

depending upon its security goals and requirements. These principles are presented as three sides of a triangle, as shown in Fig. 2.1.

Confidentiality is the first principle in the CIA Triad. It refers to the protection of secret data, objects, or resources. The goal of confidentiality is to prevent or minimize unauthorized access to data. It ensures that only authorized users can access data and resources. In simple words, confidentiality ensures the protection of data from unauthorized access, use, or disclosure while in storage, process, or transit. Several cyberattacks focus on violating confidentiality. These attacks include eavesdropping, social engineering, port scanning, stealing passwords, and capturing network traffic.

Integrity is the second principle in the CIA Triad. It ensures the correctness and reliability of data. It prevents unauthorized users from modifying data. Proper implementation of integrity means authorized changes are allowed on sensitive data. Integrity loss may result from human errors such as an authorized user making an unintentional change to data. Integrity is prone to viruses, logic bombs, unauthorized access, malicious modification, backdoors, and coding errors.

Availability is the third principle in the CIA Triad. It refers to timely and uninterrupted access to authorized objects, data, or resources. Some of the pertinent threats to the availability of data include system failures, power loss, software errors, and environmental issues (natural calamities). In addition to that, sometimes, the accidental deletion of files, overutilizing a resource, or mislabeling a classified object can also result in the unavailability of data.

In addition to the traditional CIA Triad, two new principles are added to security. These two principles include accountability (A) and authenticity (A). The addition of two new principles to the CIA Triad makes it the CIAAA principle for new researchers as shown in Fig. 2.2. Accountability and authenticity are introduced below.

Accountability is referred to as the responsibility of a person to protect an asset, material, or key information. The person is held accountable for safeguarding the equipment in his custody. If a data breach, loss, or misuse of that equipment takes place, that person is held accountable for it. Accountability is an essential part of a cybersecurity plan. For example, let us assume that an organization has a policy that

Fig. 2.2 CIAAA principle

lists legitimate software or applications that the employees can install on their computers. If an employee installs software or applications not listed in the policy, the IT administrator is held accountable for not verifying the software or applications downloaded and installed on computer systems owned by the organization.

Authenticity is the validation of messages transmitted between a sender and receiver. It ensures that an authenticated sender originates from a message, the message is authenticated, and only an authentic receiver can receive the message. It helps to prevent an unauthorized person from sending or receiving a message. In technical terms, this principle prevents an impersonator from intercepting transmission. It requires users to establish their identities before getting involved in communication. Once the sender and receiver confirm their identities, they can access the system to communicate with each other. Authenticity is established by using usernames, passwords, smart cards, biometrics, emails, and tokens.

2.4 Cybersecurity Threats

Cybersecurity threat refers to anything that can harm the computer system, server, and computer network. Cybersecurity threats may occur or not, but they have the potential to cause severe damage to the organization's assets. They can lead to cybersecurity attacks. There are several types of cybersecurity threats that organizations can face. Some of the recent cyber threats that organizations have faced include malware, ransomware, phishing, stolen passwords, cyber fraud, and disruption of essential services. Figure 2.3 highlights some important cybersecurity threat statistics from 2018 to 2020.

These statistics indicate that cybercriminals interrupt indispensable services by sending phishing emails, executing malware on target computers, demanding ransom, stealing passwords and selling them, and indulging in cyber fraud activities. The list of malicious activities never ends.

According to a survey conducted by Yahoo Finance (Yahoo Finance 2021), phishing is the most common cyber threat that attackers take advantage of. However, due to cybersecurity awareness among employees, there is a significant

Fig. 2.3 Cybersecurity threats statistics 2018–2020

decline in phishing attacks. Although phishing attacks are declining, there is a 50% surge in unique cyber threats in 2020. Overall, 389 unique threats were observed in 2019, and the numbers increased to 600 in 2020. Further, the survey found that the financial industry is the most proactive and concerned with cyber threats.

From the perspective of financial institutions, threat hunting events are becoming quite common owing to a massive increase in cyber threats across banks and other financial institutions. Financial institutions have witnessed diverse types of common and unique cyber threats such as service-specific attacks and web attacks. They are also concerned with financially motivated nation-state activities. It is intriguing to mention that most cyber breaches are caused by human errors. Most of these breaches are financially motivated, while some are motivated by espionage. Moreover, there is a strong relationship between data breaches and stolen passwords because stolen passwords are the most common causes of data breaches.

All the cyber threats discussed above are external. There are some internal sources of cyber threats. For example, a disgruntled employee who is dissatisfied with the employer may steal, delete, or modify some critical data to cause intentional harm to the organization. There are some serious attempts in which an employee exploits a vulnerability in the installed application or software to perform illegitimate and unauthorized activities that may spoil the reputation of the organization.

2.5 Cybersecurity Attacks

A cybersecurity attack or cyberattack is the intended action of an attacker to cause harm to the computer system, server, and computer network. It is a deliberate action that involves a motive and plans to attack the target. A cyberattack has more chances of success as compared to a cyber threat because it is intentional and well planned.

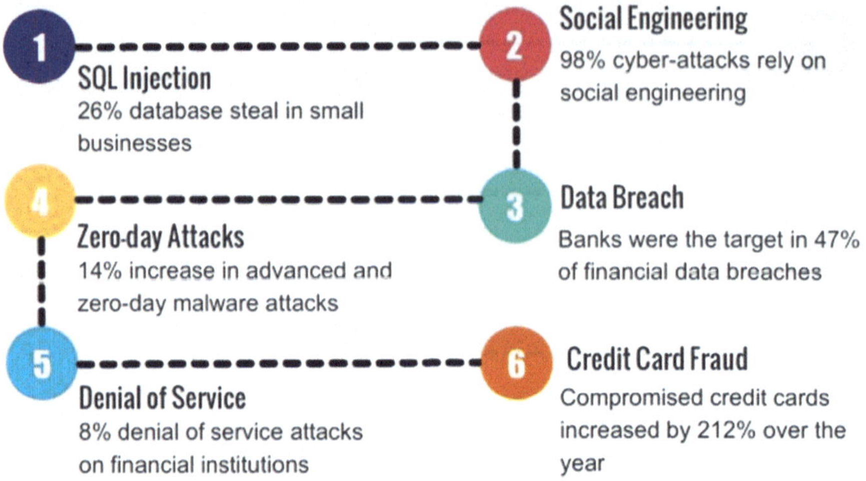

Fig. 2.4 Cyberattack statistics of 2020

Some common examples of cyberattacks include denial of service, distributed denial of service, SQL injection, social engineering, and zero-day attacks. All these attacks will be explained in detail in the coming chapters.

Cyberattacks can be politically or financially motivated. The main purpose of launching cyberattacks is to steal sensitive information, interrupt essential business services, damage reputation, and cause financial losses. Depending upon the motive of the cyberattack, attackers prepare a plan and execute it in a perfect manner to achieve their objectives.

Figure 2.4 highlights major cyberattack statistics of the year 2020 published by Purplesec (Cyber Security Statistics 2020). Credit card fraud cases are on top of cyberattacks. It is followed by data breach as a quite common cyberattack in the financial sector. Financial institutions have witnessed 85 denials of service attacks in the past year. Attackers also steal data from databases by utilizing SQL injection attacks. Further, social engineering is an important key to gathering information about the target person, computer, and company. Cyberattacks not only target computer systems, but smartphone devices have also fallen as an easy prey for them.

Apart from the financial sector, cyberattacks are prevalent in every other industry such as health care, education, federal and local government, and transportation. After the financial sector, health care is the biggest target for cyberattacks. Attackers are interested in medical records, social security numbers, and other personal data. Since the inception of the COVID-19 pandemic, there is a 238% rise in cyberattacks on banks (134 Cybersecurity Statistics and Trends for 2021 2021). Out of the increased cyberattacks, 27% targeted banks and the health care sector only. All these statistics make it paramount to analyze the current cybersecurity situation and understand its importance.

2.6 Cybersecurity Analysis

Based on the cybersecurity threats and attacks reported in recent years, cybersecurity analysis ensures whether the organization is protected against cyberattacks or not. With the use of technology, huge volumes and a variety of data are gathered. Processing big data is transforming the way companies do business. It helps to analyze historical cyberattack data to predict future cyberattacks. Nevertheless, managing big data also brings new challenges. So, how does cybersecurity analysis help in managing such a huge amount of cyberattack data?

Cybersecurity analysis does the groundwork to prepare organizations for cybersecurity challenges, forecast cybersecurity threats and vulnerabilities, perform security analytics, provide endpoint security, and protect data. Figure 2.5 provides an overview of different activities performed during cybersecurity analysis.

- **Cybersecurity challenges:** Cyberattacks have grown extremely fast in the past. Keeping in mind the rapid rate at which common and advanced cyberattacks have targeted humankind, several cybersecurity challenges are addressed by cybersecurity analysis. The most important cybersecurity challenges can be classified into three categories: disruption, distortion, and deterioration. Disruption refers to the interruption of services and flow of information. It covers denial of service, distributed denial of service, and ransomware attacks. Distortion means playing with the integrity of information. It includes data breach, modification, and deletion. Deterioration refers to lowering the ability to control information. It consists of unauthorized access to information.
- **Forecast threats and vulnerabilities:** Cybersecurity analysis examines existing threats and vulnerabilities to predict the future trends in threats and

Fig. 2.5 Activities performed during cybersecurity analysis

vulnerabilities. Threats are becoming more targeted and sophisticated. Therefore, cybersecurity analysis understands the threat landscape and forecasts threat detection to correlate threats with vulnerabilities. Although it is impossible to predict future threats as the nature of threats is always changing but cybersecurity analysis attempts to do that.

- **Security analytics:** Security analytics focuses on the analysis of data to produce proactive security measures. For example, network traffic can be monitored to identify any suspicious activity and respond appropriately to protect the network.
- **Endpoint security:** Endpoint security is provided by installing security devices such as firewalls, intrusion detection and prevention systems, and antivirus solutions. All these solutions detect malicious activities on the network and try to prevent them. For example, antivirus solutions detect a malicious file on the computer system and delete it to clean the computer system.
- **Protect data:** Cybersecurity analysis provides protection to data by encrypting data at rest and in transit. It also takes a backup of data so that an updated copy of data is available even in case of an emergency.

2.7 Why Cybersecurity Matters

Cybersecurity protects people and organizations from the evil acts of attackers. It covers the organization's critical data, resources, assets, and reputation. The purpose of securing an organization is to prevent data and financial losses. Cybersecurity incidents are politically or financially motivated. Cybersecurity incidents target the financial sector and all the critical sectors that contribute to the country's economy. For example, health care, transportation, sports, government, and trade are equally essential to building a nation. In some cases, malicious cross-border activities also tend to shut down the economy of the target country.

Beyond threatening the organization's data, cybersecurity incidents can cause harm to the functioning of communication channels, energy, and critical infrastructure. Cyberattacks on the power grid, energy sector, and health care databases are quite common. Attackers are looking for sensitive data such as medical records that contain social security numbers, credit card details, and other personal data. These data are misused to launch other cyberattacks. In some cases, cybercriminals sold the stolen data on the dark web. This data was later used for sending online advertisements.

Information theft or data leakage is the most expensive and fastest-growing cybercrime. In one of the famous data breaches, the customer data of famous restaurant chains were stolen and sold online. Another attacker group purchased that data and misused it to launch cyberattacks a few years later. Such incidents govern the importance of securing organizational and personal data.

Cyberattacks such as ransomware and phishing are so common that every data breach takes advantage of these tactics. Cybercriminals used ransomware attacks (WannaCry ransomware) in 2017 to encrypt confidential data of more than 200,000 computers across 150 countries. They demanded ransom to release the data. The total financial losses because of the WannaCry ransomware attack were estimated to be billions of dollars.

Cybersecurity encompasses everything that pertains to the security of sensitive data, personally identifiable information, health care credentials, intellectual property, personal data, and government information systems. Cybersecurity risk is governed by global connectivity. There are no boundaries to cyberattacks. The modern-day cybersecurity solutions not only include firewalls and antivirus solutions but advanced threat hunting infrastructures that can make use of detection, analysis, and correlation functions to mitigate cyber threats.

2.8 Data Science and Important Data Breachers

Data science is an emerging field of cybersecurity. It helps data scientists to ask rigorous questions, formulate theoretical structures, analyze big data, and provide a deep insight into analyzed data. With the plethora of messy data getting accumulated every day, big companies thought of extracting useful information from that data and analyzing the extracted information to dig deeper into making mappings for current and future patterns. For example, Facebook asks every user about his location to make it easier for his friends to connect to him. This data can be used to analyze global migration patterns. Similarly, users can use social media data such as Facebook friend connections to determine the cultural diversity, interests, and choices of a user.

Another simple example of data science is when YouTube suggests videos to a user based on the previously watched content on the channel. It stores every user's browsing history and performs data science operations to identify similar content or videos that the user may be interested in. All this is possible because of data science.

Although there is no definition of data science, it is most famously represented by a Venn diagram shown in Fig. 2.6. Data science is an interdisciplinary approach that collaborates with domain expertise, mathematics, and computer science. Domain expertise defines problem space, mathematics provides problem-solving theoretical structure, and computer science opens the data manipulation environment for data science.

Domain Expertise focuses on specific business environments such as finance, transportation, or healthcare. Domain experts possess sound knowledge of the business domain they belong to. The primary objective of applying data science operations in the business domain is to improve sales and increase profits. The expected outcome of applying data science to the business domain is expected to be quantified and measurable. Domain experts focus on the following exemplary questions to do so:

- Can the productivity of a specific department be improved by using heuristic data?
- Can competitiveness be improved by using product attributes?

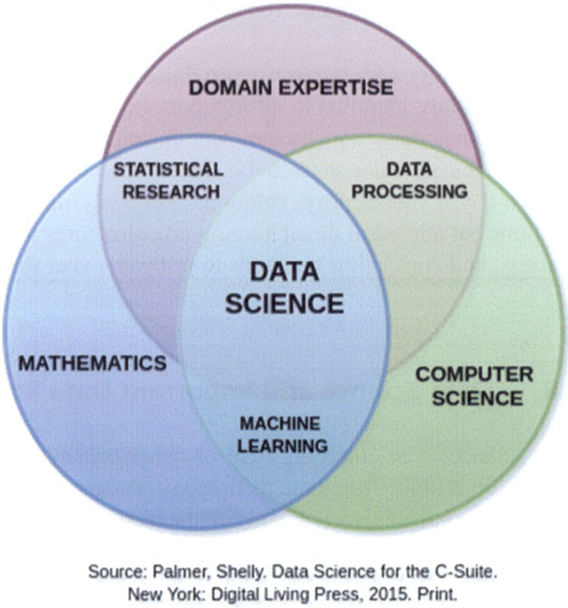

Fig. 2.6 Venn diagram presenting data science as an interdisciplinary approach

More specific questions lead to actionable results.

Mathematics provides problem-solving skills for data science operations. Mathematicians use statistical modeling, probability theory, analytics, predictions, and pattern recognition techniques to solve complex problems. Data science is meant to apply to big datasets to perform complex mathematical computations. For example, in cybersecurity, data scientists use big datasets containing malicious network traffic and apply data science operations to identify and analyze attack patterns to predict the probability of future attacks.

Computer Science provides a data manipulation environment to perform data science operations. Continuing the cybersecurity example, big datasets contain large volumes, variety, and velocity of data that cannot be handled manually. Therefore, there comes the need for computer programs or models that can automatically analyze such large datasets to yield desired predictions. Data scientists use machine learning models to automate the data analysis process. Machine learning consists of supervised and unsupervised models that can help in the classification and prediction of data, respectively.

2.8.1 Important Data Breaches

Data breach, also called data theft, is the disclosure of sensitive private/confidential information to untrusted sources. Data breach is alternatively called data leak, information leakage, and data spill. Data breaches involving millions, or billions of records are quite common across the globe. The twenty-first century has witnessed

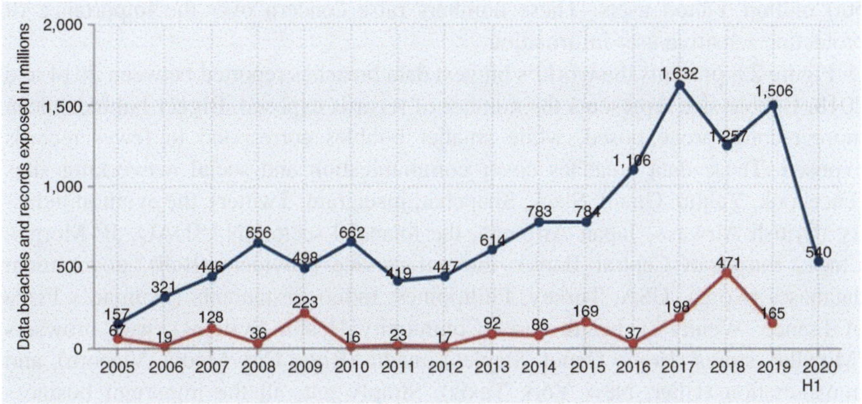

Fig. 2.7 Annual data breaches and records exposed in the USA (Statista 2020)

myriads of important data breaches that stole customers' credit card data, bank account details, and personally identifiable information (PII). Common types of data breaches include ransomware, phishing, and DoS attack.

Figure 2.7 demonstrates the annual data beaches (blue curve) and records (red curve) exposed due to those breaches in millions from 2005 to the first half of 2020. The data belongs to breaches in the USA only. The trend of data breaches has increased from 2005 to 2017. There is a sudden decline in this trend in 2018 and it jumped up again in 2019. Analyzing the records that were exposed to untrusted sources during these data breaches, it is evident that the highest number of records were exposed in 2018 even though the number of breaches in that year were comparatively less. These facts are alarming and need instant attention.

Some of the most significant data breaches of this century include big names such as Adobe, eBay, LinkedIn, Marriott International, and Yahoo. The biggest of these was related to Marriott International that spanned between 2014 and 2018. It stole the credit card data of around 100 million customers. In addition, passport numbers, guest numbers, travel information, and other personal information from 500 million customers were stolen. The breach began in 2014 in Starwood hotel brands which Marriott International acquired in 2016. It came to light in September 2018 and was officially announced in November 2018.

In another important incident, LinkedIn became the victim of social engineering attacks in 2012 and 2016. Since LinkedIn is one of the largest social networking sites for professionals, it has become an attraction for attackers. In 2012, LinkedIn announced that 6.5 million passwords were stolen by attackers. These passwords were posted on a Russian hacker forum. In 2016, the same hacker group sold the stolen passwords of around 165 million LinkedIn users. In order to reduce the impact of this breach, LinkedIn urged its users to change their passwords immediately.

In yet another important data breach, Yahoo disclosed in 2016 that it had witnessed the biggest data breach in history in 2014. The state-owned actors stole real names, email addresses, passwords, phone numbers, and the date of birth of

500 million Yahoo users. These numbers raise concern over the importance of protecting sensitive user information.

Figure 2.8 presents the world's biggest data breaches reported between 2014 and 2018. Bubble size represents the number of records exposed. Bigger bubbles mean more records are exposed, while smaller bubbles correspond to fewer records exposed. These data breaches cover communication and social networking sites (Facebook, Yahoo, Gmail, Slack, Snapchat, Instagram, Twitter), the aviation industry (British Airways, Japan Airlines), the financial sector (NASDAQ, JP Morgan Chase, European Central Bank), internet service providers (Bell), government databases (Korea, USA, Turkey, Philippines, India), restaurants (Domino's Pizza of France, Wendy's), health care (Community Health Systems), web browsers (Mozilla), stores (Home Depot, Staples), media (River City Media, Viacom), and transportation (Uber, New York Taxis). Simply put, all the important business sectors have witnessed and reported major data breaches in the last 5 years.

Most of the data breach categories reported in Fig. 2.8 include hacked, poor security, lost/stolen media, insider job, and accidentally published reports. Hacking is the dominating category that has resulted in these data breaches. The information used to plot these data breaches is publicly available. Although the excel sheet at that source contains data breaches between 2005 and 2018 but only recent data breaches are plotted here. Detailed information on worldwide data breaches is available at *bit.ly/bigdatabreaches*.

2.9 The NSA Triad for Security Assessment

The National Security Agency (NSA) provides a detailed and systematic method of assessing, evaluating, and testing security vulnerabilities from an organizational perspective. The NSA triad focuses on three main aspects of assessment, evaluation, and testing of security vulnerabilities by following Information Security (INFOSEC) Assessment Methodology (IAM) (Johnson 2004). IAM was established by experienced NSA and INFOSEC assessors in the USA in 1997. However, it became known in 2001.

IAM serves the purpose of assessing the security vulnerabilities of an organization and providing detailed information on what to look for in a security assessment. It also raises security awareness among organizations. Without going into more details of NSA IAM, this section lays stress on three main activities performed by this triad: assessment, evaluation, and testing (Miles et al. 2004).

Before starting the security assessment process, it is imperative to understand what needs assessment. For example, an organization has several critical resources that may be attacked. Does the organization want all of them assessed? The answer to this question is a three-level top-down approach that starts with assessment at the top, followed by evaluation in the middle, and attack and penetration testing at the bottom. Since it is a top-down approach, every level adds more details and concrete information to the security assessment process.

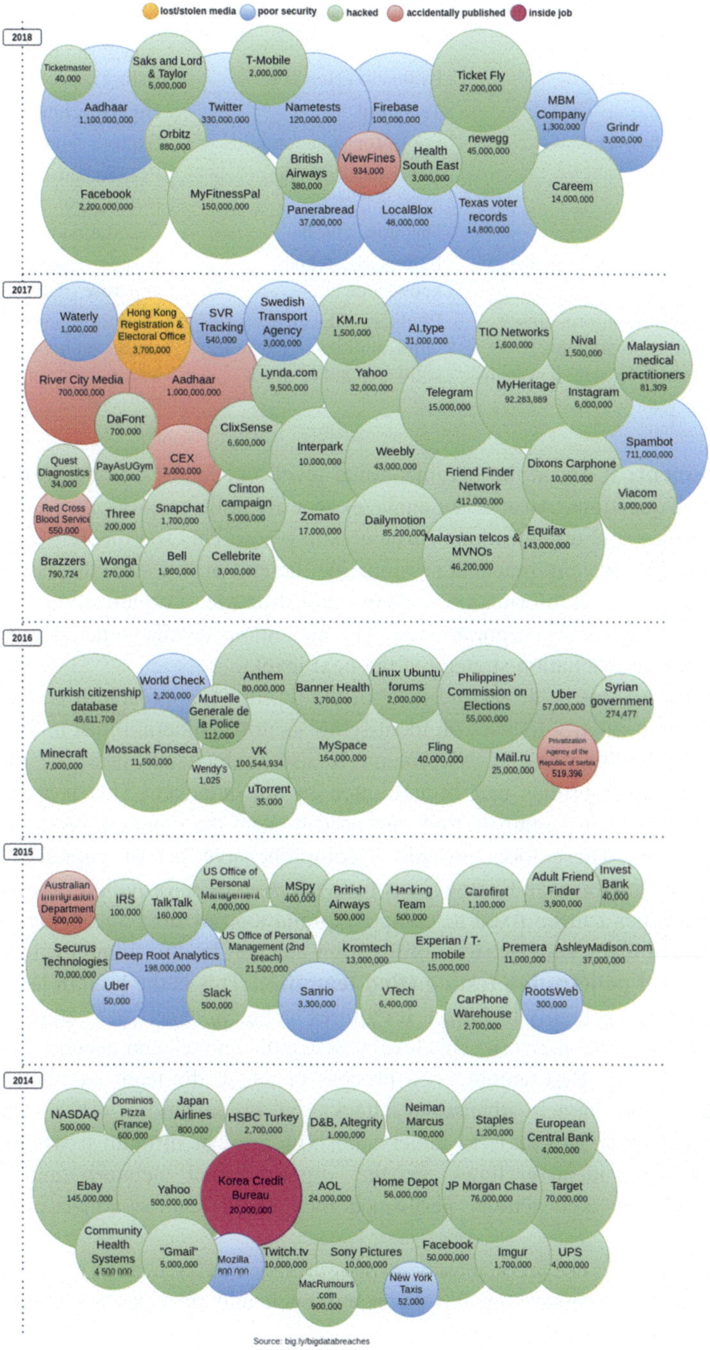

Fig. 2.8 World's biggest data breaches between 2014 and 2018 (Information is Beautiful: Data Breaches (public) 2018)

Table 2.1 NSA's top-down approach for security assessment

Assessment (Level I)	Evaluation (Level II)	Attack and penetration testing (Level III)
Nontechnical	Technical	Highly technical
Provides a high-level view	Looks for vulnerabilities.	Exploits vulnerabilities
Theoretical	Hands-on scanning	Practical attacks and penetration
No use of tools	Diagnostic tools	Penetration tools
Intermediate expertise to gather information	Intermediate/expert knowledge	Requires special expertise (red team)
Produces concrete information about organization structure, resources, and information systems	Produces a detailed list of vulnerabilities in hardware, software, and network	Produces hands-on results on how adversaries can attack the network

- **Assessment:** It lies at the organizational level and focuses on addressing non-technical questions. An assessor analyzes security policies, procedures, standards, architecture, and organizational structures in place. This is a theoretical step and does not involve any practical sessions. At the end of this step, the assessor can understand critical information, systems, and structure of organization. This level provides a high-level corporate view. The meticulous details gathered at this level help draft an evaluation strategy at the next level.
- **Evaluation:** This is the second level of the top-down approach. It is a technical round that primarily focuses on identifying security vulnerabilities in the critical systems identified in the assessment. It also understands how the identified security vulnerabilities can be exploited by the attacker. This is a hands-on process in which diagnostic tools are used to scan the computer systems in the organization. These tools provide a comprehensive list of vulnerabilities in hardware, software, and network. It further provides information on how these vulnerabilities can be fixed to escape exploitation. At the end of this step, the assessment team has extensive information that can lead to future evaluations.
- **Attack and penetration testing (Red teaming):** This is the bottom level of the approach and is highly technical. It requires technical expertise to attack and test the organizational network. This level is also called attack and penetration testing or red teaming. Red teaming is a process in which the team members imitate attackers and launch adversarial attacks on organizations. The purpose of launching these attacks is to understand how easy or difficult it would be for attackers to identify flaws in the organizational network and exploit vulnerabilities. The activity performed by the red team is called penetration testing.

Table 2.1 summarizes the top-down approach and provides a comparison of activities performed at each level.

2.10 Data-Centric Security Management

Data breaches have become more frequent and have created a burden on financial sources to protect data. As the volume of data grows, traditional network-based security models become incapable of detecting data breaches. The reason for the failure of traditional network security models is that they are focused on the location of data. That means these models concentrate on where the data is located. Data-centric security management is different from traditional network security models because it protects from data breaches irrespective of where the data is located.

Data-centric security management no longer considers borders, perimeters, and endpoint security of network data. It emphasizes data-centric characteristics that apply protection to data itself. As soon as new data is created or existing data is modified on a computer system and server, the data-centric security management system scans the computer system to verify whether the data contains sensitive information. A data-centric security management system protects confidentiality, integrity, and availability of information, assets, and resources from threats and vulnerabilities.

2.10.1 Data-Centric Security Cycle

Data-centric security is a five-step cyclic model that includes data protection, transfer, control, access, and measurement as shown in Fig. 2.9 (Nicho and Advani 2012).

- **Protect** data from unauthorized use irrespective of where it is stored. Data protection is achieved by using encryption and passwords. Only encrypted data

Fig. 2.9 Data-centric security cycle model

can be transmitted between a sender and receiver. Encrypting data ensures that data cannot be stolen by adversaries. A data-centric solution provides persistent protection of data at rest, in transit, and in use.
- **Transfer** means delivering and sharing sensitive information stored in files. Information can be shared within or outside the network.
- **Control** access to sensitive information even after it is shared and transmitted. This ensures that access rights are properly applied to sensitive information files. Access rights are used to control who has access to files. Only the authorized person can make changes to the sensitive information. Three types of access rights are assigned to every user: administrator, user, and guest. This concept puts data control in the hands of data administrators (data owners) and provides a clear distinction between activities performed by administrators, users, and guests.
- **Access** permissions on sensitive information can be revoked any time after transmission. This is a continuous process that is completed on a regular basis.
- **Measure** the activities performed by users and perform regular audits to verify that the required control measures are in place.

2.10.2 Characteristics of Data-Centric Security Management

Data-centric security management is designed with the following characteristics to protect data theft (PKWARE 2020):

- **Centralized control:** Data-centric approach follows a centralized control for data protection. The centralized control keeps track of any changes to data in the database records. As soon as sensitive information is identified, data protection is applied to it. Sensitive information is encrypted and passwords to protect data are stored safely and shared with recipients.
- **Automation:** With the increasing volume of data, it becomes unmanageable to apply a centralized data protection approach in an effective manner. Automated data protection is the key to encrypting data and preventing data theft.
- **Adaptable:** Every organization has a distinct size and type of data and data protection policies. Further, these characteristics vary within an organization as well. A good data-centric security management system must be adaptable to cater for all these requirements.
- **Gapless protection:** Data-centric security considers gaps in data storage and transmission. Data may be stored and transmitted without encryption. However, a data-centric approach makes sure that such gaps are identified and taken care of.

2.10.3 Problems with Data-Centric Security Management

Despite managing four main characteristics of data-centric security, there are the following problems with the system (Armoni 2002):

- **Inefficient distributed systems:** Data-centric security management is a centralized approach, but it becomes inefficient in a distributed (non-centralized) system. In a distributed system, there are several protection points that increase the complexity of the system. Furthermore, the process becomes cumbersome for manually updated systems.
- **Human behavior:** Data-centric uses encryption and passwords to protect data. However, it is human behavior to use the same password over again. Reusing the same password creates another problem for data-centric systems.

2.11 Chapter Summary

This chapter introduces the basic principles of cybersecurity. After understanding cybersecurity and the three principles of protecting data, the motivation to carry out cyberattacks is put forward. The CIA triad is an inseparable part of cybersecurity that ensures confidentiality, integrity, and availability of data. It is extended by adding two more principles of accountability and authenticity. Several data breaches reported in the last couple of years are listed. Analysis of data breach information reveals that data breaches are quite common, and they result in exposure to millions of data records. Further, data breaches affect financial institutions (banks, stock market, and capitalists) and FinTech startups (payment systems, lending, wealth management, crowdfunding, insurance companies, and stock markets) in the FinTech ecosystem.

The top-down approach to assess the security of an organization using the NSA IAM process is introduced. The process obtains meticulous information about the organization at the first level, gathers more critical information related to vulnerabilities in organization and how they can be exploited by scanning the network, and then a red team performs adversarial attacks to understand how the attacker can exploit the vulnerabilities in the organization network. Finally, various aspects of securing information are brought forward at the end of the chapter. After understanding all the fundamental concepts, the following questions are addressed in this chapter:

- What are the motivations to launch a cybersecurity attack?
- What are the essential elements of the CIAAA principle?
- What is the importance of cybersecurity?
- What are important data breaches that how do they impact the financial sector?
- How can the security of an organization be assessed?
- How can data-centric security be managed?

References

134 Cybersecurity Statistics and Trends for 2021. (2021). https://www.varonis.com/blog/cybersecurity-statistics/.

Armoni, A. (2002). Data security management in distributed computer systems. *Informing Science, 5*(1), 19–27.

Boer, M., & Vazquez, J. (2017). Cyber security & financial stability: How cyber-attacks could materially impact the global financial system, *Institute of International Finance*, pp. 1–9.

Cyber Security Statistics. (2020). https://purplesec.us/resources/cyber-security-statistics/.

Information is Beautiful: Data Breaches (public). (2018). bit.ly/bigdatabreaches.

Johnson, B. C. (2004). *National Security Agency (NSA) INFOSEC Assessment Methodology (IAM)* (pp. 1–6). https://systemexperts.com/pdf/NSAIAM.pdf

Miles, G., Rogers, R., Fuller, E., Hoagberg, M. P., & Dykstra, T. (2004). *Security assessment: Case studies for implementing NSA IAM*. Rockland: Syngress.

Nicho, M., & Advani, A. (2012). A data centric Security cycle model for data loss prevention of custodial data and company intellectual property. *SECURWARE 2012: The sixth international conference on emerging security information, systems and technologies* (pp. 134–141).

PKWARE. (2020). *A blueprint for data-centric security, whitepaper*. PKWARE. https://www.pkware.com/data-centric-security-whitepaper

Statista. (2020). *Annual number of data breaches and exposed records in the United States from 2005 to 1st half 2020*, Statista. https://www.statista.com/statistics/273550/data-breaches-recorded-in-the-united-states-by-number-of-breaches-and-records-exposed/.

Vaidya, T. (2015). *2001–2013: Survey and analysis of major cyberattacks* (pp. 1–25). https://arxiv.org/abs/1507.06673.

Yahoo Finance. (2021). *Over 50% increase of unique cyber threats in the wild in 2020, cymulate's continuous security testing report reveals*. New York: Yahoo Finance. https://finance.yahoo.com/news/over-50-increase-unique-cyber-130000675.html.

Information Security Governance in FinTech

3

Cyberattacks are inevitable. Sophistication and persistence of attacks depend on the importance of information available within the organization. It is the information that attracts attackers to target that organization. The prime targets in the organization are its information-based assets. In the techno-savvy world, threats originating from script kiddies are replaced by professionally trained and skilled attackers, who use advanced tools to conduct sophisticated covert cyberattacks. With the rising sophistication, the threats to information-based assets are much higher than in the past. With the advancement of technology, tools to gain unauthorized access have also become powerful. This increases the need to secure information as an asset.

After understanding the importance of cybersecurity in a financial institution, it is imperative to get ourselves equipped with the significance of information security. Information is the key to success in the contemporary era. Organizations safeguard the information to protect it from getting stolen and misused. Attackers seek information to take advantage of potential flaws in the organizations that they can exploit to gain money. Thereby, information can be secured by governing an information security system.

This chapter introduces the concept of information security governance. It provides an overview of policies and standards used to profile information security governance and elaborates available security governance models. It further presents an integrated framework for information security governance which is widely adopted by the developed countries. Based on the integrated security framework, a general information security governance framework for FinTech is proposed toward the end of the chapter.

3.1 What Is Information Security Governance?

Information technology is an integral part of establishing businesses in the current era. It has become a vital resource in setting up competitive business practices. This is the reason why organizations invest heavily in information technology.

G. Kaur et al., *Understanding Cybersecurity Management in FinTech*, Future of Business and Finance, https://doi.org/10.1007/978-3-030-79915-1_3

Investment is not the only part of a successful working solution for information technology. Organizations need to govern business practices. It includes drafting policies and standards, assessing strategies, setting up directions, and deciding tools required to follow such practices. The portfolio of performing these activities is called information technology governance (Asgarkhani et al. 2017). Information technology governance involves both strategies and operations.

Information security ensures that personal, private, confidential, and sensitive information is protected. Governance is the set of responsibilities and practices exercised by responsible individuals in an organization. Combining these two definitions, information security governance is the practice of ensuring information security by responsible individuals by exercising a set of responsibilities and practices.

In other words, information security governance is a practice of ensuring that the information (personal, sensitive, and confidential) is managed effectively in compliance with the accountability structures, governance policies, procedures, staff, and resources. In addition to these attributes of effective information security, risk management is also an important part of information security governance. Risk management is associated with different domains such as finance, legal, information security, and regulatory compliance. Furthermore, managing risks for different domains requires different experts.

Therefore, a comprehensive definition of information security governance is: *"Information security governance is the practice of securing information and managing cyber risks to protect any kind of information required for effective working of the organization in compliance with the information security policy and risk management strategy."*

There are multiple definitions of information security governance across organizations. All the definitions have their own modifications, but information security and risk management are two common components of all the definitions. The Institute of Internal Auditors' (IIA) International Professional Practices Framework (IPPF) provides the following definition of Information Technology Governance: *"Information Technology Governance consists of leadership, organizational structures, and processes that ensure the enterprise's information technology sustains and supports the organization's strategies and objectives."*

The most common way of depicting information security governance is presented in Fig. 3.1 (Love et al. 2010). Information security is an important part of enterprise-level security governance. It interacts with information technology (IT) operations, IT projects, and IT governance, where IT operations are considered the current state of IT and IT projects are considered the future state of IT. This way, it interacts with the current and future state of IT. At the top level of the enterprise exists corporate governance which evaluates the standards and policies. It also directs the middle- and low-level management consisting of IT governance, information security, IT operations, and IT projects. On the contrary, the bottom-up approach monitors the governance activities for corporate governance.

Although various organizations have their own definition for IT governance, all of them agree that IT governance promotes good practices with clear direction and

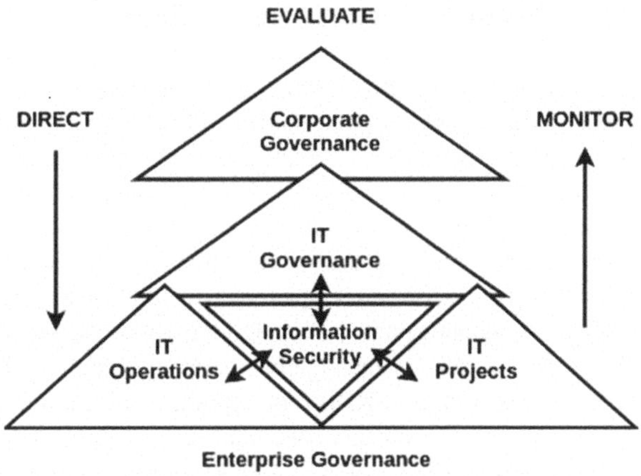

Fig. 3.1 Information security governance

understanding from the top. It controls security risks associated with each domain of the business, sustains information security activities, and risk appetite levels. Overall, information security governance performs the following activities (Love et al. 2010):

- Promotes valuable information security practices with a clear direction from top to bottom.
- Controls the risk appetite of the enterprise by considering different domains such as legal, finance, information technology, and regulatory compliance.
- Creates an overall information security activity that reflects the organization's needs and risk appetite levels.
- Monitors corporate governance policies and standards for managing information security governance standards.

3.2 Security Governance Solution

A security governance solution provides insight into the core components of a security governance framework. It includes risk management, finance management, asset management, and threat management. These management systems help to develop strategies to perform multifaceted tasks such as auditing, risk controls, and decision-making. Information security governance is important because it facilitates financial payoffs, supports new technologies, serves multiple performance goals, and evaluates the maturity level of the enterprise. This section sheds light on security governance profiling, policies and standards, roles and responsibilities, assets management, and security governance assessment.

3.2.1 Security Governance Profiling

Profiling a good security governance solution is a three-step process: (1) create governance, (2) deliver governance, and (3) review it on an ongoing basis as shown in Fig. 3.2. Governance is created in a top-down approach in which the board of directors are placed at the top. Other individuals involved in governance solutions include chief officers for various departments including finance, law, risk, and information technology. These individuals develop and implement risk management policies and establish a risk appetite structure for the organization.

The risk management policy is aligned to the business requirements and processes. An overall risk management strategy as defined in the IT Security Executive Risk Review Board (ERRB), incorporates the current risk structure (CGI Group 2015). Governance creates roles and responsibilities for appropriate personnel to perform activities that collaboratively support profiling security governance. These individuals also draft an audit and review policy to validate changing risks.

Delivering governance identifies assets, threats, risks, and critical information associated with the organization. It delivers a series of security controls and associated procedures for risk management. Security awareness programs are organized so that personnel can understand their responsibilities. This makes risk management more effective. Finally, the policies are reviewed after a regular interval so that risks are properly managed (CGI Group 2015).

3.2.2 Security Policies and Standards

Information security policies outline management's position on information security. An organization's security policy comprises three levels: operational, tactical, and strategic. Operational level policies lie at the bottom of the organization chart. Tactical policies are designed for middle-level management, while strategic policies

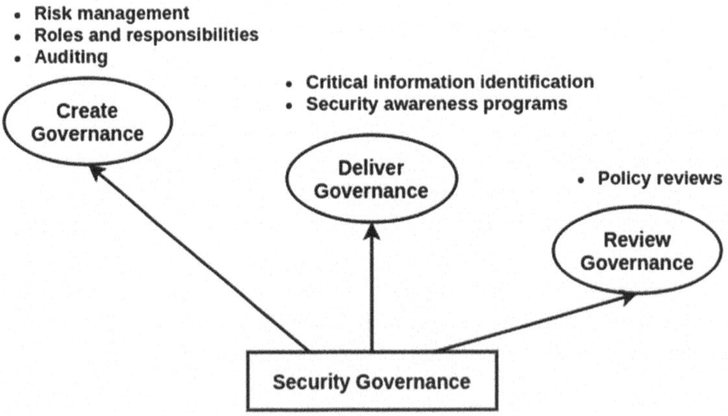

Fig. 3.2 Security governance profiling steps

are meant for upper-level management. Strategic policies, as evident from the name, create strategies that are implemented at the lower level of the organization by middle-level management. These policies are also referred to as issue-specific policies because they handle a specific information security issue in the organization. Some common examples of strategic policies include internet and email usage, disaster and business continuity planning, and protection against malware (Von Solms et al. 2011). Chapter 8 discusses security policies and strategies management in more detail.

Tactical policies are implemented at the middle level and are subparts of strategic policies. Operational policies target technical people such as IT administrators who monitor and report security incidents. Overall, security policies cover the following areas for every level of management (Information Security Governance Policy 2016):

- Establishment of an information security organization and its services.
- Access management to networks, applications, and other information systems in the organization.
- Managing cryptographic controls to secure information.
- Managing security operations related to IT operations, malware detection, event management, vulnerability management, security response and monitoring, and endpoint security.
- Managing communication security.
- Managing confidentiality, integrity, and availability of information systems.
- Managing information security incidents.
- Planning business continuity and recovering from information disasters.
- Management of information technology risk and compliance.

There are specific practices and security standards that ensure that the strategic objectives of the organization are achieved. Some of these standards include ISO27001, BS7799, Payment Card Industry Data Security Standard (PCIDSS), Information Technology Infrastructure Library (ITIL), Control Objectives for Information and Technology (COBIT), ISO27002: 2007/ISO 7799:2005, and ANSI/ISA-99.02.01–2009.

3.2.3 Security Strategic Planning

Information security governance provides four basic outcomes when properly implemented: strategic alignment, value delivery, risk management, and performance measurement. Strategic alignment incorporates aligning the security requirements with the enterprise requirements. Not only security requirements but security solutions must also fit in with the enterprise processes. Further, proper security strategic planning ensures that investment in information security is aligned with the enterprise strategy and risk profile. Risk profile represents an acceptable risk appetite for the enterprise (Williams 2001).

Strategic planning covers high-level steps. To begin strategic planning for the enterprise, the board of directors and executives collect critical information related to benchmarks, maturity models, gap analysis, and continuous performance reports. This information helps policymakers to prepare a strategy in compliance with practiced security standards and policies. Further, it is important to consider that risk levels always change, and so does the enterprise's risk appetite. Analysis gaps in current and acceptable risk levels are necessary to bridge this gap. In addition to that, executives consider annual risk reports, and a brainstorming session is organized to discuss the actionable conclusions prepared by the internal auditors. These conclusions are reviewed by the upper management, and follow-ups are conducted until the audit reports are closed.

A critical aspect of strategic planning is Business Continuity Planning (BCP). Whatever be the situation of risks to the enterprise, the business must not stop. Business continuity planning recovers the information systems from potential threats and protects assets in the event of a disaster. BCP determines the effect of risks on operations and implements safeguards to mitigate risks. It also reviews the processes to verify that they are up to date. Finally, it ensures that testing procedures are working correctly.

Strategic planning aims to address a successful information security program. It should be linked to the enterprise's long- and short-term objectives. It is associated with policies and standards that direct and control the use of technology and protect its information. Many organizations measure the effectiveness of their strategic planning by using metrics (Ula et al. 2011).

3.2.4 Security Roles and Responsibilities

Security governance in an organization is split into three levels. It is headed by the board of directors at the top level. There are nine groups of personnel involved in the information security governance framework. Every group has its own unique roles and responsibilities which are described below:

1. **Board of directors:** These are the top-level personnel who take strategic decisions and approve policies and standards for the enterprise. They understand the need for an information security governance program, address threats and risks, and take board and senior-level decisions.
2. **Senior officers:** It includes upper management personnel such as Chief Executive Officer (CEO), President, and Chief Operating Officer (COO).
3. **Cross-organizational security steering council:** It comprises general counsel, Chief Information Officer, Chief Security Officer and/or Chief Risk Officer, Chief Privacy Officer, Chief Financial Officer, Deans/academic unit executives and/or other unit executives, Communications executives/public relations, and Director of Human resources. The council personnel set security policies, procedures, programs, and training sessions. Chief Information Officer is involved in incident management, compliance, and audit coordination.

Table 3.1 Activities performed by management personnel

Management individuals	Activities
Chief executive officer (CEO)	• Planning overall strategic and operational control. • Considering information technology as the most important resource for planning.
Chief financial officer (CFO)	• Responsible for overall financial matters. • Use of financial management to support corporate objectives. • Understanding of information technology tools to make financial decisions.
Chief information officer (CIO)	• Overall responsible for use of information technology in the organization.
Chief security officer (CSO)	• Overall responsible for the security of the organization. • Support activities such as vulnerability management. • Aligns technical risks with business risks.
Chief legal counsel (CLC)	• Acts as a legal advisor to the organization.
Chief risk officer (CRO)	• Concerned with managing risks across the organization.

4. **Asset owners:** They identify critical assets in the enterprise that are prone to risks and the information systems cannot work without them.
5. **Business managers:** They perform multiple functions from managing the other workers to ensuring financial targets of the enterprise.
6. **Operational personnel:** Operational personnel are the workers who perform operations at the lower management level. They are responsible for the day-to-day operations of the enterprise.
7. **Certification agent:** The authority acts as the policy authority that is responsible for the establishment, distribution, maintenance, promotion, and policy enforcement.
8. **Board audit committee:** The committee consists of auditors who oversee the financial reporting and disclosure process. They monitor accounting policies and principles.
9. **Internal and external audit personnel:** Auditors (internal and external) validate that the policies and procedures in the documentation are implemented properly and there is no gap in implementation.

Table 3.1 provides the list of activities performed by management to comply with governance frameworks (IT Governance Institute 2006).

3.2.5 Security Governance of Assets

An asset is defined as "an item of value." Every asset in the institution accounts for information security governance. Some important assets in an institution are IT hardware, software, data, information systems, storage media, and system documentation. Security governance of assets is identifying, tracking, classifying, and assigning ownership for the most important assets in the institution.

Table 3.2 Asset rating

Rating	Meaning
1	Critical is always available and protected
2	Very important this asset is available and protected
3	Important if this asset is available and protected
4	Good if this asset is available with minimal protection

To begin with, an asset inventory is prepared that contains the list of all assets, their location, and responsible personnel in the institution. Responsible personnel can be the asset owner or custodian. An asset owner is responsible for the security of the assets while the custodian makes sure that the assets are adequately managed as per the owner's guidelines. Data owners have direct responsibility for the management of the data. Identifying the owners will help determine who is responsible for carrying out the protective measures (Asset and Data Management 2019).

All assets add value to the organization. However, the value of assets is not equal. Some assets contribute more than the value of other assets. Therefore, a rating of assets is created (highest to lowest) to label assets for classification purposes, as presented in Table 3.2.

After assigning asset ratings, it is mandatory to draft an acceptable use policy for the assets. The acceptable use policy defines and documents the rules that clarify the acceptable use of assets associated with information and information processing facilities. The policy is communicated to all users within the organization and third-party users residing outside the organization.

The most important aspect of information security governance is to protect assets. Different assets have different impacts on the reputation and continuity of business. Once the importance of assets is determined, the process of protecting the assets begins. There are various methods of protecting assets, such as technical security controls and legislative mandates. Protecting measures range from addressing managing access to ensuring the physical security of the assets.

3.2.6 Governance Structure Appropriate to the Organization

Information security governance combines technical and managerial functions under one roof. It is imperative in the modern era to secure information as it is the key to success. The key players in the enterprise perform their designated tasks to achieve the unanimous goal of security information. Information security must comply with standards, institutional policy, and law to effectively control information security. Overall, it is pertinent to design an appropriate governance structure for the organization.

An unorganized and uncoordinated structure poses great challenges for the organization regarding security, compliance, privacy, identity, and other regulations. Moreover, it is also inefficient. An effective governance structure consists of several committees such as a top-level steering committee, advisory committee, and

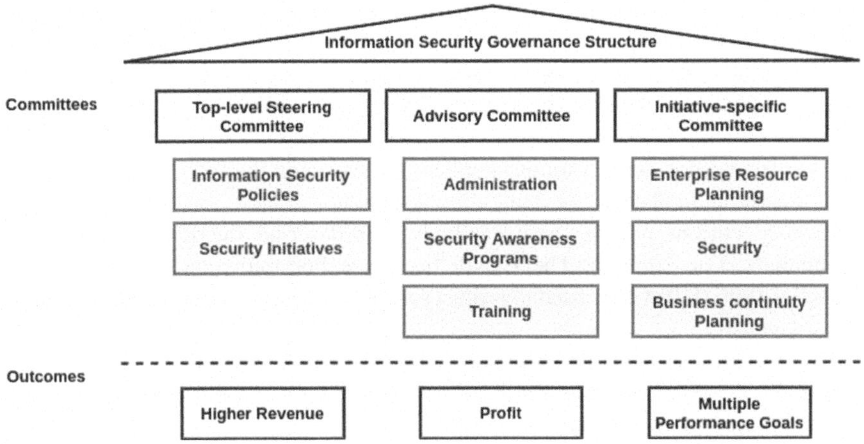

Fig. 3.3 Core components of an appropriate information security governance structure

initiative-specific committee. The steering committee provides oversights of major information security policies and initiatives. The advisory committee is responsible for administration, security awareness programs, and training. The initiative-specific committee indulges in enterprise resource planning, security, and business continuity planning.

Based on this information, an appropriate information security governance structure for an organization consists of the following core components as shown in Fig. 3.3.

Every organization has a different governance structure that depends on the desired outcomes of an enterprise. The desired outcomes can be higher revenue, profit, or multiple performance goals. Increased revenue is decentralized to promote customer responsiveness and innovation. Profit can be centralized to promote sharing, reuse, and efficient asset utilization. Finally, multiple performance goals can be centralized or decentralized. It may be a mix of both.

3.2.7 Third Parties and Suppliers

Businesses are turning out to third-party vendors for IT services, assets, and operations. The use of third parties and suppliers not only extends the operational services of the business but increases the risk of security. The true cost of outsourcing can be identified once the risks are identified and managed. In order to manage the risks, regulatory and compliance requirements need to be fulfilled by the third parties (KPMG 2019).

External suppliers are a vital component of business operations. They may have access to a wide range of information from the supported organization. When information is accessed by suppliers, direct control of this information is lost.

Therefore, appropriate technical controls and mitigation processes are established with all external suppliers.

To commence the evaluation process for suppliers, the following information is needed (Vendor and Third-Party Management 2019):

- Identify and document various suppliers to determine the information that they access or manipulate.
- Identify current policies and standards that describe the responsibilities of suppliers. For example, The Health Insurance Portability and Accountability Act of 1996 (HIPAA) is used to protect sensitive patient information in the health care industry.
- Review data classification standards and their relation to suppliers.
- Review or develop a supplier life cycle process that includes initial reviews, monitoring, validation, and assessments.

3.2.8 Information Security Governance Assessment Tools

An assessment tool evaluates the information security governance programs using the International Organization for Standardization (ISO) 27,002:2013 "*Information Technology Security Techniques. Code of Practice for Information Security Management*" as the framework. It maps to the common standards and frameworks such as ISO 27002:2013, NIST 800–53 r4 Controls, NIST 800–171 r1 Controls, the NIST Cybersecurity Framework, and the CIS 20 Critical Security Controls.

An assessment tool can be used in a single unit or the entire organization. Assessment is performed by the Chief Information Officer or Chief Information Security Officer, unless otherwise stated. In general, self-assessment is completed every year. The frequency of assessment may be altered at the discretion of the enterprise. A typical assessment tool provides a six-point scale to measure the maturity of the information security governance program as shown in Fig. 3.4. The assessment tool uses ISO 21827:2008 framework for scoring maturity which scales from 0 to 5, 5 being the highest level of maturity.

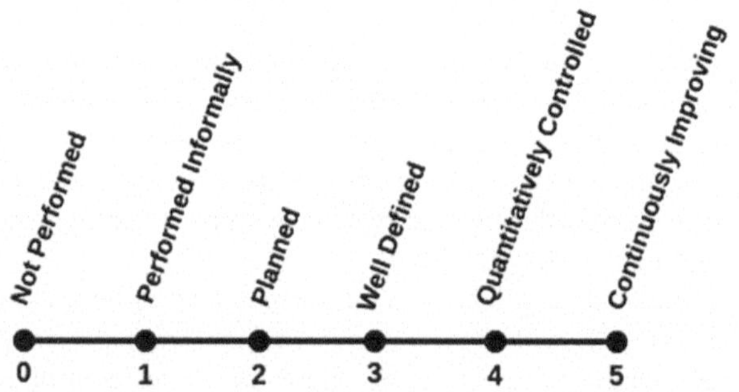

Fig. 3.4 Maturity level of the information security governance program

In order to compute the score, a scale is selected (between 0 and 5) for every question. For example, a sample assessment tool contains the following questions (Information Security Program Assessment Tool 2015):

- **Question 1: Information Security Policies**—It assesses how an institution expresses its intent regarding information security.
- **Question 2: Organization of Information Security**—It assesses how an institution manages its information security across the entire enterprise, including how the institutional leadership commits its support and provides overall direction.
- **Question 3: Asset Management**—It assesses an institution's asset management program. Does it include ways to identify, track, classify, and assign ownership for the most important assets to ensure they are adequately protected?

The Chief Information Officer selects a scale for each question to answer it as per the enterprise's information security governance policy. Finally, all answers are added, and an average score is computed for the enterprise. This score represents the maturity of the information security governance program at that enterprise.

A sample assessment tool for information security governance is presented in (Information Security Governance Assessment Tool for Higher Education 2006). The tool evaluates the organization's risk management, people, processes, and technology score to compute an overall security assessment score for the organization. The tool considers the characteristics of the organization by posing certain questions related to the size of the organization, the number of assets, and its dependency on information technology. It divides the questionnaire into four sections for computing risk, people, process, and technology score. Every section has specific questions that are answered on a scale between 0 and 4, where 0—not implemented, 1—planning stages, 2—partially implemented, 3—close to completion, and 4—fully implemented. Based on the answer scale for each questionnaire, the score of every section is added up. Finally, total risk score, total people score, total processes score, and total technology score are added to obtain the enterprise's total security assessment score. Based on this final score, a security evaluation rating is assigned to the organization. This rating also mentions the quality of maturity level of the organization.

3.3 Available Information Security Governance Models

This section provides extensive details on available information security governance models. It begins with the basic model and proceeds with extended models.

3.3.1 Basic Information Security Governance Model

A basic information security governance model comprises three levels of management: strategic (upper management), tactical (middle management), and operational

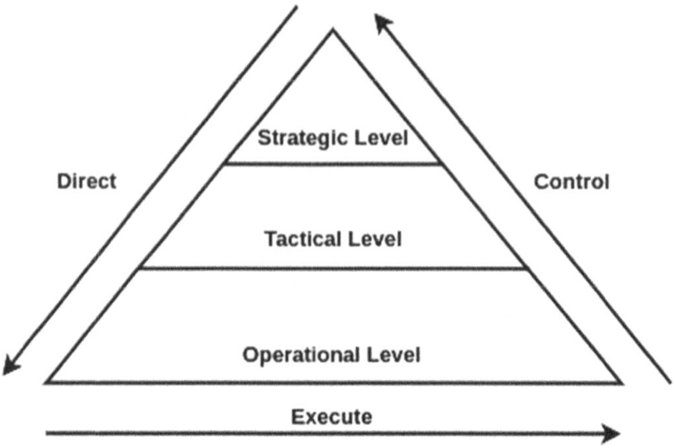

Fig. 3.5 Basic information security governance model (Von Solms et al. 2011)

(lower management) as shown in Fig. 3.5. Security governance generally comprises two main processes: directing and controlling. These processes are facilitated through strategic directives. Directing occurs when upper management gives directives to achieve an organization's objectives. Controlling occurs when the directives given by upper management are followed.

Directing is pointed from top to bottom, and controlling is pointed in the reverse direction to indicate the operations' provider and executor, respectively. Directing and controlling occurs at all levels of management. At the strategic level, executive management indicates the importance of valuable assets. At the tactical level, directives from the strategic level are used to plan policies and create organizational standards. These policies and standards are implemented at the operational level (Von Solms et al. 2011). If information security governance practices are correctly applied, the executive must be able to trace the directives from the strategic to operational level.

3.3.2 Extended Information Security Governance Model

The basic model is extended to add more functions to each level and add a technical level at the bottom as shown in Fig. 3.6. The primary functions of strategic level management are planning information security strategy, providing leadership and monetary support (sponsorship) to organization, commitment to protect assets, direct and control an organization, proposing policies and standards to facilitate directing and controlling, preparing security metrics to evaluate the security governance model of the organization, and running an internal and external audit program to validate the information security governance in the organization.

Tactical and operational levels are merged to represent senior managers and operational managers in the extended model. This level addresses user awareness

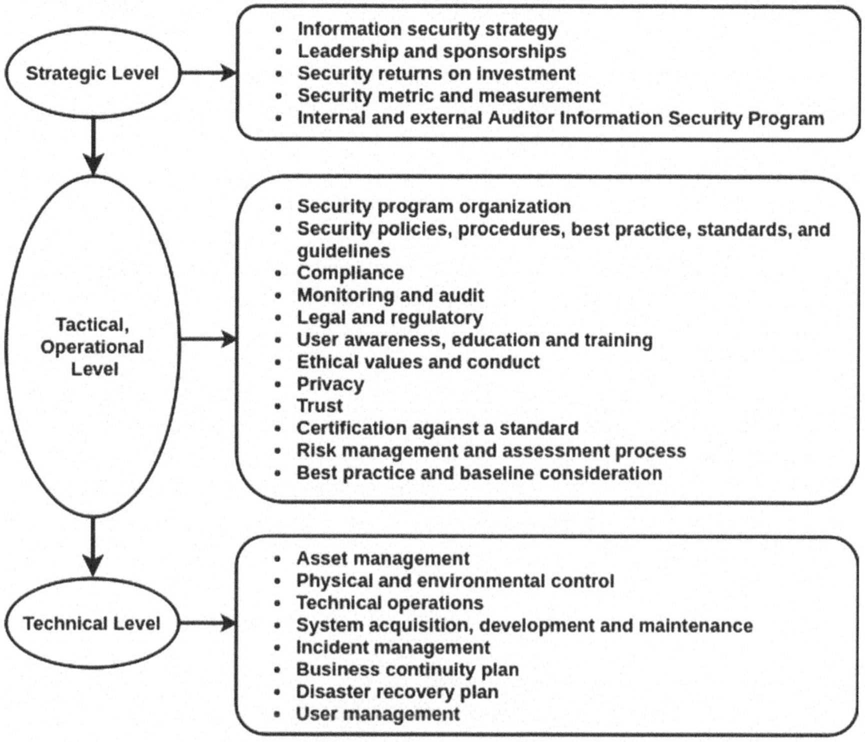

Fig. 3.6 Extended information security governance model (Ula et al. 2011)

programs, education and training, creating and monitoring security programs, monitoring user behavior to ensure compliance with information security standards, and risk management process. There is a contradiction among researchers to include privacy, trust, and ethical values at this level. Privacy and trust management deal with concerns of information security and unauthorized access to data. Special emphasis is given to maintaining a trusting relationship among traders and stakeholders of the organization. Ethical conduct must be addressed by the management to reduce risks. In addition to that, a baseline is prepared by senior managers to follow the directives provided by strategic personnel.

The technical level is a new level added to the extended model. It includes all employees. It involves technical and physical mechanisms to secure the IT environment. The activities undertaken by technical level personnel include asset management, technical operations, security incident management, business continuity plan, disaster recovery plan, and user management. It is essential that the technical environment is monitored to identify risks of technology changes (Ula et al. 2011). Nevertheless, the addition of technical level to the information security governance model is not widely accepted by different organizations.

3.3.3 Comprehensive Information Security Governance Model

This model contains three levels like the basic model. Strategic level consists of a board of directors and executive management who gives directives. Tactical level consists of senior and middle management who draft policies and company standards by following directives. Operational level consists of lower management and administration who follow procedures and implementation of policies and standards.

Figure 3.7 presents the added functions to the basic model to design a comprehensive information security model adopted by developed countries. The directing part starts at strategic management. The directives provided by executive management depend on several internal and external factors such as risks, regulatory aspects, and business requirements. These factors, in turn, offer input to the security directives. In addition, the model facilitates aids such as executive-level directive exercise (indicated by (A) in Fig. 3.7). The output of these directives is clearly defined directive questions that reflect the expectations of the executive management (Coertze and von Solms 2013).

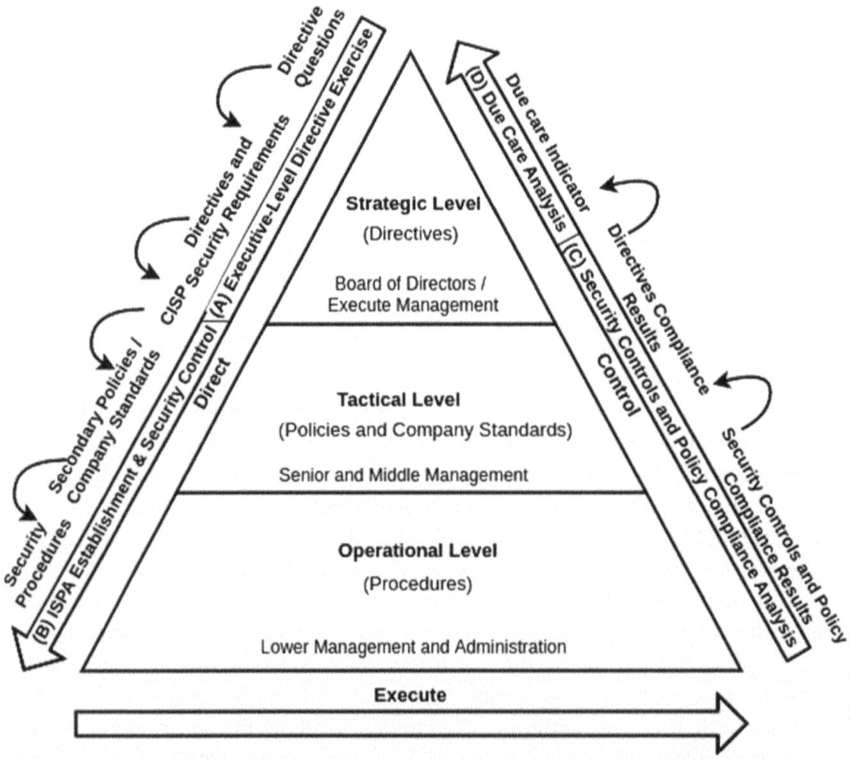

Fig. 3.7 Comprehensive information security governance model adopted by developed countries

The next big thing is the security requirements, including confidentiality, availability, integrity, authentication, and audibility. The corporate information security policy (CISP) defines the high-level security statements that specify roles, directives, and vision of information security governance. CISP is supported by various company standards, which offer adherence to lower management and operational staff. There are secondary policies and company standards that are followed under Information Security Policy Architecture (ISPA) establishment and security control (indicated by (B) in Fig. 3.7). These policies and security procedures are used in day-to-day operations (Coertze and von Solms 2013).

On the controlling side, security controls and policy compliance analysis (indicated by (C) in Fig. 3.7) and due care analysis (indicated by (D) in Fig. 3.7) is conducted. The implementation of security controls and procedures must be analyzed to identify any gaps. Secondly, the duties of executive management should be constantly evaluated to determine if due care is exercised regarding information security. The control action starts at the operational level. The model suggests that the security controls and policy compliance analysis is conducted at the tactical and operational level while the due care analysis is conducted at the strategic level (Coertze and von Solms 2013). At the end of due care analysis, strategic management can determine any mismanagement in the successful implementation of information security governance.

3.4 What Is Effective and Efficient Information Security Governance?

Effective information security governance has several characteristics such as involving appropriate organizational personnel, a governance framework, risk management, deliverables, and tackling changing risk levels.

Appropriate Organizational Personnel Appropriate organizational personnel include the board of directors, executive management, business managers, and internal auditors. These personnel are involved in designing governance policies, implementing them throughout the organization, and perform internal auditing so that compliance with governance standards can be validated. These individuals lead from the front to provide an insight into the corporate culture, provide leadership, dedicate resources, contribute to the implementation of information security activities, validate them, and recommend improvements.

There are several governance bodies such as the audit committee, governance committee, risk management committee, and finance committee. There are leaders such as Chief Executive Officer (CEO), Chief Financial Officer (CFO), Chief Information Officer (CIO), Chief Security Officer (CSO), Chief Legal Counsel (CLC), and Chief Risk Officer (CRO) who lead these committees to accomplish information security objectives. They are responsible for effective information security governance. Table 3.3 details the activities performed by these committees and individuals leading the committees (Love et al. 2010).

Table 3.3 Committees and their activities

Committee	Activities
Audit	• Oversight of financial issues • Internal audit assessment • Risk management • Ethics
Governance	• Selecting board members • Assessment • Leadership of board's operations
Risk management	• Risk analysis and assessment • Risk response • Risk monitoring
Finance	• Review financial statements • Cash flow operations • Investment management • Making financial decisions • Generate financial reports • Understand information technology to ensure accuracy of information

Governance Framework A governance framework provides guidelines for the board of directors and executive management to develop an audit plan. These frameworks help the organization to operate in a structured, consistent, and effective manner such that it can be explained easily to all stakeholders, regulatory agencies, service providers, and other parties in the business. Well-planned governance frameworks can help guide future business changes and activities.

Risk Management Like all business risks, technical risks are equally important. Deploying a risk management tool to analyze, assess, mitigate, monitor, and review risks is important to establish a threshold to tackle risks on time. Some of the risks are avoided, some are accepted, some are transferred, and the rest are mitigated. It all depends on the risk appetite policy of the organization. Since every organization has different risk levels and different financial resources to tackle risks, the mitigation measures also vary. However, maintaining proper resources and finance to mitigate risks is the key for every organization.

Deliverables Information security governance produces qualitative and quantitative deliverables. Qualitative deliverables are useful in measuring management activities while quantitative deliverables are used for tracking capabilities that are not feasible with qualitative measures. Quantitative deliverables could include several policies and standards delivered, a number of security events, and result of corporate training and security programs. This does not diminish the value of qualitative deliverables. In general, a mixture of both qualitative and quantitative deliverables is used in an organization.

Tackling Changing Risk Levels Risk management is used by the authorities to tackle risks, set up a risk appetite for the organization, and cope with the changing nature of risk levels. The risk appetite policy is updated with changing technological and informational assets. These changes are validated with an audit plan.

3.5 Integrated Governance Mechanisms

Integrated governance mechanisms combine information security governance, risk management, and compliance (GRC) together in a single framework. Integration is important from two perspectives: (1) how information systems coordinate integrated governance, risks, and compliance, and (2) how integrated GRC can be applied to the information technology landscape (Racz et al. 2010). In general, the main perspective is how well this integration is carried out and supported in an organization.

3.5.1 The Role of Governance

Integrated governance plays the following important roles (Park et al. 2006; Selig 2016):

- The framework integrates strategies, controls, securities, performance, and communities together.
- It specifies the decision-making authority and accountability to encourage desirable outcomes in terms of profits and cost analysis.
- Robust governance standards create productivity gains and cost-effectiveness.
- It establishes accountability and decision rights.
- It manages risks, change, and contingencies proactively.
- It improves performance, compliance, maturity, and staff development in the enterprise.
- It improves customer service and overall responsiveness.
- It manages, prioritizes, funds, monitors, and measures deliverables and IT resources. It also ensures maximum utilization of assets.
- It aligns IT investments and priorities more closely with the business.

3.5.2 Corporate Governance

Corporate governance is defined as a system of rules, practices, and processes by which an organization is directed and controlled. It essentially involves balancing the interests of several stakeholders, such as shareholders, management, board of directors, customers, suppliers, employees, the government, and the community. Governance has become an important part of corporate vocabulary after failures and scandals of the late 1980s and early 1990s. Corporate governance was encouraged by the Cadbury report of 1992. A corporate governance structure is accountable for managing the best practices in the enterprise.

The objective of corporate governance is to improve standards of corporate behavior, strengthen security controls, and ensure accountability. It also maintains the essential spirit of the corporate (Williams 2001). The role of corporate governance was extended later to include the audit committee. It reiterated that the board must maintain a sound system of internal control to safeguard the shareholder's interests. The key principle of corporate governance is to maintain shareholder primacy. The Board of directors is the primary force behind enforcing corporate governance.

The major task of corporate governance is to make everybody accountable for their activities. For example, the government is accountable for compliance; the board of directors and executive management is responsible for directives; employees are accountable for day-to-day operational tasks, and the media is responsible for endorsements. As a part of accountability, the board regularly reports financial information to the shareholders, which reflects the policy of transparency in corporate governance.

Poor corporate governance occurs when stakeholders share foggy information, making them less accountable for the activities. It can cast doubtful corporate operations and profitability. Types of poor governance practices include (Chen 2021):

- Poorly structured boards that make it difficult for shareholders to communicate.
- Poorly designed executive compensation packages that fail to generate incentives for corporates.
- Poor communication with auditors results in the publication of fake or noncompliant financial documents.

3.5.3 Principles of Good Governance

Based on a discussion on poor practices in corporate governance and directing and controlling as the two main functions of information security governance, following are the principles of good governance (Stallings 2018):

- **Accountability and responsibility:** Every stakeholder in the enterprise must be accountable for the activities performed by him. This principle ensures that individuals are doing their best to achieve the organization's objectives. Top management should ensure accountability and responsibility throughout the organization.
- **Transparency:** Every stakeholder shares some information in the form of documents, reports, or financial statements that reveals the outcomes of his activities. This ensures transparency in the enterprise.
- **Strategic decision-making:** Investments support governance objectives. Security governance ensures that information security is integrated with existing organization processes to make strategic decisions.

- **Risk management:** Based on resources and assets in the organization, risks are identified, analyzed, monitored, and mitigated. Risk-centric security governance helps identify the risk appetite of the organization by considering compliance, liability risks, operational losses, disruptions, and reputational harm.
- **Performance review:** Security governance impacts the overall objectives and goals of the enterprise. It must review performance through financial statements, audit reports, and risk management reports to find areas of improvement.
- **Conformance with requirements:** Security governance must conform to internal and external requirements. External requirements include mandatory legislation, regulations, standards, and contracts. Internal requirements include organizational goals and objectives. Conformance is monitored through security audits.

3.5.4 Principles of Undertaking Governance Review

The purpose of governance is to ensure that the board of directors have ample oversight in performing their responsibilities. It also makes sure that delegated powers of the board of directors are exercised appropriately. The governance review is undertaken to clarify the expectations from the outputs of the meetings. It also assures that there is no duplication and adds value to the structure of each meeting. The integrated governance structure acts as the platform to develop a systemic approach to map assurance against key strategic and operational risks. It identifies the gaps in security controls. Finally, it supports long-term sustainability by inspiring process and system improvements (Integrated Governance Handbook 2015).

3.6 Comprehensive Security Governance

This section introduces the approaches that act as a driving force for creating comprehensive security governance. It entails strategic integration, cybersecurity risk mitigation, and adaptability and agility of decisions that vary for every organization based on its preparedness of facing threats.

3.6.1 Strategic Integration

Strategic integration addresses the extent to which cybersecurity policy is integrated into the information security governance of the enterprise. It can be "not at all integrated" or "fully integrated." The level of integration entirely depends on the cybersecurity policy of the enterprise. For "not at all integration," each program or business process implements its own strategy. The second level of strategic integration is "consistency," in which accountable personnel make sure that execution of strategy in one domain does not impact the strategy in other domains. The third level of strategic integration is "coordination", in which accountable personnel work

Table 3.4 Strategic integration within organization (Bodeau et al. 2010)

Preparation level (high to low)	Strategic integration with other strategies in the organization
Pervasive agility	Full integration of cybersecurity into organization's mission strategy.
Architectural resilience	Coordination of architectural and acquisition strategies with cybersecurity strategies.
Responsive awareness	Consistency between architectural, acquisition, and cybersecurity strategies.
Critical information protection	Coordination of information security with business continuity.
Perimeter defense	No integration

Table 3.5 Strategic integration beyond organization

Preparation level (high to low)	Degree of integration
Pervasive agility	Coordinate with cybersecurity counterparts in other organizations and business partners, suppliers, and customers.
Architectural resilience	Coordinate with partner, supplier, and customer organization to support a shared response to threats.
Responsive awareness	Engage with cybersecurity counterparts in other organizations (partner, supplier, and customer) to support shared awareness of threats and detect incidents.
Critical information protection	Share information with partner and supplier organizations to support shared awareness of threats and detect incidents.
Perimeter defense	Share information with security needs and concerns with cybersecurity staff in supplier organization.

together to utilize the resources. The final level of strategic integration is "full integration," in which strategies for different domains are included to accomplish the enterprise-wide mission strategy (Bodeau et al. 2010).

Strategic integration can be conducted within the organization or beyond it by integrating various preparation levels. It includes strategies in the area of acquisition and/or program management, architecture, business continuity, and mission assurance, as presented in Table 3.4.

Strategic integration beyond organization reflects the way in which the organization engages with suppliers, customers, third-party vendors, and business partners. Table 3.5 provides glimpses of this integration.

3.6.2 Cyber Risk Mitigation Approach

Cyber risk mitigation approach reflects the priorities of the organization regarding compliance with standards of good practices and proactive mitigation techniques. The approach to cyber risk mitigation must consider motivations behind adversarial tactics, techniques, and procedures. It must also investigate soaring cyber risks after

Table 3.6 Cyber risk mitigation approach (Bodeau et al. 2010)

Preparation level (high to low)	Approach
Pervasive agility	Cybersecurity builds on standards of good practice but ensures continuity in the face of an innovative adversary.
Architectural resilience	Cybersecurity builds on standards of good practice but incorporates state-of-the-art techniques.
Responsive awareness	Cybersecurity includes conformance with standards of good practice but addresses advanced threats.
Critical information protection	Information security is identified in compliance with standards of good practice in the context of broader risk management.
Perimeter defense	Information security is identified with compliance with standards of good practice.

Table 3.7 Approach to adaptability and agility (Bodeau et al. 2010)

Preparation level (high to low)	Approach to adaptability and agility
Pervasive agility	A defined, implemented, and exercised process to provide critical decision-making in case of a cyber incident. It also delegates responsibilities for a long-term service disruption as a result of cyber threats.
Architectural resilience	A defined and implemented process to provide critical decision-making in case of a cyber incident. It also delegates responsibilities for a long-term service disruption as a result of cyber threats.
Responsive awareness	A process that defines support for limited alternative decision-making process in case of a cyber incident.
Critical information protection	An informal decision-making process to provide short-time alternative support in case of a cyber incident.
Perimeter defense	Decision-making process in case of minor disruption of services and processes as a result of adversarial action.

integrating different domains and processes. Table 3.6 summarizes the approaches used for cyber risk mitigation in the enterprise.

3.6.3 Adaptability and Agility

Adversarial threats can disrupt businesses across the organization. Handling cybersecurity incidents is a part of security governance practices. However, business continuity planning does not usually address adversarial activities. Therefore, there is a need for adaptability and agility to make decisions and provide alternative modes of communications, control, and processing. Table 3.7 presents the approach to adaptability and agility as used by the organization.

3.6.4 Reporting Framework for Good Governance

A reporting framework for good governance consists of two core components: overarching principles and up-to-date documents. These components ensure that meetings are effective, timely, attended by the right people, and recorded (Bradford District Care 2020).

(a) **Overarching principles**
The overarching principles ensure that information gathered, analyzed, and presented in the framework can answer the questions raised by committee members. Three overarching principles for a reporting framework are mentioned below:
- **Style guide:** The documentation guide must follow a standard format and must be written in predominantly the same font size and style.
- **Circulation of agenda and papers:** Agenda and meeting papers must be circulated well in advance so that members get ample time to prepare for the points to be discussed in the meeting. The ideal time for circulation is five working days before the meeting.
- **Verbal items and tabled papers:** Substantive agenda items must be verbal and tabled in exceptional circumstances. It is essential that every member in the meeting has time to prepare for their answers. Documents support the decision-making process and the rationale to take an appropriate decision.

(b) **Up to date documents**
Several documents are needed for the meeting including agenda template, meeting template, action notes, action log, annual work plan, and supporting documents. The type of information contained in these documents is briefed in Table 3.8.

Table 3.8 Documents required for a reporting framework (Bradford District Care 2020)

Type of document	Information contained
Agenda	Items to be discussed in the meeting.
Minutes	A clear format of official summary of discussions in the meeting.
Action notes	Actions agreed in the meeting. It is a record of the meeting.
Action log	Actions captured in the meeting in a different format to that of action notes.
Terms of reference	Information about committee members, attendees, and their duties.
Annual work plan	Drawing up future agendas.
Cover sheet	Standard information about each agenda item such as paper presentations in the meeting.
Supporting papers	Any information in addition to the one not mentioned in the cover sheet.

3.7 Effectively Implementing a Sustainable Strategy

Sustainability has become an equally important concept for organizations. It helps organizations to take competitive advantages by engaging employees in profit-making and satisfying customers. Thus, it creates value for a business. Sustainability not only helps companies avoid the backlash faced from the governments, but it also makes business sense (Garza 2013).

Effective implementation of sustainable strategy requires committed leadership, clear direction, and strategic influence. Following are the considerations for effectively implementing sustainable strategy (Eapen 2017):

- **Committed leaders:** Committed leadership is the foundation of a sustainable strategy. It demonstrates an enterprise's seriousness.
- **Accountability:** It ensures that sustainability is integrated with business goals.
- **Structured alignment:** Sustainable structures that align with business goals, performance reviews, and organizational structures are more successful.
- **Flexibility:** Flexibility to adapt and build sustainable programs across the business units in the enterprise assures employee engagement.

The best structure in place for obtaining sustainability includes the following:

- **Head:** Head of sustainability assures seriousness and acts as a driving force to continuously work to meet the objectives. It also signals the company's commitment.
- **Formal board:** Board committee is a formal method of educating the board on sustainability issues. There can be several formal board committees, or a dedicated committee can also serve the purpose.
- **Cross-functional executive committee:** Below the board committee, having a cross-functional executive committee would engage leadership across business units. It performs many functions such as risk management, supply chain, operations and facilities, marketing, and communication.
- **Sustainability teams:** These teams work under the guidance of a cross-functional committee to coordinate daily activities.
- **Supporting structures:** These groups support the integration of strategy and goals. The members in these groups are responsible for implementing strategies, tracking performance, and engaging employees.
- **External advisory:** External advisory committee is not an official part of the sustainability strategy, but it can serve as a valuable mechanism to advance the company's agenda.

A sustainable society is one that meets the needs of the current generations without sacrificing the needs of the future generations. Sustainable strategy earns financial benefits, customer loyalty, and employee engagement. It is associated with financial performance, especially access to finance. The financial performance of a firm declines in the absence of a sustainable strategy (Integrated Governance 2014).

3.8 Integrated Governance Framework

There are three main views of an integrated governance framework: architecture, domain, and presentation. Table 3.9 summarizes the requirements of the integrated governance framework (Park et al. 2006).

The security governance framework consists of three domains: community, security, and performance. Every domain has several objects that perform the functions. There are two relationships among the domains: harmonization and flywheel. The harmonization category governs the relationships between three domains and deals with social, organizational, and human factors of enterprise security. The flywheel category governs the relationship between performance and security domain and deals with the virtuous cycle of enterprise security (Park et al. 2006). Figure 3.8 presents the integrated security governance framework.

The framework integrates government, shareholders and management, media and customers, and employee and supplier to perform four major tasks. The government creates the standards and policies that the enterprise works in compliance with, media and customers endorse security programs, employees and suppliers are bound to agreements with the enterprise, and shareholders and management align themselves with the security standards and policies of the enterprise.

The community domain contains people such as shareholders and management who give directives and are directly affected by the profits and losses in the enterprise. Performance domain performs cost and benefit analysis based on the availability of resources and their competitive value. As already mentioned, every resource brings a competitive value to the business. The security domain deals with risks and their value to impact the security of the enterprise. It also consists of an enterprise strategy to produce value to resources.

3.9 The Integrated Framework Assessment

Assessing an integrated framework is oriented around governance structure, management structure, operations/infrastructure, and compensation/funds flow.

Table 3.9 Requirements of the integrated security governance framework

View	Requirements
Architecture	• Clear relationships among domains • Partitioning the domains in enterprise security
Domain	• Consider every participant of the enterprise security • Characteristics of business information • Cost and benefit analysis • Subdivisions of security controls and strategies
Presentation	• Bird-eye view of security governance framework • Structured presentation of every object in enterprise security

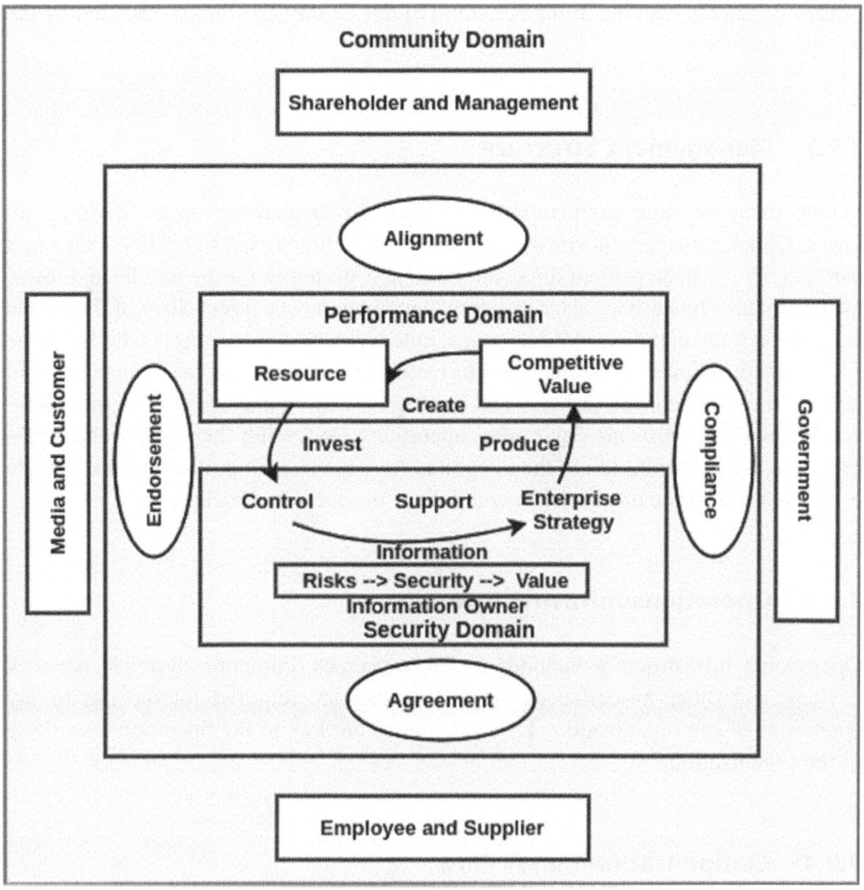

Fig. 3.8 Integrated security governance framework (Park et al. 2006)

3.9.1 Governance Structure

The governance structure is used interchangeably with the governance framework as they both refer to the structure of the governance of an organization. It reflects the interrelated relationship, factors, and other influences upon the enterprise. It governs and manages various roles in the organization. It also sets rules, procedures, and other informational guidelines for various business units in the enterprise. In addition to that, it defines, guides, and provides for the enforcement of business processes.

Organizations adopt a governance structure to secure their information assets. The governance structure is considered a corporate governance issue that spans across the entire enterprise. As mentioned earlier, corporate governance can be modeled using the direct and control cycle. Directing starts at the top management level and proceeds downwards while controlling follows the reverse direction.

Controlling deals with the implementation of day-to-day operations designed by the top management.

3.9.2 Management Structure

Management structure comprises three levels of management: upper, middle, and lower. Upper management consists of the board of directors, CEO, CFO, COO, and partners. Upper management directs policies and strategies for the middle and lower management. The individuals in upper management have a direct share of the profits and losses of the company. Middle management consists of managers who bring the documented policies and strategies into reality. They direct the lower management people to implement the policies and strategies. Lower management is the operational force that performs day-to-day operations. Assessing the levels of management and their contribution to the integrated framework is important as these people bring business to the organization and deliver products to the clients.

3.9.3 Operations/Infrastructure

Operational infrastructure includes assets, resources, computer systems, network devices, and other miscellaneous resources that are required for the day-to-day operations of the organization. These resources are key to the operational working of the organization.

3.9.4 Compensation/Funds Flow

Compensation and cash flow mandate that bonuses are paid out for the right reason. As a result, executives are asked to report on cash flow, working capital, and return on investment. The other side of cash flow is earnings and revenues. There needs to be a balance between the total expenditures and total earnings which is maintained by recording every transaction in a balance sheet (Bodeau et al. 2010). Assessing the compensation or cash flow ensures that the organization has sufficient funds to invest in a business.

3.10 A General Information Security Governance Model for FinTech

The integrated security governance framework lays the foundation of a general information security governance model for FinTech. Working on the same pattern, an information security governance model for FinTech is proposed and presented in Fig. 3.9. It comprises three domains (community, performance, and security) and

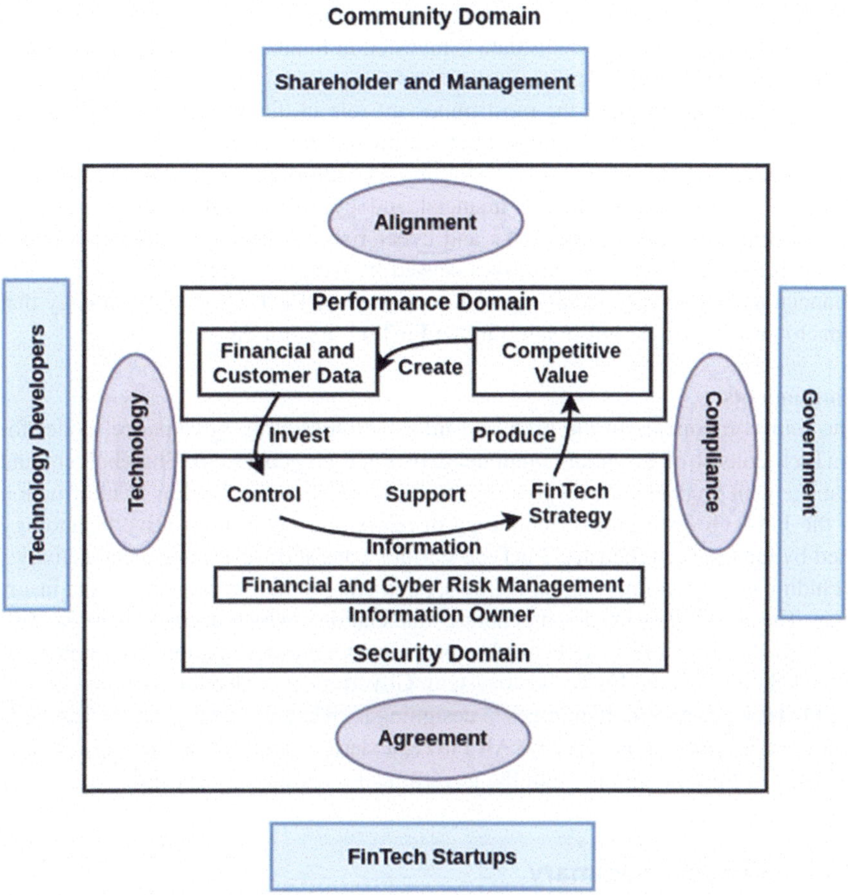

Fig. 3.9 A general information security governance model for FinTech

four main components (shareholders and management, technology developers, FinTech startups, and government).

Domains

Community domain consists of shareholders and management personnel who take directives and pass them to the bottom level of the FinTech institution. These directives include security policies and strategies that help protect financial information. Shareholders are directly impacted by the profits and losses of the financial institution. Members of the community domain must align the business objectives of the FinTech institution with the security objectives. Performance domain contains financial and customer data such as expenditure, income, participating entities (buyers and sellers), customers, and payments, to name a few. Every data is counted as a resource for the FinTech institution, and it adds value to the overall institutional assets. Since it adds value to an institution, it is considered a competitive data and needs protection. Moreover, this data is invested in financial transactions performed by the participating entities.

The third domain plays the most important role in this model as it protects the information, assets, and resources. FinTech institutions are prone to financial risks which may lead to cyber risks. Therefore, the information security governance model must consider managing financial and cyber risks. It needs to map the relationship between financial risks and cyber risks. A detailed mapping between financial risks and security objectives caused by them is provided in Chap. 7. The financial and cyber risk management is supported by FinTech security strategy that aims to protect critical information in the FinTech institution.

Components

The four components in the proposed information security governance model for FinTech consist of essential components of FinTech ecosystem. Shareholders and management prepare security policies and strategies to direct the flow of information in the FinTech institution. Technology developers develop innovative technology used by the FinTech industry. FinTech startups consist of several financial activities including crowdfunding, capital markets, payments, wealth management, and insurance. These activities need and generate financial data which needs to be protected. FinTech startups work in agreement to provide a secure information environment to all stakeholders in the FinTech ecosystem. Government is also an important part of the FinTech ecosystem. It indulges in designing legislatures and regulatory standards that govern information security. All FinTech startups and managerial policies in a FinTech institution comply with the government's regulatory standards.

3.11 Chapter Summary

This chapter introduces information security governance, various policies and standards used to profile information security governance, and available security governance models. It provides insight into the roles and responsibilities of various personnel in three levels of management in an organization. Based on the levels of management, a security governance framework comprises directing and controlling as two main function lines that are supported by the execution of policies and strategies by lower management. The chapter further presents an integrated framework for information security governance which consists of important domains, components, individuals, their activities, and outcomes. Based on the integrated security framework, a general information security governance framework for FinTech is proposed toward the end of the chapter.

Information security governance can be linked to government, traditional financial institutions, and FinTech startup components of the FinTech ecosystem. Government drafts the legislatures and regulations for a governance program. Financial institutions and FinTech startups have the three levels of management just like any other organization. The following questions are addressed in this chapter:

- What is information security governance and why is it important for an organization to secure information?
- Who are the people involved in an organization and what are their roles and responsibilities?
- Which information security governance models are available?
- What are the characteristics of effective information security governance?
- What are the important components of comprehensive security governance?
- What is an integrated governance framework and how can we assess it?

References

Asgarkhani, M., Correia, E., & Sarkar, A. (2017). An overview of information security governance. In *2017 International Conference on Algorithms, Methodology, Models and Applications in Emerging Technologies (ICAMMAET)* (pp. 1–4). India: IEEE.

Asset and Data Management. (2019). https://www.educause.edu/focus-areas-and-initiatives/policy-and-security/cybersecurity-program/resources/information-security-guide/asset-and-data-management#AssetandDataManagement-Assets.

Bodeau, D., Boyle, S., Fabius-Greene, J., & Graubart, R. (2010). *Cyber security governance, a component of MITRE's cyber prep methodology, Mitre technical report*, pp. 1–45.

Bradford District Care. (2020). *Integrated governance guide: Supporting high-quality governance standards for our colleagues and their teams* (pp. 1–27). Bradford: Bradford District Care.

CGI Group. (2015). *IT security governance – a holistic approach* (pp. 1–8). Montreal: CGI Group.

Chen, J. (2021). Corporate governance, Investopedia. https://www.investopedia.com/terms/c/corporategovernance.asp.

Coertze, J., & von Solms, R. (2013). A model for information security governance in developing countries. In K. Jonas, I. A. Rai, & M. Tchuente (Eds.), *e-infrastructure and e-services for developing countries. AFRICOMM 2012. Lecture notes of the Institute for Computer Sciences, social informatics and telecommunications engineering* (Vol. 119, pp. 279–288). Berlin, Heidelberg: Springer.

Eapen, S. (2017). *How to build effective sustainability Governance structures*. https://www.bsr.org/en/our-insights/blog-view/how-to-build-effective-sustainability-governance-structures.

Garza, F. A. (2013). A framework for strategic sustainability in organizations: A three-pronged approach. *Journal of Comparative International Management, 16*(1), 23–36.

Information Security Governance Assessment Tool for Higher Education. (2006). https://er.educause.edu/-/media/files/articles/2006/1/sec0421.pdf?la=en&hash=8F3053026C559CD17E351E87BCD9B57BE73BA686#:~:text=The%20Information%20Security%20Governance%20(ISG,strategic%20level%20within%20their%20institution.

Information Security Governance Policy. (2016). *IT-INFOSEC-CP001*, pp. 1–2.

Information Security Program Assessment Tool. (2015). https://library.educause.edu/resources/2015/11/information-security-program-assessment-tool.

Integrated Governance. (2014). *A new model of Governance for sustainability, a report by the Asset management working group of the united nations environment Programmer finance initiative*, pp. 1–64.

Integrated Governance Handbook. (2015). *Lancashire Care*, pp. 1–21.

IT Governance Institute. (2006). *Information security governance: guidance for boards of directors and executive management* (2nd ed.). Rolling Meadows, Ill: IT Governance Institute.

KPMG. (2019). *Third party governance/cloud compliance* (pp. 1–2). Amsterdam: KPMG.

Love, P., Reinhard, J., Schwab, A. J., & Spafford, G. (2010). *Information security governance, IPPF – Practice guide* (pp. 1–28).

Park, H., Kim, S., & Lee, H. J. (2006). *General drawing of the integrated framework for security governance, knowledge-based intelligent information and engineering systems* (pp. 1234–1241). Berlin, Heidelberg: Springer-Verlag.

Racz, N., Weippl, E., & Seufert, A. (2010). *A process model for integrated IT governance, risk, and compliance management.*

Selig, G. J. (2016). IT governance-an integrated framework and roadmap: how to plan, deploy and sustain for improved effectiveness. *Journal of International Technology and Information Management, 25*(1, Art 4):55–76.

Stallings, W. (2018). *Understanding information security governance, inform IT.* https://www.informit.com/articles/article.aspx?p=2931571&seqNum=2.

Ula, M., Ismail, Z. B. T., & Sidek, Z. M. (2011). A framework for the Governance of information Security in banking system. *Journal of Information Assurance & Cybersecurity, 2011*, 1–12.

Vendor and Third-Party Management. (2019). https://www.educause.edu/focus-areas-and-initiatives/policy-and-security/cybersecurity-program/resources/information-security-guide/vendor-and-thirdparty-management

Von Solms, R., Thomson, K.-L., & Maninjwa, M. (2011). Information security governance control through comprehensive policy architectures. *Information Security for South Africa*, 1–6.

Williams, A. P. (2001). Information security governance. *Information Security Technical Report, 6* (3), 60–70.

Cybersecurity Threats in FinTech

4

With the use of a plethora of digital wallet methods, financial cyber risks such as fraudulent transactions, extortion, denial of service attacks, and credit card fraud have also become frequent. These cyberattacks are capable enough to cause systemic risk to the financial sector. Some of the most prominent cyberattacks that the financial sector has witnessed so far have impacted critical economic infrastructures such as messaging systems. These attacks have the potential to deliberately destroy hardware and compromise sensitive business data to adversely impact services.

Data breach and distributed denial of service (DDoS) are the two most common cyberattacks that have been recorded on a regular basis in the timeline of cyber risks and threats on FinTech across the globe. Figure 4.1 highlights the reported cyberattacks and threats that incurred major monetary losses to financial institutions and banks between 2007 and 2019. It is evident that cyber threats pose severe risks to FinTech over the years.

Out of the reported cyberattacks, data breaches, malware, DDoS attack, and hacking are the most popular ones. Attackers steal passwords and sensitive information to perform data breaches. On the more technical side, SQL injections are a common and popular method to steal data from the database server. SQL (Structured Query Language) is a language used to select, insert, delete, and manipulate data stored in a database. Attackers use SQL queries and inject malicious parameters into them to steal data from the database.

Ransomware attacks such as WannaCry and NoPetya have created havoc in the financial stability of leading FinTech companies. Attackers used cross-site scripting (XSS) to exploit web application vulnerabilities to steal sensitive financial data on several occasions. In addition, cybercriminals also used spear-phishing emails to infect bank's computer systems in the Carbanak attack in 2013 (Johnson 2016). In spear-phishing emails, attackers target a specific group of recipients, such as a business group, to steal sensitive information.

In one of the popular examples, JPMorgan Chase, ranked sixth-largest American bank in the world, reported a data breach of over 7 million small businesses and 76 million households in 2014. This data breach is considered one of the most

G. Kaur et al., *Understanding Cybersecurity Management in FinTech*, Future of Business and Finance, https://doi.org/10.1007/978-3-030-79915-1_4

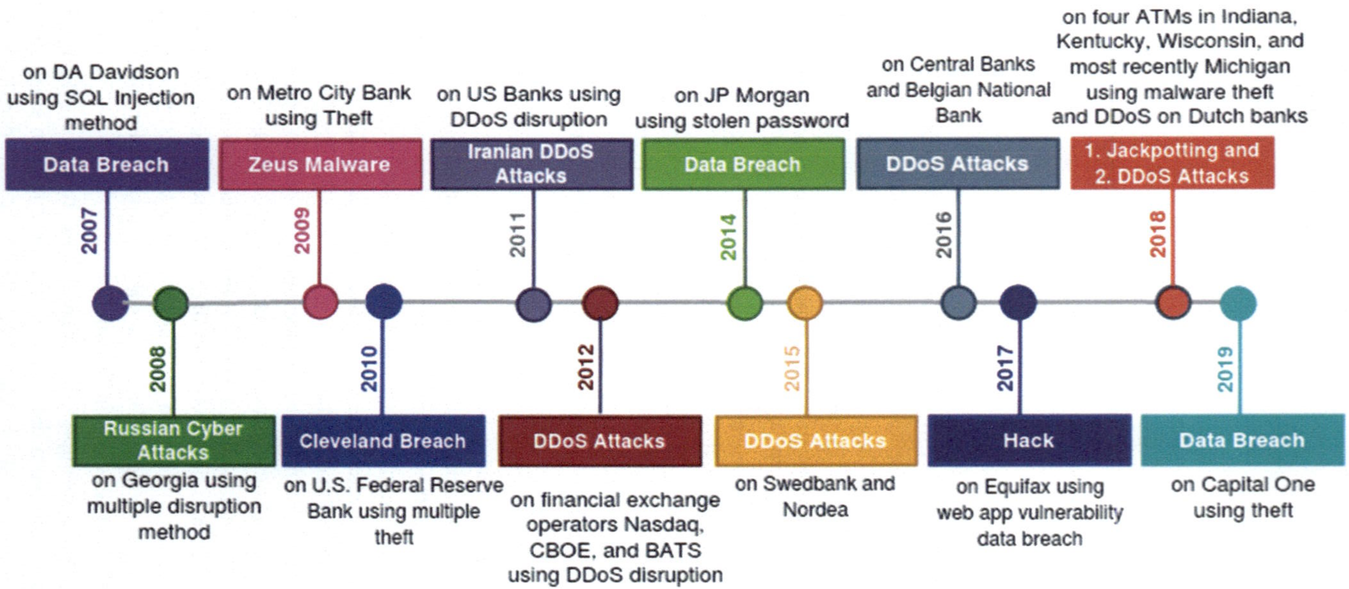

Fig. 4.1 Timeline of cyber risks and threats on FinTech across the globe (Timeline of Cyber Incidents Involving Financial Institutions 2021)

serious intrusions into one of the world's highly secure banking infrastructures. The hackers stole personally identifiable information, including email, phone numbers, names, and postal addresses associated with bank accounts. However, the bank denied that passwords were stolen in the breach (Morgan 2014).

Similarly, Capital One, the world's tenth-largest American bank, is the recent victim of the data breach. In the attack, a hacker gained access to over 100 million customers' bank accounts and credit card applications in 2019. The hacker was blamed for sharing the stolen social security numbers, social insurance numbers, and bank account numbers with others online (McLean 2019). These incidents quote the severity and intensity with which cybercriminals have targeted FinTech companies to gain financial benefits and disrupt financial services.

To summarize, the FinTech industry is afraid of cyberattacks that intend to cause harm to various aspects of the business. Cyberattacks steal data, cause financial losses, result in reputation loss, and tarnish the industrial image. All these activities pose severe threats to the Fintech industry.

This chapter introduces a new paradigm of cybersecurity that helps understand cybersecurity threats, actions of an adversary, and different threat categories for FinTech. After knowing the fundamental details, the next section will lead the path to introduce the threat landscape by getting familiar with distinct types of threat actors, threat intelligence, and threat modeling.

4.1 Understanding Cybersecurity Threats

The word "cyber" derives its origin from cybernetics—the science of understanding the movement of machines. In the current era, the term is used to describe information security matters. A cyber threat is a malicious act to steal sensitive data, disrupt normal operations, damage data, or make it unavailable to use. Cyber threats are caused by unauthorized personnel (commonly cyberattackers) attempting to access authorized information. Some common cyberattacks include malware, ransomware, DoS, DDoS, data breach, and phishing.

It is also not always true that cyber threats result from illegitimate acts of unauthorized personnel only. Authorized personnel can also pose serious cyber threats by misusing their authority and privileges. In some cases, organizational employees can cause potential damage unintentionally. For example, an employee can be a victim of a phishing attack if he clicks a malicious link that secretly downloads malware on his workstation/computer to create a backdoor.

According to the FinTech security analysis report of 2017 (NSFocus 2017), by the end of 2021, cybercrime damages to the world will be increased by USD 3 trillion to reach USD 6 trillion when compared to 2015. Since financial institutions have been incorporated into the Internet, they are a major target of cyber attackers. According to the same report, 60% of financial institutions use cloud services, most of which are private clouds.

Understanding the threat landscape is the need of the hour as cyber threats are becoming more sophisticated with increased variety and volume of attacks. The manifestation of cyber threats results in a security incident that compromises the confidentiality, integrity, or availability of data. These results confirm the disclosure of sensitive financial information to unauthorized external or authorized internal personnel.

Cyber threats represent adverse effects on assets. Therefore, it is pertinent to accurately identify potential threats that pose significant challenges to financial assets. Despite its rapid growth, privacy and security are the biggest threats to FinTech companies that store overly sensitive personal and organizational information such as credit cards, social security numbers, bank account numbers, and income details.

With emerging technologies such as artificial intelligence and machine learning, perpetrators can launch more sophisticated cyberattacks which can take autonomous decisions and possess self-learning capabilities to identify and exploit system weaknesses. Some of the important threat categories for FinTech are discussed in the forthcoming subsections.

4.2 Understanding the Adversary

Oxford dictionary defines an adversary as "a person that somebody is opposed to and competing with in an argument or a battle." Similarly, in cybersecurity, an adversary is an attacker who uses various tactics, techniques, and procedures (TTPs) to breach the security of an organizational network. The ultimate objective of the adversary is to install rootkits and backdoors to return to the network without being noticed to steal data, make essential operations unavailable to legitimate users, disrupt services, and avoid detection.

From the viewpoint of the cybersecurity team, knowing the enemy is important as it helps to identify attackers' motives and types of threats. In the next step, it aids to create a prioritized list of detection and prevention capabilities that need to be in place to stop the adversary.

> *Know that enemy and know yourself; in a hundred battles, you will never be defeated. When you are ignorant of the enemy but know yourself, your chances of winning or losing are equal. If ignorant both of your enemy and of yourself, you are sure to be defeated in every battle.*—Sun Tzu.

This famous quote holds true in cyber warfare also. According to CrowdStrike's Global Security Survey (Global Security Attitude Survey 2019), only 19% of UK respondents believe that it is important to understand the tactics of attackers. This is alarming because security professionals overlook the importance of knowing their adversaries and understanding their motives. Understanding the adversary helps to streamline the following information:

- Determine the weaknesses in the system.
- Chalk out the threats that can exploit those weaknesses.

- Who can exploit the identified weaknesses and how?
- Identify indicators of compromise (IOCs) and attack vectors.

Indicators of compromise aid security professionals to detect malicious infections, data breaches, or other threats. Some important parameters used as indicators of compromise include log entries, hashes of files, unusual outgoing network traffic, and suspicious file changes.

An attack vector presents the method used by an attacker to breach the security of the network. Some common attack vectors include unpatched software, social engineering, phishing, reused passwords, and misconfigurations.

This information is indispensable to improve the security of the organization and foresee future attacks. Simply put, this information will help organizations to protect their assets and limit potential damage from a cyberattack.

4.3 Threat Categories for FinTech

FinTech companies face the most prevalent cyber threats. This section defines paramount cyber threats to FinTech startups.

- **Malware:** Malware is malicious software specially designed to disrupt, damage, or gain unauthorized access to a computer system to steal sensitive information. Malware can be classified as Adware, Ransomware, Riskware, Scareware, Spyware, Trojan horse, Virus, Worm, and Zero-day. Every form of malware can perform divergent functions such as stealing information, encrypting files and directories on infected computers, deleting data, altering registry files, and illicitly monitoring user information.
- **Adware:** Adware represents advertisement malware. It is a malicious application that throws unwanted advertisements on the user's screen, especially when accessing web services. Adware lures the user toward flashing advertisements that offer lucrative products and attract them to click on the advertisement. Once a user clicks on the advertisement, revenue is generated by the developer of this unwanted application. Some common examples of adware include weight loss programs, making money in less time, and bogus virus warnings on screen. This is not the only way that adware attacks users. Some adware samples are downloaded when any software or application is installed on the smartphone.
- **Ransomware:** Ransomware is malware that encrypts files and directories on the machine to make them inaccessible to users. It asks for a handsome amount of ransom to provide the decryption key that is used to unlock the data. Ransoms are often paid for bitcoins. Certain incidents, however, have confirmed that some users were unable to get their data back after paying the ransom. Some of them reported receiving incomplete files. At times, files simply vanished. One cannot confirm that paying a ransom is helpful. Android ransomware has evolved significantly, and new variants are emerging. Some ransomware samples masquerade as popular apps and manage to escape detection.

- **Riskware:** Riskware is a legitimate program that poses potential risks to the security vulnerabilities on the device. Although it is a genuine program, it is used to steal information from the device and redirect users to malicious websites. It can be alternatively termed as risky software that performs functions at the cost of device security. Riskware families collect personal and phone information, send/receive SMSs, steal network information, connect to malicious websites, install malicious content on devices, show malicious advertisements, and modify system settings and files on the device.
- **Scareware:** Scareware is a fear coaxer that raises fear in users' minds to download or buy malicious apps. For example, convincing users to install a fake application that pretends to safeguard the device. Scareware families attempt to collect device information and Global Positioning System (GPS) location and install malicious code on the device.
- **Spyware:** Spyware is malicious software that can steal sensitive information once installed on the device. The data collected by spyware is passed to advertisers, external agencies, or firms. This data is later used to carry out malicious activities. Android asks users to provide permission to access device information such as location, camera, and settings, but spyware is installed without the user's authorization. Spyware families collect personal information, send/receive SMSs, collect phone information and device location, steal network information such as Wi-Fi connections to which the device is connected, and access system files and settings to modify them.
- **Trojan:** Trojans are sneaky impersonators that behave like legitimate programs. They can hide in the background and steal information from the device. It is the biggest malware category that represents several malware categories including trojan-banker, trojan-dropper, trojan-SMS, and trojan-spy. Trojans often engage in removing, changing, blocking, and copying data to disrupt services provided by the operating system.
- **Virus:** Virus is a computer program that replicates itself by changing other programs and inserting its own code. Computer viruses require a host program. The virus writes its own code into the host program. When the host program is run, the malicious part of the program is executed first to infect the computer system.
- **Worm:** Worm is a computer program that does not require a host program. It replicates itself to spread to other computer systems. A worm uses the target machine to infect other machines on the network.
- **Zero-day:** Zero-day is a vulnerability that is unknown to the security community. Zero-day is referred to as the duration in which the vulnerability is not known to people and a malicious program is developed to exploit the vulnerability. Once the vulnerability is made public, vendors develop the patch to fix it.
- **Data Breach:** Data breach is the act of leaking sensitive or confidential data either intentionally or unintentionally to any untrusted party. It is also called data leak, information leakage, and data spill. Most of the time, it has targeted banks and credit cards across the globe. Figure 4.1 demonstrates major FinTech data breaches detected in the last couple of years.

- **Denial of Service:** Denial of Service (DoS) is a targeted attack launched against a computer system, server, or network to make the services unavailable to legitimate clients.
- **Distributed Denial of Service:** Distributed Denial of Service (DDoS) is one of the lethal and targeted attacks involving multiple attackers and multiple compromised systems. The DDoS attacks have impacted all the major economies of the world ever since their origin. It leverages client/server architecture to use several computers to target a specific computer to flood it with requests so that it is unable to render its services to legitimate clients. The main difference between a DoS and DDoS attack is that in a DoS attack, a single attacker targets a single computer while in a DDoS attack, multiple attackers target a single computer.
- **Cryptojacking:** Cryptojacking is the unauthorized use of someone else's computer to mine cryptocurrency. Attackers do this by luring the victim to click on a malicious link in a phishing email. Clicking the link automatically loads the malicious code into the victim machine.
- **Digital vandalism:** Digital vandalism is the act of defacing the digital assets of a company or individual to cause damage or nuisance. It is not a fundamental problem, but the number of instances has increased in recent years. Digital vandalism is a modern form of physical vandalism. Hackers hack the technology to disrupt the availability of digital assets of a person or company. In a digital vandal incident in 2015, Google organized a map creation event on its Map Maker. Digital vandals created an illustration of an Android mascot urinating on Apple's logo which was visible to the public. It was removed by Google later.
- **Cyber fraud and forgery:** Cyber fraud and forgery is the act of making unauthentic digital documents and using them to commit a crime. Cybercriminals counterfeit the documents, create forged documents that appear indistinguishable from the original documents, and use these documents as proof to avoid safeguarding cyber documents.
- **Spamming:** Spamming is the process of sending unwanted messages or emails to a person or group of people. Spam messages include offers, advertisements, brochures, and pamphlets. The purpose of spamming is commercial advertising. Phishing is an example of spamming.
- **Man-In-The-Middle (MITM) attack:** In a MITM attack, an interceptor listens to the communication between a sender and receiver and attempts to modify the data transmitted between the two parties.
- **Insider threats:** Insider attacks involve authorized personnel within the organization who attempt to exploit security issues. The seriousness of this attack can be estimated from the fact that authorized insiders are the trusted users of an organization and if they breach the code of conduct to exploit the potential resources of their employer, it may bring more financial or reputation damage to the organization.
- **Cloud-based threats:** Cloud-based attacks are launched to take control of user's data stored on the cloud.
- **Phishing:** Phishing is a cyberattack in which the attacker sends emails to victims so that the recipients click on some malicious link in an attachment or fill a form

containing their sensitive data. Phishing can be classified as spear phishing, vishing, and whaling.

Table 4.1 presents several instances of cyberattacks launched against financial institutions between 2007 and 2020. The intensity of the attack is estimated to be based on financial damage associated with it. It is imperative to mention that these threats are reported publicly. The actual number is certainly extremely high since many cyber threats in the financial sector are never reported in lieu of reputation and business loss.

Apart from the reported attacks in Table 4.1, some other recent cyber threat attempts include hijacking famous Twitter accounts for bitcoin (USA), Scotia Bank data breach (Canada), ransomware attacks (USA), GoldenSpy malware in tax software (China), DDoS attacks (Europe), dForce cryptocurrency (China), and DDoS extortion (Australia). To sum up, cyberattacks have targeted financial institutions and banks all over the world.

4.4 Threat Actors

Threat actors are the unauthorized individuals or groups behind launching cyberattacks on any organization. Although the alleged personnel remain the same for every organization, yet a special workforce of attackers is observed for financial institutions. Some of the prominent threat actors identified based on the history of cyberattacks targeting the financial sector are listed below:

- **Malicious insiders:** Malicious insiders have always proved to be one of the most dangerous threat actors. These are authorized people who have the rights and permissions to access, read, write, and transfer critical private and proprietary data of a financial institution, especially in banks. There are several examples of malicious insiders exploiting known vulnerabilities to steal sensitive data and share it with business rivals for their personal financial gain and to lower the business reputation of the employer. Furthermore, he can provide a cybercriminal with knowledge about how the system functions and where to find the critical data. The severe aspect of malicious insiders is that they may go unnoticed for a long time. According to IBM's Cost of a Data Breach Report 2020 (IBM 2020), the average cost of data breaches is $6.71 million. It includes both system glitches and human error. Additionally, the average cost of cyber incidents, across different sectors, is $4.37 million. In HSBC bank's internal fraud case in 2008 (Timeline of Cyber Incidents Involving Financial Institutions 2021), a clerk at its headquarters in London fraudulently wired €90 million to accounts in Manchester and Morocco. The clerk used passwords stolen from his colleagues to execute these transactions. However, he was arrested later and was sent to jail for 9 years.
- **Hacktivists:** Hacktivists perform politically or religiously motivated activities to misuse a computer system or network. The act of performing such activities is called hacktivism. Hacktivists are also called hackers in simple terms. They act in

Table 4.1 Reported cyber risks and attacks on FinTech (2007–2020) (Timeline of Cyber Incidents Involving Financial Institutions 2021; Marsh and McLennan Companies 2018)

Attack category	Examples	Year	Country	Intensity
Malware	ATMDtrack	2019	India	3
	GozNym	2019	Bulgaria	3
			Germany	
			Georgia	
			Moldova	
			Ukraine	
			USA	
	Metel	2015	Russia	2
	NoPetya	2017	Australia	2
			Europe	
			Ukraine	
			USA	
	Ploutus	2013	Connecticut	3
			Mexico	
			Rhode Island	
			USA	
	Retefe	2019	Germany	3
			Switzerland	
	Skimer	2009	Multiple	2
	Ursnif	2019	Japan	3
	WannaCry	2017	China	2
			Russia	
			UK	
			USA	
	Zeus	2009	Multiple	2
	Cerberus	2020	Spain	2
Data Breach	SQL Injection	2007	USA	4
	Stolen Credit Card	2020	Indonesia	3
			Malaysia	
			Philippines	
			Singapore	
			Thailand	
			Vietnam	
	Stolen Password	2014	USA	4
	Theft	2010	Japan	4
		2019	UK	4
			USA	
Distributed Denial of Service	Ransomware	2007	Estonia	2
	Pinch Malware	2008	Georgia	2
		2009	South Korea	2
			USA	
			USA	2

(continued)

Table 4.1 (continued)

Attack category	Examples	Year	Country	Intensity
		2011/12		
		2013	China	2
		2015	Greece	2
		2016	Russia	2
		2020	Australia	2
Insider	Insider Hack	2008	UK	5
	Fraud	2016	USA	5
Cloud-based	Data Breach/Theft	2019	Canada	5
			USA	
Phishing	Spear Phishing	2015	USA	5
		2019	USA	5
		2020	USA	2
	ThreadKit—an exploit builder kit	2018	Belarus	4
			Bulgaria	
			Czech Republic	
			Hungary	
			Moldova	
			Poland	
			Romania	
			Slovakia	
			Ukraine	

groups and collaborate to coordinate a politically acclaimed cyberattack on major financial institutions of the country. Hackers are curious to know innovative ways of breaching security and follow a defined procedure to launch attacks. In a related incident in 2016, some anonymous hacktivists took down the website of the Bank of Greece, and the central banks of Mexico, Panama, Kenya, Bosnia, and Herzegovina by launching a DDoS attack (Timeline of Cyber Incidents Involving Financial Institutions 2021). One of the infamous hacktivist groups is "Anonymous," which carried out Operation Payback (Fowler 2016), comprising hundreds of DDoS attacks to disrupt web services, preventing users from accessing them.

- **Cybercriminals:** Cybercriminals are individuals or groups of techno-savvy professionals who use technology to commit malicious activities on digital systems or networks to steal sensitive data for financial gains. They are popular for accessing underground markets found on the dark web to trade illegitimate goods and services such as weapons, banned medicines, adult content, and narcotics. Cybercriminals infiltrate computer systems with the intention of finding useful information to launch targeted attacks. They focus on multiple systems or networks rather than concentrating on a single system. They are unlikely to follow defined steps or procedures that fulfill their malicious deeds. To instantiate, an international group of cybercriminals used GozNym malware to steal $100 million from over 40,000 victims, including bank accounts, law firms, small businesses, international corporations, and nonprofit organizations in 2019 (Timeline of Cyber Incidents Involving Financial Institutions 2021).

- **Third party:** Several financial firms use cloud-based services to store their customer data. Cloud services can be private, public, or hybrid. Based on the type of cloud services purchased by the firm, it is prone to several types of threats. The cloud services provided by the third party could be hacked by various threat actors including malicious insiders, hacktivists, and cybercriminals. In 2019, Capital One bank suffered a data breach by a software engineer who hacked into the cloud-based server compromising credit card applications of around 100 million customers. These applications contained sensitive customer data including name, address, social insurance number, date of birth, credit scores, and contact information. The hacker exploited a misconfigured firewall to access a database of personal information hosted by Amazon Web Services (AWS).
- **Nation-states:** Nation-state actors or state-sponsored actors are well funded and sophisticated. They are sponsored by a government entity. They are long-term players in the sense that they perform tactics and techniques to deploy attack payload on targeted systems. They are experts in being unnoticed for months or years and quietly carry out malicious activities. Nation-state activities in the past include DDoS attacks, destructive malware, and cyber reconnaissance of critical infrastructure. One of the recent nation-state attacks is the NoPetya ransomware outbreak in 2017 that targeted Australia, Europe, Ukraine, and the USA. NoPetya is considered the fastest propagating malware ever. The attack originated because of conflict between Russia and Ukraine. Russian military hacking groups deployed NoPetya to target Ukraine, but it impacted several other countries too.
- **Cyber terrorists:** Cyber terrorists are involved in carrying out malicious activities to shut down the critical infrastructure (energy, transportation, and government operations) of the target. These activities fall under cyber terrorism which is considered the new cyberwar. Cyber terrorists are politically motivated organized criminals who cover a broad threat landscape to conduct online terrorist activities such as vandalism, deliberately disrupting services, sending phishing emails, and deploying malware. The purpose of cyber terrorists is to cause massive damage to government systems, hospital data, and national security of a country to spread terror. Researchers classify NoPetya and WannaCry ransomware as an act of cyber terrorism.
- **Script kiddies:** Script kiddies are beginners or unskilled people who are lured to cybercrime activities but are inefficient to write their own code. Therefore, they search the internet to use already developed code. Script kiddies leave significant fingerprints of their activities when they do something for a thrilling experience.

Table 4.2 compares several types of threat actors based on their target and motivation and proposes the best defense strategy against their activities.

Table 4.2 Comparison of several types of threat actors

Threat actor	Target	Motivation	Best defense
Malicious insiders	Local employer organization	Dissatisfaction, rivalry	Separation of duties, lease privilege to resources
Hacktivists	Government, corporations, or individuals	Political, social, religious, and economic	Understanding tactics, techniques, and practices
Cybercriminal	Enterprises	Financial gain	Good cyber practices
Third party	Enterprises	Data breach for financial gain or reputation loss	Good cyber practices, intrusion detection, and prevention tools
Nation-states	Any computer	Cyberwarfare for political, economic, or military agenda	Patch and vulnerability management
Cyber terrorists	Government, military, critical infrastructure	Political, religious, economic, military agenda	Vulnerability management and threat hunting
Script kiddies	Any computer	Reputation among peers	Defensive tools

4.5 Threat Intelligence

Threat intelligence is a term used to represent information about threats and threat actors. Cyber threat intelligence refers to information related to cyber threats and cyber threat actors. Information sources for gathering threat intelligence include human intelligence, technology, social media, and open-source intelligence. Threat intelligence also considers dark web and deep web information. For the purpose of introducing this concept, we will start with the basic information.

Cybersecurity professionals use diverse types of tactics, operations, and strategies to collect intelligent information that may prove helpful in mitigating the threats before the onslaught. Figure 4.2 demonstrates three types of threat intelligence.

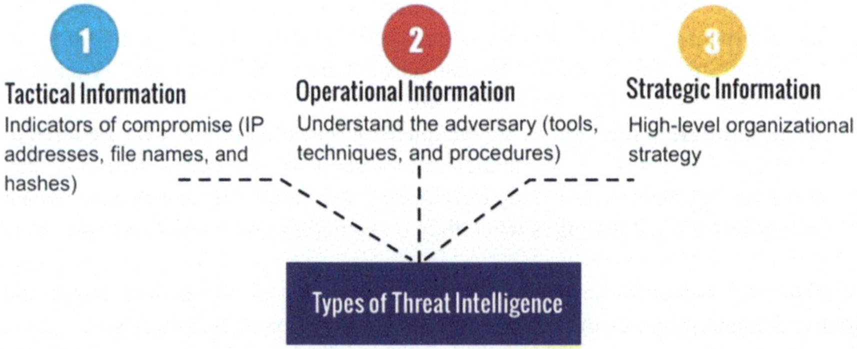

Fig. 4.2 Three types of threat Intelligence

- **Tactical information:** It includes technical information collected by using technology and tools. Tactical information includes indicators of compromise such as IP addresses, file names, and hashes. This information is helpful in identifying the threat actors.
- **Operational information:** Operational information collects the details of understanding the adversary by identifying his tools, techniques, and procedures. It also aids to determine the motivations behind carrying out a cyberattack.
- **Strategic information:** It maps the risks associated with cyber threats to create a high-level organizational strategy. The strategy outlines the risks associated with the organization and plans to accept, avoid, detect, prevent, or deny a risk.

After collecting multifaceted information from distinct types of threat intelligence methods, security professionals empower organizations to develop a proactive cybersecurity posture and reframe their policies to include risk management. The following are the benefits of cyber threat intelligence:

- **Better risk management:** Organizations include risk management as a part of their planning process. This makes them understand and predict the risks that may prove dangerous in the future and how to tackle those risks.
- **Improved decisions:** Foreseeing the risks helps in a better and informed decision-making process. This way organizations can prevent cyber threats and intrusions.
- **Proactive cybersecurity posture:** Threat intelligence facilitates organizations to empower a proactive cybersecurity posture which includes advanced threat detection and prevention tools. It prepares organizations for future cyberattacks by learning from the historic and present data.
- **Improved threat detection:** Collecting useful threat information in advance proves extremely helpful to detect threats before they exploit the vulnerabilities and cause potential damage.
- **Know the enemy:** Threat intelligence collects operational information that reveals the motivations of attackers to launch cyberattacks. Understanding the adversary and his moves in a war allows the defender to update his strategy and protect crucial assets. The same is true in cybersecurity warfare.

4.6 Structural Approach to FinTech Threat Modeling

FinTech threat modeling follows a structural approach to identify, categorize, and analyze cyber threats. It can be performed as a proactive or reactive measure. It comprises a series of events starting from the design of a plan to the implementation and review of a threat plan. The goals of the threat plan are to reduce threats and consequences of the aftermath. In other words, it attempts to reduce the vulnerabilities and their impact on the FinTech institution.

A proactive threat modeling approach is also called a defensive approach that aims to defend the FinTech institutions against cyberattacks. It is based on predicting threats so that early warnings can be issued, and resources can be secured. However, it is impossible to predict all cyber threats in real time. This fact makes the proactive approach less practical. Therefore, the proactive threat modeling approach is ineffective to protect FinTech institutions from all kinds of cyber threats.

Alternatively, the reactive threat modeling approach protects against adversarial attacks by taking appropriate actions to prevent a cyber threat. It is also known as the adversarial approach and includes ethical hacking and penetration testing techniques.

The primary objective of both approaches is to accurately identify potential threats that can exploit vulnerabilities in the FinTech institution and result in huge financial losses. In order to achieve this objective, FinTech institutions focus on assets, attackers, or software. The selection of an appropriate structural approach entirely depends on the type of FinTech, its size, and investment in a business.

4.6.1 Focusing on Assets

This method uses asset valuation results to identify threats to valuable assets. For example, a specific asset is evaluated to determine if it is vulnerable to cyber threats. If the asset holds sensitive information or user data, it is susceptible to a data breach as a cyber threat. Lost data causes data availability issues. Similarly, modified or tampered data causes data integrity issues. Other than that, unauthorized access to such data causes confidentiality issues (Nweke and Wolthusen 2020).

4.6.2 Focusing on Attackers

Some FinTech institutions focus on identifying attackers that can launch cyberattacks to exploit vulnerabilities in the software systems and applications used by FinTech (Moeckel 2020). For example, a cybercrime gang named "*OldGremlin*" targeted a Russian bank with a ransomware attack in 2020. The gang used spear-phishing emails to enter the bank's network and then encrypted its data. The gang demanded a ransom of around USD 50,000 to provide the decryption key (Timeline of Cyber Incidents Involving Financial Institutions 2021). Infamous attacker groups are known for their frequent and repeated attempts to launch cyberattacks against FinTech institutions over the years.

4.6.3 Focusing on Software

FinTech institutions transform the traditional financial industry into digital platforms by using software, applications, and mobile apps. They use websites, web apps, and software to perform financial transactions. These software and applications may have flaws in design, code, and implementation. These flaws are identified by attackers to exploit them. Therefore, threat modeling approaches focus on identifying vulnerabilities in such software systems to fix them before the attackers exploit them (Potteiger et al. 2016).

4.7 Threat Modeling

Threat modeling is the process of identifying, categorizing, and analyzing potential threats. It can be performed as a proactive measure during the design and development of a reactive measure once a product has been deployed. The process identifies the potential harm that a threat poses, the probability of occurrence of that threat, and mitigation measures to reduce the impact of that harm. Once a threat is identified, it is compared to the list of vulnerabilities to match which threat can exploit which vulnerabilities and pose risk to the financial institution.

As illustrated in Fig. 4.3, a high-level threat modeling framework for financial institutions designed for the Department of Homeland Security identifies essential components of threat modeling and relationship among them (Fox et al. 2018). It is based on the National Institute of Standards and Technology (NIST) 800–30 Revision 1 framework (National Institute of Standards and Technology 2012). The high-level threat modeling framework identifies threat sources, threat events caused by threat sources, threat types and their characteristics, threat scenarios involved in threat sources, consequences of threats, the likelihood of occurrence, and its effect on financial institutions.

The framework provides an entity-relationship diagram that shows different entities and their relationships with each other. For example, a threat source has a threat type, and it causes threat events.

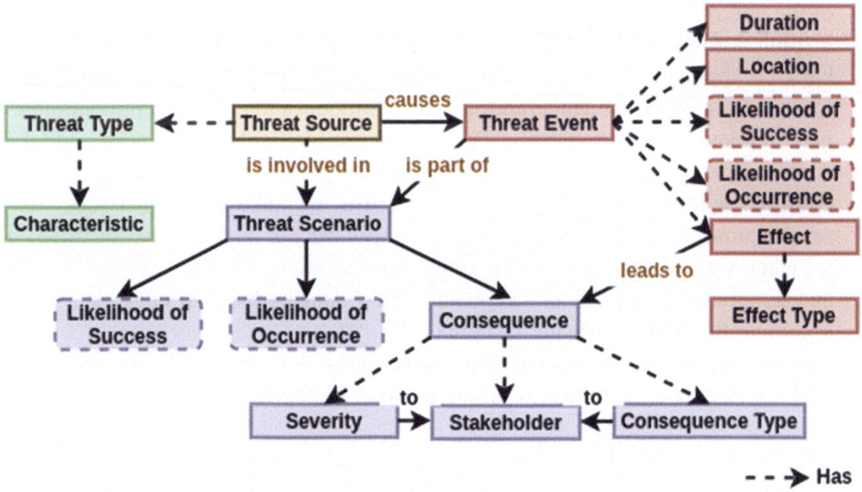

Fig. 4.3 Essential components of a threat modeling framework designed for the Department of Homeland Security

Threat Source The threat source is involved in a threat scenario. The consequences of the threat eventually lead to a negative impact on stakeholders.

Threat Type Threat type is a classification of threats. For example, a threat in FinTech is classified as phishing, DoS, DDoS, malware, and cloud-based transactions. Every threat type also has some characteristics.

Threat Scenario Threat scenario is attributed to likelihood of success, the likelihood of occurrence, and consequences. Consequences have a type and a severity value assigned to them. Stakeholders are impacted by the consequences of the threat.

Threat Events Threat events are the step-by-step actions taken by the adversary to launch a cyberattack. Threat events are caused by the threat source and are also a part of the threat scenario. Every threat event has some important characteristics such as duration of threat, location, the likelihood of its success and occurrence, and its effect on the financial institution. The high-level framework for threat modeling includes a list of 66 adversarial threat events in Appendix E (National Institute of Standards and Technology 2012). Some prominent threat events for FinTech include:

- **Crafting a phishing attack:** A phishing attack is used to acquire username, passwords, or social security numbers. This event occurs via email, instant messaging, or directing users to illegitimate websites that look legitimate. In 2020, researchers identified a new variant of the *IceID* banking trojan that used COVID-19 related phishing information. The variant is equipped with anti-detection capabilities and lures the customers to click the link.
- **Deliver targeted malware for control of internal systems and data exfiltration:** Adversary installs malware in the internal network to take control of the internal systems and steal sensitive information.
- **Exploit known vulnerabilities in smartphones:** Since most of the FinTech banking applications are installed on smartphones, they can be an easy target for attackers. They use vulnerabilities in smartphones to collect additional information related to those systems. This can be used to exploit the device and take control of it.
- **Conduct a DoS/DDoS attack:** Adversary tries to make an internet-accessible service unavailable to intended users, temporarily or indefinitely. In 2015, a teenager was sentenced to community service after carrying out four DDoS attacks against Nordea and Swedbank. These attacks blocked customers from accessing the bank's website for hours.
- **Cause integrity loss by corrupting critical data:** Adversary accesses, modifies, or deletes some critical data, resulting in loss of integrity.

The high-level modeling framework emphasizes the identification of adversary characteristics that allows adversary profiling capabilities. An adversary profile describes an attacker's motives, threat sources, capabilities, opportunities available to him, motivations to launch attack, timeframe of attack, stealth and persistence of

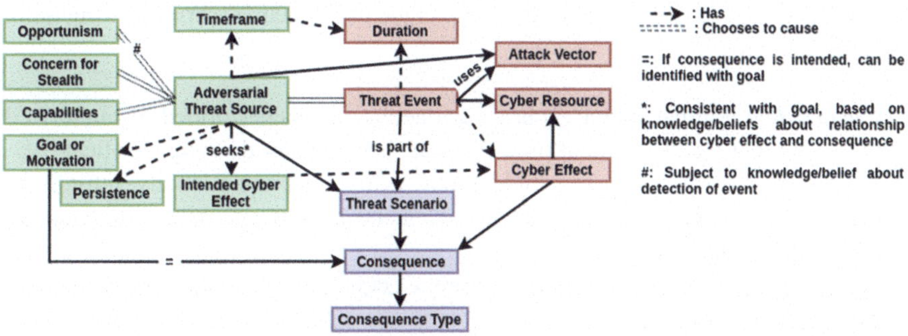

Fig. 4.4 Adversary characteristics by Department of Homeland Security (Fox et al. 2018)

attack, and consequences of attack on business. As presented in Fig. 4.4, it highlights the intentions of the attacker in terms of how likely he chooses to cause a threat to a particular source.

If the consequence of an attack is intended, it can be identified with a goal or motivation. The more knowledge the adversary has about the target network, the more effective the attack would be. Acquiring the know-how of the target allows the adversary to be consistent with his goals and evade detection. It also helps him to perform cleanup operations after the attack to remove his fingerprints. The threat event uses some attack vectors and cyber resources that provide initial information about the target. The threat event causes cyber effects as explained earlier in this section.

Cyberattack Vectors Following are the potential attack vectors for a threat scenario:

- Maintenance environments
- External network connections such as the internet, smartphone applications, and worldwide web services
- Internal networks such as the intranet and local area network
- Trusted or partner network connections such as secure shell connection to a partner's server, and third-party cloud services for data storage
- Actions of non-privileged or privileged users
- Physical attack vectors including physical damage to a facility on network premises
- Humans attack vectors including personal vulnerabilities, cyber awareness, and lack of cyber education.

Threat Sources Threat sources are characterized by type, description, and risk factors associated with them. The characteristics include likelihood and impact of a threat source on financial institutions. Adversarial threat sources choose to cause concern for stealth of attack. It has some motivation and possesses the capabilities to achieve its goals. Types of threat sources include accidental, adversarial, structural, and environmental:

- *The accidental* threat source includes erroneous actions performed by authorized personnel that lead to a threat. For example, accidentally deleting a critical file.
- *Adversarial* threat sources include threat actors that intentionally intrude on organizations. These sources include attackers, hacktivists, nation-state actors, and script kiddies, etc.
- *Structural* threat sources comprise failure of equipment, resource depletion, and expiring software.
- *Environmental* threat sources consist of natural disasters such as earthquakes, hurricanes, tsunami, and tornadoes, etc.

Accidental and adversarial threat sources are more common in financial institutions. Structural threat sources are encountered when the license of software of application used for financial management expires. Every hardware device also has an end of life (EOL) date. For example, data storage media reaches its end of life and cannot be used anymore. Environmental threat sources are exceedingly rare because a plan is prepared to establish a business unit at a physical location that is least prone to natural disasters. Nobody wants to build his business site on a red earthquake zone that is prone to witness earthquakes of high magnitude.

4.8 The Best Threat Modeling Methodology for FinTech

Several popular threat modeling methodologies exist that model threats in an enterprise. This section outlines the most popularly used threat models, such as STRIDE, Trike, and VAST. Finally, it introduces PASTA which is the best threat model for FinTech. The following text briefly introduces these models.

4.8.1 STRIDE

Microsoft developed STRIDE, a threat model used to assess threats against applications and operating systems. STRIDE is an acronym that stands for Spoofing (S), Tampering (T), Repudiation (R), Information disclosure (I), Denial of service (D), and Elevation of privileges (E). Although it is designed for application threats, it is also suitable for assessing host-based and network-based threats. Figure 4.5 presents glimpses of the STRIDE model.

- **Spoofing:** It is an attack with the goal of gaining access to the target computer by using a false or fake identity. It can be done with IP address, MAC address, usernames, system names, wireless networks, email addresses, and other types of logical identities. Spoofing is done to bypass authentication and authorization by attackers. It is followed by subsequent attacks targeting data, service disruption, and denial of service.

Property Violated	Threat	Threat Definition
Authentication	Spoofing	Pretending to be something or someone else
Integrity	Tampering	Modifying data stored on disk, memory, network, or storage
Non-repudiation	Repudiation	Claiming that you did not do something; not taking responsibility
Confidentiality	Information Disclosure	Providing information to unauthorized person
Availability	Denial of Service	Exhausting resources to provide service to legitimate users
Authorization	Elevation of Privilege	Allowing unauthorized persons to do something with higher privileges

Fig. 4.5 STRIDE model

- **Tampering:** Any action resulting in unauthorized changes to the data is called tampering. Tampering violates the integrity of data.
- **Repudiation:** The ability of the attacker to deny performing illegitimate activities is called repudiation. Attackers are not held responsible in repudiation.
- **Information Disclosure:** Disclosure of information to unauthorized parties violates confidentiality. It can include any type of information such as customer identification, financial information, or business operations details.
- **Denial of Service:** It is an attack that exhausts the resources so that legitimate users are unable to access them. The main motivation behind this attack is the disruption of services. This attack can be launched by flooding the target with unnecessary requests, connection overloading, and exploitation of network flaws. A more severe form of this attack is called distributed denial of service. It violates the availability of data and services.
- **Elevation of Privilege:** In this attack, a limited user account is transformed into a privileged account with access to critical resources and data. It might be accomplished with data or credential theft.

4.8.2 Trike

Trike is another threat model based on a risk-centric approach. It provides a method of performing security audits in a reliable and repeated procedure. It is a unique threat modeling process focused on satisfying the security auditing process from a

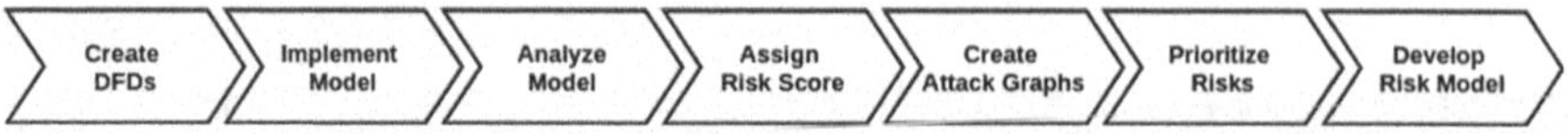

Fig. 4.6 Trike threat model

cyber risk management perspective. It provides a centric risk management approach with unique implementation and risk modeling process. It is based on "requirements model" that ensures the assigned level of risk for each asset is acceptable for the organization. The next step in trike model is to create Data Flow Diagrams (DFDs) to communicate system, its components, and flows between those components. After creating DFDs, the model is implemented to represent actions that a user in the system can perform. The implementation model is then analyzed to identify threats. Every threat is assigned a risk score which is used to create an attack graph. The threats are then prioritized to understand which threats need a preference for mitigation. Finally, users develop a risk model based on assets, roles, actions, and threat exposure. Figure 4.6 presents an overview of the trike threat model.

4.8.3 VAST

Visual, Agile, and Simple Threat (VAST) is another threat model based on agile programming principles. The objective of the VAST model is to integrate threat and risk management into Agile programming environments on a scalable basis. This model is focused on enterprise-level risk. It was conceived after reviewing the shortcomings and challenges faced by other threat modeling techniques. It is based on the principle that threat modeling techniques must be scaled at the enterprise level and must integrate Agile programming to it. It aims to produce actionable, accurate, and consistent outputs for developers, security teams, and senior executives. The fundamental difference that makes this threat model stand out is its practical approach. The VAST model comes in two types: application and operational threat model. Application VAST threat model creates Process Flow Diagrams (PFDs) to map the features and communication between processes. It is designed for developers. An operational VAST threat model is designed for infrastructure teams. It is like traditional DFDs that represent flows from an attacker's perspective. Figure 4.7 presents an overview of VAST threat model.

4.8.4 PASTA

Process for Attack Simulation and Threat Analysis (PASTA) is a seven-stage threat model based on a risk-centric approach. Each stage of the model focuses on specific objectives. Figure 4.8 presents the seven stages of PASTA.

Each stage performs multiple activities as illustrated below.

Stage 1:

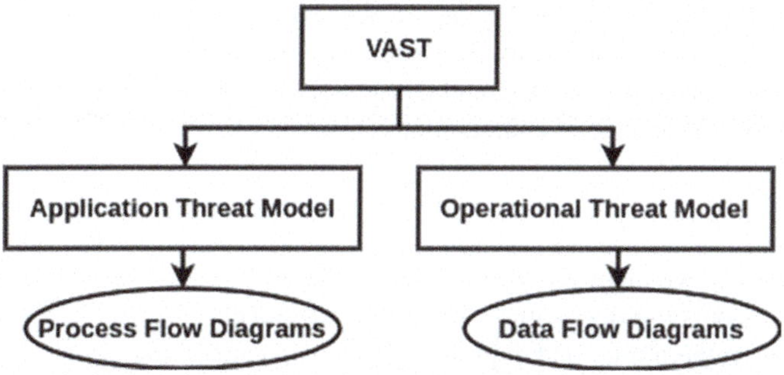

Fig. 4.7 VAST threat model

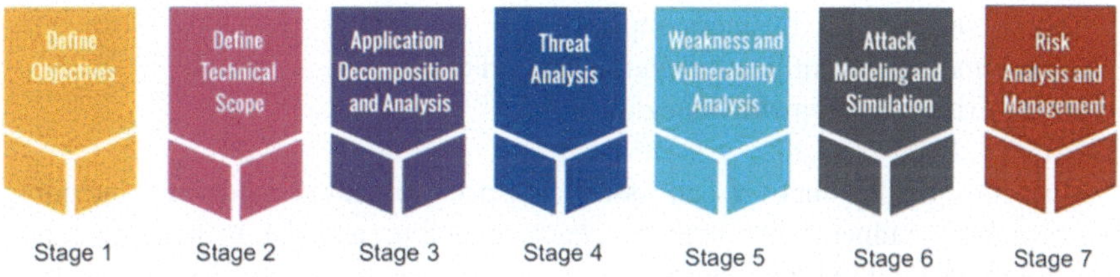

Fig. 4.8 Seven stages of PASTA model

- Identify business objectives
- Identify security and compliance requirements
- Business impact analysis

Stage 2:

- Capture the boundaries of the technical environment
- Capture infrastructure | applications | software dependencies

Stage 3:

- Identify use cases | define application entry points and trust levels
- Identify actors | assets | services | roles | data sources
- Data Flow Diagrams (DFDs) | trust boundaries

Stage 4:

- Probabilistic attack scenario analysis
- Regression analysis on security events
- Threat intelligence correlation and analytics

Stage 5:

- Queries of existing vulnerability reports and issue tracking
- Threat to existing vulnerability mapping using threat trees
- Design flaw analysis using use and abuse cases
- Scorings (CVSS/CWSS) | enumerations (CWE/CVE)

Stage 6:

- Attack on surface analysis
- Attack tree development | attack library management
- Attack on vulnerability and exploit analysis using attack trees

Stage 7:

- Qualify and quantify business impact
- Countermeasure identification and residual risk analysis
- Identify risk management strategies

Since this model uncovers all essential aspects of threat modeling, including threat analysis, vulnerability analysis, attack modeling, and risk management, it is best suited for the FinTech industry.

4.9 Chapter Summary

This chapter introduces cyber threats in the FinTech industry and answers the question: why are we afraid of cyber threats? It is important to know the adversary, his motivations, tools, techniques, and moves in advance so that a defense strategy can be prepared. This chapter puts forward the types of threat actors and categories of potential threats to FinTech. Toward the end of the chapter, threat intelligence and threat modeling are brought into picture. Threat intelligence gathers essential information to understand indicators of compromise, motivation behind launching cyberattacks and formulate an informed decision-making process that inculcates risk management as one of the important components.

Cybersecurity threats impact almost all the components in the FinTech ecosystem. They may pose potential exposure to various financial institutions that use technology, FinTech startups, and financial customers in the FinTech ecosystem. Technology developers are also related to cybersecurity threats as they need to be aware of potential threats that can exercise vulnerabilities and flaws in the technology that they are developing. Overall, the following questions are answered in this chapter:

- Which cybersecurity threats pose challenges to the FinTech industry?
- Why is it important to know the adversary and his motivations?
- What are the different threat categories and how intense are the cyber threats in real-world examples?

- What are the several types of threat actors and how do they differ from each other?
- What is threat intelligence and what are the types of methods used to collect adversary's information?
- How can we model cyber threats?
- Which threat models exist for mitigating threats?

References

Fowler, K. (2016). Chapter 1 – an overview of data breaches. *Data breach preparation and response* (pp. 1–26).

Fox, D. B., Arnoth, E. I., Skorupka, C. W., McCollum, C. D., & Bodeau, D. J. (2018). Enhanced cyber threat model for financial services sector (FSS) institutions – threat model ATT&CK/ CAPEC version. *Department of Homeland Security*, 1–118.

Global Security Attitude Survey. (2019). https://www.crowdstrike.com/resources/reports/global-security-attitude-survey-2019/.

IBM. (2020). *Cost of a data breach report*. IBM. https://www.ibm.com/security/data-breach.

Johnson, A. L. (2016). Cybersecurity for financial institutions: The integral role of information sharing in cyber attack mitigation. *North Carolina Banking Institute, 20*, 277.

Marsh & McLennan Companies. (2018). *Cyber risk management: response and recovery* (pp. 1–20). New York: Marsh & McLennan Companies.

McLean, R. (2019). *A hacker gained access to 100 million Capital one credit card applications and accounts*. CNN Business. https://www.cnn.com/2019/07/29/business/capital-one-data-breach/index.html.

Moeckel, C. (2020). Attacker-centric thinking in Security — Perspectives from financial services practitioners. *Proceedings of the 15th international conference on availability, reliability and Security, Ireland* (pp. 1–10).

Morgan, J. P. (2014). *Chase reveals massive data breach affecting 76m households*. The Guardian. https://www.theguardian.com/business/2014/oct/02/jp-morgan-76m-households-affected-data-breach.

National Institute of Standards and Technology. (2012). *Guide for conducting risk assessments, National Institute of Standards and Technology*, NIST SP 800–30 Revision 1, pp. 1–95.

NSFocus. (2017). *Fintech security analysis report* (pp. 1–32). Beijing: NSFocus Technologies.

Nweke, L. O., & Wolthusen, S. (2020). A review of asset-centric threat modelling approaches. *International Journal of Advanced Computer Science and Applications, 11*(2), 1–7.

Potteiger, B., Martins, G., & Koutsoukos, X. (2016). Software and attack centric integrated threat modeling for quantitative risk assessment. In *Proceedings of the Symposium and Bootcamp on the Science of Security* (pp. 99–108). Pittsburgh: ACM.

Timeline of Cyber Incidents Involving Financial Institutions. (2021). https://carnegieendowment.org/specialprojects/protectingfinancialstability/timeline.

Cybersecurity Vulnerabilities in FinTech 5

FinTech revolves around technologies such as cloud, blockchain, AI, and mobile devices that are used for financial transaction payments, cryptocurrencies, money transfers, trading, and regulatory compliance. With so much monetary value associated with all these technologies, the perpetrators are always lured to breach security by exploiting the vulnerabilities that exist in these technologies.

A vulnerability is defined as a weakness that can be exploited by a cyberattack launched by a threat actor. In other words, vulnerability is a flaw, loophole, error, limitation, oversight, or susceptibility in any aspect of FinTech, especially the IT environment. If a vulnerability is exploited, it can cause severe losses or damage to the assets.

Since startups are a prominent element of the FinTech ecosystem, these companies do not emphasize strong cybersecurity solutions. Thereby, they become easy victims for lone-wolf cybercriminals and nation-state hackers. There are three essential components to every FinTech industry: technology, humans, and transactions. All these components can be described in a single statement as follows.

FinTech uses *technology* that allows *humans* to perform monetary *transactions* in a much faster and efficient manner. All these components are vulnerable to threats and these vulnerabilities can be classified into various categories. This chapter begins with shedding light on some of the common cybersecurity vulnerabilities in FinTech and proceeds with specific vulnerabilities related to technology, humans, and transactions that were exploited in the past.

5.1 General Cybersecurity Vulnerabilities in FinTech

FinTech has evolved a lot in recent years and this success can be attributed to evolving technologies. However, it cannot overshadow the fact that these innovative technologies also bring the fear of exposing several vulnerabilities that can be exploited at no extra cost. Some of the general vulnerabilities in the technologies,

G. Kaur et al., *Understanding Cybersecurity Management in FinTech*, Future of Business and Finance, https://doi.org/10.1007/978-3-030-79915-1_5

platforms, frameworks, and related solutions used by FinTech are summarized below:

- **URL redirection:** It is a simple vulnerability that allows a threat actor to redirect or forward a legitimate URL (Uniform Resource Locator) to make it available under one or more URL addresses. It is also referred to as URL forwarding. When a web browser attempts to open a redirected web page, a web page with a different URL is opened. It is a worldwide web technique designed to prevent broken links when web pages are moved. However, it is misused to redirect to malicious websites linked to phishing attacks and malware distribution attempts.
- **Crafted URL redirection:** It is a modified version of URL redirection in which a URL is specially crafted or created to mislead the users and destine them to a different web page designed to conduct illegal activities.
- **Remote code execution:** It is performed by executing a code remotely through an automated script. The aim of exploiting this vulnerability is to provide the administrative privilege of a vulnerable system to a remote user. Once the attacker gains the administrative privileges on the vulnerable system, he tries to hide his identity and existence on the compromised system and uses it to launch remote code execution on other hosts.
- **Microsoft exchange memory corruption:** It is a remote code execution vulnerability that exists in Microsoft Exchange software. This vulnerability is triggered when the software fails to handle an object in memory. By exploiting this vulnerability, an attacker can run arbitrary code in memory to perform actions such as installing programs, modifying permissions to files and directories, or creating new accounts.
- **Information disclosure:** It is a vulnerability in which sensitive information is revealed intentionally or unintentionally to unauthorized personnel. Some organizations refer to the term information leakage as an alternative to information disclosure. However, Common Weakness Enumeration (CWE) discourages the use of this term as leakage refers to several other aspects of leaks such as memory leak due to out-of-bound writing.
- **DLL hijacking:** It is a vulnerability in Windows operating systems that allows attackers to execute unexpected code to exploit a vulnerable Dynamic Link Library (DLL). DLL is the implementation of a shared library where the DLL files may contain code, data, or resources, like portable executable file format. This vulnerability allows the attackers to load and execute a malicious DLL file contained in the same directory as that of data files opened by that application. It was first discovered in 2000 but is still active. It targets programs or applications that are run from unsafe locations such as *Downloads* or *Temp* Directory.
- **Ransomware:** It is a type of malware that encrypts files and directories on that target computer to disrupt authorized access and demand a handsome amount of ransom to provide the decryption key. Several famous ransomware attacks including *WannaCry* and *CryptoWall* have created havoc by bringing down business across multiple continents.

- **Command injection:** It allows executing arbitrary commands on the host operating system through a vulnerable application. Command injection is possible when a user passes unsafe data to a system shell. This unsafe data may comprise forms, cookies, and HTTP headers, etc. Simply put, the attacker supplies operating system commands that are executed with the privilege of vulnerable applications that fail to support input validation.
- **Out-of-bounds write:** As apparent from the name itself, it is a vulnerability in which data is written either before the beginning or after the end of the intended buffer assigned to an application. This vulnerability can be corrected by checking the input bounds or validating the input.
- **Cross-site Scripting (XSS):** It is a type of injection vulnerability in which a malicious code is injected into a benign web page. The attacker uses a web application to send malicious code, in the form of a script, to a different end user. Since the script appears to come from a trusted website, the end user has no idea of suspecting it. Therefore, he executes it, and the script can access cookies, session tokens, or other sensitive data retained by the web browser during that session.
- **Microsoft Office SharePoint XSS:** This vulnerability exists when the Microsoft SharePoint server does not properly sanitize the specially crafted web request to an affected SharePoint server. Once the vulnerability is exploited, the attacker can send cross-site scripting attacks to other systems also. As a result, the attacker gets access to an authorized content not intended for him.
- **Elevated privileges:** A normal user has zero administrative rights in any capacity. However, when an attacker exploits a vulnerability, the next step is to elevate privileges to obtain administrative rights to perform certain authorized activities for illicit purposes. Once the attacker gains administrative or root privileges, the severity of damage done by his activities may include the working of the kernel of the operating system.
- **Brute-force authentication:** In a brute-force attack, the attacker tries a combination of several passwords or passphrases to guess the correct password. He performs an exhaustive key search to discover the correct password to authenticate a system. In simple words, the attacker tries every combination of passwords to make up the correct password. The time and computational power to find the correct password increases exponentially with the length of the password.
- **Execute a maliciously crafted file:** A maliciously crafted file can cause a buffer overflow which allows an attacker to inject malicious code into a legitimate code and execute it alongside.
- **Remote hijacking:** It exploits the legitimate features of the Remote Desktop Protocol (RDP) service in a Windows operating system. In this vulnerability, the attacker attempts to resume a previously disconnected remote session. This allows him to get elevated privileges without stealing any authentication credentials.
- **DNS amplification:** It is a type of DDoS attack in which an attacker leverages the functionality of an open DNS resolver to exhaust the target server with a voluminous amount of DNS traffic. This amplified traffic renders the DNS server

inaccessible to legitimate DNS client requests. A DNS amplification attack is launched with the help of bots to generate such a huge amount of spoofed DNS requests.

- **Directory traversal:** It is a web security vulnerability that allows an attacker to read arbitrary files on the server. In some cases, the attacker may be able to write these files.
- **Arbitrary file overwrite:** This vulnerability allows the attacker to replace existing files or create new files. It is alternatively called Zip-Slip vulnerability. By modifying arbitrary files on the server, the attacker may be successful in changing the behavior of the application running these files or comprising the server itself.
- **Money laundering:** Most of the financial institutions are vulnerable to money laundering. The term is used to refer to making substantial amounts of money through illegal activities and processing it to make it clean and come from a legitimate source. In other words, money laundering attempts to hide the origin of money obtained by illegal means.
- **Phone verification without OTP:** This vulnerability bypasses the authentication process of confirming a One-Time Password (OTP) generated as a part of the financial transaction.

5.2 Specific Cybersecurity Vulnerabilities in FinTech

After getting familiar with general cybersecurity vulnerabilities in FinTech, let us dig deeper into specific cybersecurity vulnerabilities in FinTech that can be divided into three categories as presented in Fig. 5.1.

The following subsections elaborate on these vulnerabilities one by one.

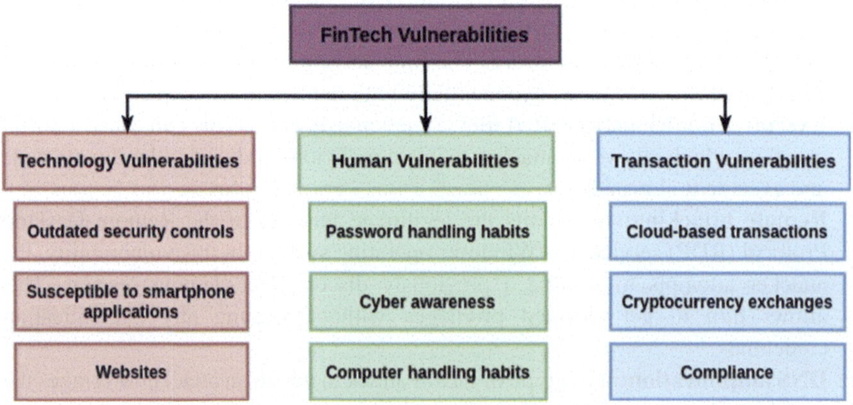

Fig. 5.1 Specific cybersecurity vulnerabilities in FinTech

5.2.1 Technology Vulnerabilities

Technology vulnerabilities refer to the specific vulnerabilities in the technologies used by financial institutions. Most of these vulnerabilities are related to startup companies because they do not have a sufficient budget to invest in strong cybersecurity solutions. Since startups face immense pressure to establish themselves among the traditional financial giants, they lure customers with innovative websites and mobile applications, without caring much about protecting technology. Some of the most common technology-related vulnerabilities exhibited by financial startups are highlighted below.

Outdated Security Controls

- *Outdated antivirus version:* One of the common mistakes committed by startup companies is not updating the antivirus solutions used to monitor malicious applications. Outdated antivirus protection software represents a false sense of safety and is as risky as no protection.
- *Unpatched operating system and applications:* Unpatched operating systems and applications expose vulnerabilities to attackers who are always peeping into the security flaws. Security breaches due to exploitation of vulnerabilities exposed by unpatched software can run rampant on business owners by reducing productivity and economic stability.
- *Installing applications and software from a spurious source:* Installing software from unreliable sources, without matching hashes, is like inviting malware to break in and create havoc. Applications downloaded from such websites may contain hidden malware samples that are triggered when the downloaded application is executed on the host computer.
- *Weak endpoint security devices:* Endpoint security devices such as firewalls and intrusion detection and protection systems filter malicious traffic and prevent it from entering the network. Even the next-generation firewalls can protect against zero-day malware. Nevertheless, weak security policies and incorrect filter rules can result in underrated performance by these devices.

Susceptible to Smartphone Applications

- *Injecting malware to steal login credentials and other important data:* The use of smartphones for online banking and payment is an essential application of FinTech. These applications have brought a revolution to the FinTech industry by promoting digital wallets. These applications store critical user data such as bank account number, credit amount, user contact, social insurance number, and other personal details. However, these applications are also prone to certain malware infections. Attackers inject malicious code into mobile applications to steal login credentials and use them to perform financial frauds, especially credit card frauds. In addition to that, the stolen personal data is misused or sold online to cyber criminals who use it to sell/purchase illegal items on the dark web.
- *Insecure connection to server:* The Norton cyber security report reveals that 978 million people in 20 countries were affected by cybercrimes in 2017 (Norton

Cyber Security Insights Report Global Results, Symantec 2017). Thirty-eight percent of the affected people were victims of credit card fraud resulting from insecure storage of data on the server. According to the same report, these victims lost $172 billion in global cybercrime. Transferring and storing data in an insecure manner by the financial servers can have catastrophic ramifications because sensitive personal data of users is involved in such transactions.
- *Device verification without OTP:* Most of the digital platforms support two-step authentication involving login credentials and OTP sent to the registered mobile number of the customer. In such a case, if the attacker succeeds in login theft, he still must do more stuff to obtain OTP to successfully log in to the system. Nonetheless, if two-step authentication is not adopted by the financial institution, stealing the login credentials will do the trick for cybercriminals.

Websites

According to *ImmuniWeb* findings, XSS (Cross-Site Scripting) is the most popular website vulnerability as described by the Online Web Application Security Project (OWASP) A7), Sensitive Data Exposure (OWASP A3), and Security Misconfiguration (OWASP A6) (Study says fintech startups vulnerable to web or mobile app attacks 2019). Other website vulnerabilities include:

- *URL redirection to malicious web page: Attackers* make use of phishing attacks and adware to force the user to click on malicious links. Adware lures the customers by offering them financial benefits and gifts related to their searched content and once the customer clicks on the malicious link prompted on screen, he is redirected to a malicious web page used to surf objectionable content. In some instances, these malicious links forwarded the user to his bank account web page stored in session cookies and a handsome amount was debited from his bank account automatically.
- *Typosquatting:* Type squatting is based on the fundamental idea of URL hijacking. Cybercriminals target users who incorrectly type the URL of a genuine website. In one of the audacious examples of type squatting ever, a Canadian youngster named Mike Rowe published his website *www.MikeRoweSoft.com, which sounded* like *www. MicroSoft.com* to promote his design business. As a result, Microsoft took on him and the rift ended in redirecting to *www.Microsoft.com*.

5.2.2 Human Vulnerabilities

Human vulnerabilities refer to general mistakes made by users as a part of human error or human nature, whichever describes the situation best. Human vulnerabilities are more dangerous than technology vulnerabilities. Consider a situation in which a customer wants to transfer money through an e-Interac facility. Even if the mobile banking application is protected and funds are transferred in a secure manner, a human error in typing the receiver's email may result in an incorrect fund transfer.

The following are some of the most common human vulnerabilities identified from the real-time cyberattacks on FinTech.

Password Handling Habits

- *Auto-saving login credentials:* Some users prefer to save their login credentials rather than remembering them. The web browser stores the session cookies and the username and password used to log in to the system. If an attacker hijacks the session, he can easily steal login details. Another common habit observed in human beings is to write passwords on paper to remember them. A malicious insider can perform social engineering tactics or shoulder surfing to see the written password.
- *Using the same password for multiple accounts:* Humans are habitual to use the same password for multiple user accounts. If one of the password hashes for an account is hacked by the criminals, the other unhacked accounts with the same passwords are also at the same risk.
- *Frequency of changing password:* For the sake of remembering a password, users are reluctant to change their password. Although some of the institutions' policies make it mandatory for users to change their password every 90 days (about 3 months) or so.
- *Password strength and length:* Some users select simple and short passwords. This compromises with the strength and complexity of a password. It is also observed that breaking smaller passwords requires less time and computational power.
- *Sharing passwords with friends or colleagues:* Sharing passwords with friends and family members poses the same vulnerability of using the same passwords for multiple accounts, social engineering, and shoulder surfing.
- *Throwing documents containing sensitive information in trash:* It is a general trend in financial institutions to tear the papers and send them in the trash. However, attackers may use social engineering tactics to grab sensitive information from trash and misuse it.

Cyber Awareness

- *Clicking suspicious emails and filling up personal identifiable information in suspicious forms:* Many users reveal personally identifiable information such as date of birth and social insurance number to irrelevant forms such as for grabbing shopping vouchers. In addition, opening external emails from the official email account needs great care as phishing emails contain suspicious links that, when clicked, lead to malicious web pages.
- *Clicking malicious links pertaining to free offers:* Adware targets users by offering them free gifts, vouchers, and vacation offers. These fake offers intend to click on fake advertisements that redirect to malicious websites.
- *Lack of cyber education:* Most people are not aware of the kind of response to cryptic cyberattacks such as phishing and social engineering. People trust their friends, colleagues, and family members. That is why social engineering attacks such as tailgating, and shoulder surfing succeed in real life. There is a lack of

cyber education and training among common people so that they can be made aware of what vulnerable situations are and how to respond to those situations to stay protected.

Computer Handling Habits

- *Keeping the unattended computer or workstation unlocked:* Employees leave their computers unlocked when they temporarily move away from their office. To make it worse, many of them do not use automatic screen lock features to lock their monitor after being idle for some time. This encourages social engineering attacks.
- *Trusting malicious insiders:* Malicious insiders pose a severe threat to every organization, especially if they are dissatisfied with the policies and work environment. They possess the potential to cause intentional damage to the organization in one way or the other. Trusting such insiders and sharing job responsibilities with them can provide a breakthrough in breaching sensitive data or credentials and sharing it with other threat actors outside the organization.
- *Bring Your Own Device (BYOD):* Some organizations follow a BYOD policy according to which employees can use their personal laptops and smart devices for office work. Different devices are vulnerable to different cyberattacks. This increases the cyber risk for the organization.
- *Computer literacy:* With the transformation in the FinTech industry, manual systems of daily operations are successfully replaced by modern technology and software. However, there is still a section of employees who prefer traditional work culture and are reluctant to get trained in innovative technology. Such employees are a serious threat to the institution as they are not computer literate to tackle simple situations to prevent privacy breaches.

5.2.3 Transaction Vulnerabilities

Most of the financial transactions are completed through cloud-based servers nowadays. Since the business is growing, the FinTech industry is seeking the services of several prominent cloud-based servers hosted by the big business giants. These services allow startups and medium-sized financial companies to use the platform, software, and infrastructure owned by a third party and pay as per their usage. In addition, these companies are exempted from the burden of investment in purchasing these services and training or hiring technical staff to operate and manage these services. Nonetheless, cloud-based transactions are vulnerable to several threats mentioned below.

Cloud-Based Transactions

- *Compromising cloud security:* Cloud customers use a set of Application Programming Interfaces (APIs) to interact with cloud services. These APIs contain the same software vulnerabilities just as the operating systems and libraries. Once the attackers find these vulnerabilities, they exploit them to launch a successful

cyberattack to compromise the security of cloud data. Thus, every piece of data sent or received through the cloud server can be breached.
- *Storing sensitive data in plaintext:* There are several instances when cloud data was stored in plaintext form by the cloud service provider. Once cloud security is compromised, sensitive data stored in plaintext can be stolen.

Cryptocurrency Exchanges
- *Susceptibility to phishing attacks:* Cryptocurrency exchanges are susceptible to phishing attacks. To illustrate, Bitstamp, a bitcoin exchange, observed phishing attacks for several weeks in 2015 resulting in steals worth USD5 million. The cybercriminal persuaded one of the employees at Bitstamp to download a file that contained a VBA script. When the file was opened, there was a malicious file on the compromised machine.
- *Anonymous customer transactions:* Cryptocurrency transactions make use of signatures that may be manipulated before the transaction is posted. In one of the largest hacks in the history of cryptocurrency, named "*Mt. Gox hack*," the hackers changed the code before the initial transaction was posted. It resulted in a loss of USD473 million and went bankrupt with the hacked exchange.
- *Software bugs in cryptocurrency platforms:* Cryptocurrency platforms also contain software bugs just like other operating systems and APIs. These bugs are vulnerable to several cyber threats.

Compliance
- *Noncompliance with organization policy:* Every financial institution has its own crypto-compliance policy to abide by the rules and guidelines laid out to protect against FinTech crimes such as money laundering, financial terrorism, and malicious cryptocurrency exchange. Noncompliance with the institution's policy can yield devastating results.

5.3 Assessing the FinTech Cybersecurity Vulnerabilities

A vulnerability assessment looks for vulnerabilities in the system, network, and processes. It is helpful to understand the performance of cyber solutions, provide guidance on future strategies, maintain compliance, protect against cyber threats, and propose remedial measures (Sheshadri 2019). In order to assess the three types of FinTech vulnerabilities, the following strategies are useful (Wu 2019):

- **Identify assets:** This is one of the key steps. Most of the organizations struggle to identify their critical assets that are exposed to cyber risks. An inventory list is prepared that contains every bit of information related to assets, their location, and usability.
- **Align business with IT strategies:** Every cybersecurity vulnerability starts with a FinTech institution's long-term objectives. There needs to be communication

between business and IT departments to continue business operations. It acts as a foundational step to effective security.

- **Identify inherent risks:** Inherent risks are associated with business or FinTech industry. For example, the geographic location of the FinTech industry may be prone to natural disasters such as earthquakes. Such types of risks are counted when assessing vulnerabilities.
- **Monitor risk tolerance levels:** Every FinTech firm has a default capacity to tolerate risks. It can avoid, accept, mitigate, or transfer risks based on its risk appetite or tolerance level.
- **Establish a continuous monitoring program:** Adversaries are always innovative in using technologies and changing threat methodologies. A continuous monitoring program keeps a check on the most common threat vectors, especially zero-day malware and ransomware that affect the FinTech industry the most.

Cybersecurity vulnerabilities are growing at a rapid rate. This growth is causing operational risks for banks and financial institutions. However, many FinTech institutions have adopted cybersecurity vulnerability assessment program that has following key steps (Uddin et al. 2020):

1. **Planning:** The program starts with identifying the systems and networks which would be assessed. For example, systems that contain sensitive customer information need assessment (Goldman 2019).
2. **Scanning:** After obtaining the list of systems and networks, a vulnerability scan is initiated manually or through automated tools. There are many popular open-source and commercial vulnerability assessment tools available in the market. These tools provide a comprehensive view of the type of vulnerabilities on every system scanned.
3. **Analysis:** In the next step, these vulnerabilities are analyzed to determine how they can impact the system, level of severity, and suggested mitigation methods. Every vulnerability is associated with a severity rank that specifies the priority order in which identified vulnerabilities are mitigated.
4. **Remediation:** Finally, remediation measures are taken to fix the vulnerabilities. For example, some vulnerabilities can be fixed by updating the application or software in which they are identified.
5. **Repeat:** Vulnerability assessment is a continuous process that watches for any cybersecurity vulnerability in the systems and networks over and again.

5.4 General Policies to Mitigate FinTech Cybersecurity Vulnerabilities

Based on the types of vulnerabilities discussed in the previous subsection, every FinTech institution designs a policy to implement basic regulations to avoid or treat the identified vulnerabilities. These policies are based on factors influencing the budget, market value, infrastructure cost, and reputation of the institution. Some essential policies for providing fundamental security for the financial work of an institution are streamlined below. For easy understanding, these policies are based on the types of cybersecurity vulnerabilities identified earlier.

Technology Vulnerabilities

- *Cost of software failure:* FinTech business is conducted through cloud servers nowadays. FinTech companies avail themselves of third-party cloud services to store their sensitive data. Failure of Software as a Service (SaaS) makes data unavailable for use and costs heavily to the business.
- *Dependency between impact and security controls:* Security controls protect confidentiality, integrity, and availability of data. There exists a dependency between security controls and the impact of their failure on business. Technology-related policy considers the relationship between impact and security controls.

Human Vulnerabilities

- *Password complexity:* Password complexity rule includes choosing a password with a combination of lowercase and uppercase alphabets, numbers, and special characters.
- *Minimum password length: It ensures s*etting a minimum length of the password. For example, Windows 10 allows a password between 1 and 14 characters.
- *Minimum and maximum password age:* It determines the minimum and maximum number of days after which the password must be changed. For Windows 10, the minimum password age can be set to 0 and the maximum password age is 998 days. A user can select any value between these days to reset his password.
- *Time and frequency of login:* Most of the websites use a maximum number of attempts to enter the correct credentials for login. If the user does not enter correct information within those attempts, his access is blocked for a temporary duration as a safety rule.
- *Removable device usage:* Personal removable devices may inject malware into office computers and workstations. Therefore, it is a common policy to prohibit the use of removable storage media such as USB drives in office machines.
- *Download frequency and size:* Some organizations set a maximum file size for download. In these cases, an employee is not allowed to download large files from the Internet. In other words, it is a measure designed to use the internet for official work only. Some administrators even restrict the frequency of download.
- *Click on hyperlinks in email:* All the employees must be educated about phishing attacks and opening links in emails received from outside the organization. External emails need to be opened carefully and employees must know that they must not click any hyperlinks in the luring emails.
- *Open email attachments:* Malware may be transmitted through attached files in emails that pretend to be sent by the high-rank officer in the organization. If these files are downloaded, they can execute the malware on the compromised machine and can initiate a covert financial transaction resulting in huge financial losses.

- *File access logs:* Some organizations verify the file access logs to determine who has accessed sensitive files and at what time and for what duration. A logbook is maintained to record all the entries related to accessing a confidential file.
- *Web server access logs:* Like file access logs, server access logs can also be maintained to record who has accessed the server, time of access, duration of access, and activities performed during that time.
- *Applications used:* Some organizations specify a list of applications to use in office hours. They expect their employees to use only those applications for office work.
- *Visited website:* System administrators keep an eye on the websites/URLs visited by the employees to identify any malicious activity from inside the organization. This policy also ensures that blacklisted websites are not used by the employees through proxy services.

Transaction Vulnerabilities

- *Transaction history:* A comprehensive security policy records the transaction history to keep an eye on who is performing financial transactions and when.
- *Cost of infrastructure failure:* Like software (SaaS) failure, Infrastructure as a service (IaaS) failure also impacts the finances. A secure transaction policy estimates the cost of infrastructure failure, whether it is in-house or owned by the third party.
- *Cost of nonfunctional cloud server:* Cost of nonfunctional cloud server includes SaaS, IaaS, and Platform as a Service (PaaS).
- *Dependency between common vulnerabilities:* Vulnerability in one software may be dependent on vulnerability in another software. This dependency between common vulnerabilities such as critical software needs to be considered to draft a policy for secure FinTech transactions.

General Guidelines

- *Computer literacy:* Educate users to understand common cyber threats, especially phishing, eavesdropping, and social engineering tactics.
- *Social media interactions:* Users must also be aware of the extent of social media interactions which include posting professional or work-related information on personal accounts and accepting friend requests sent by strangers or acquaintances.
- *Physical security:* Physical security must be provided to the perimeters of the institution by using fences, lighting, fire alarms, security guards, and bollards.
- *Background check:* One of the important aspects of recruiting a new employee is to have a background check. It facilitates financial institutions to investigate a candidate's education, criminal background, and employment history.
- *Administrative duties:* Employees must be assigned responsibilities based on their capability. Some duties require dual control from more than one employee. In addition, employees must be given limited access to the resources through the Acceptable Use Policy (AUP).

- *Termination:* Employee exit policy must be designed carefully. The terminated employee must hand over smart cards, keys, and essential documents immediately. He must be escorted to the exit door after an exit interview is conducted and must not be allowed to visit his office premises alone. All the accounts and credentials handled by the terminated employee must be suspended with immediate effect.

5.5 Chapter Summary

This chapter instigates cybersecurity vulnerabilities in FinTech. It brings forward some general and specific cybersecurity vulnerabilities that were exploited in the past. Specific FinTech cybersecurity vulnerabilities are divided into three categories: technology, human, and transactions. Technology vulnerabilities deal with outdated security controls, susceptibility to smartphone applications used in FinTech, and websites used for the same. Human vulnerabilities involve computer and password handling habits. Finally, transaction vulnerabilities consist of cloud-based transactions, cryptocurrency exchanges, and noncompliance with security standards.

Cybersecurity vulnerabilities exist in every technology, tool, software, and application. They impact almost all the components in the FinTech ecosystem, especially various financial institutions that use innovative technology, FinTech startups that transform traditional financial institutions into contemporary FinTech institutions, and financial customers in the FinTech ecosystem. Technology developers are also related to cybersecurity vulnerabilities as they need to be aware of potential threats that can exercise vulnerabilities and flaws in the technology that they are developing. Overall, the following questions are answered in this chapter:

- Is FinTech vulnerable to cyber threats?
- What are the types of cybersecurity vulnerabilities in FinTech?
- What are the vulnerabilities in technology and how can they be exploited?
- What are the vulnerabilities in humans who operate FinTech services and how can they be exploited?
- What are the vulnerabilities in transactions and how can they be exploited?
- How can one mitigate cybersecurity vulnerabilities in FinTech?

References

Goldman, J. (2019). *How to conduct a vulnerability assessment: 5 steps toward better cybersecurity*. https://www.esecurityplanet.com/networks/how-to-conduct-a-vulnerability-assessment-steps-toward-better-cybersecurity/.

Norton Cyber Security Insights Report Global Results, Symantec. (2017). https://www.nortonlifelock.com/us/en/newsroom/press-kits/ncsir-2017/.

Sheshadri, V. (2019). *How to conduct a vulnerability assessment (in cybersecurity).* https://riversafe.co.uk/tech-blog/how-to-conduct-a-vulnerability-assessment-in-cybersecurity/.

Study says fintech startups vulnerable to web or mobile app attacks. (2019). https://www.itworldcanada.com/article/fintech-startups-vulnerable-to-web-or-mobile-app-attacks-vendor-study/421134.

Uddin, M. H., Ali, M. H., & Hassan, M. K. (2020). Cybersecurity hazards and financial system vulnerability: a synthesis of literature. *Risk Management, 22*, 239–309.

Wu, M. (2019). *6 strategies for creating your cyber vulnerability assessment.* https://securityscorecard.com/blog/strategies-for-creating-cyber-vulnerability-assessment.

Cybersecurity Risk in FinTech

6

Security threats disrupt business and hence, financial stability. The attractiveness of financial gain and access to confidential data are the two most important reasons for making the financial sector one of the biggest targets. Therefore, cybersecurity risk management is vital to every financial organization in combating these security threats. As with other financial risks, firms must decide how to manage their exposure to cyber threats. The risk identified, analyzed, and evaluated in the risk assessment needs to be actively managed, including reducing, transferring, and avoiding risk.

The essential component of the risk management model is to identify threats and vulnerabilities, evaluate or assess the risk to determine monetary and nonmonetary assets and compute approximate loss to these assets, and vulnerable systems in the organization. This step uses standard risk assessment methods designed to rate the risk on a scale to determine its importance and prioritizes it based on the probability of occurrence and its impact on critical resources.

This chapter defines cybersecurity risk and introduces various cybersecurity risks faced by FinTech. It proceeds with the cyber risk life cycle and provides a comprehensive discussion of risk assessment, analysis, mitigation, monitoring, and review steps. It further presents challenges faced by the cybersecurity risk management process in FinTech. Finally, it analyzes various uncertainties in Fintech risk management and proposes solutions to deal with those uncertainties.

6.1 What Is Risk?

In general terms, the risk is the possibility of mishappening. It is related to uncertainty in different domains of a person's day-to-day activities. For example, a businessperson considers falling prices as a risk to his business revenue. A new car driver assumes accidents are a risk as they may cause damage to his vehicle. Risk always focuses on the negative impacts of a single or series of incidents.

G. Kaur et al., *Understanding Cybersecurity Management in FinTech*, Future of Business and Finance, https://doi.org/10.1007/978-3-030-79915-1_6

In computer science, risk is anything that damages the computer system or steals data from it. To elaborate, when malware exploits a computer system, it results in potential damage to the computer system and may steal some data from it. The situation is considered a risk to the computer system.

NIST SP 800-28 Version 2

A measure of the likelihood and the consequence of events or acts that could cause a system compromise, including the unauthorized disclosure, destruction, removal, modification, or interruption of system assets.

6.2 What Is the Cybersecurity Risk?

Based on the understanding of cybersecurity and risk definition, cybersecurity risk may be defined as the probability of exposure resulting from the data breach by malicious insiders or cybercriminals. From an organizational perspective, cybersecurity risk is a potential loss or harm caused by cyberattacks related to an organization's critical infrastructure. The critical infrastructure includes tangible and intangible assets such as technology, reputation, and intellectual property. Since organizations are becoming more dependent on computers, networks, and social media, the probability of cyber exploits is also surging at a much faster rate.

Figure 6.1 highlights the timeline of cyber risk trends in the global economy. Apparently, cyber risk began to trend in the third quarter of 2014 and then declined till the first quarter of 2016. It remained stable in 2016 and started to increase gradually until the third quarter of 2017. With a consistent value in 2018, it has been decreasing since 2019. The continuous decline in cyber risk trends in the global economy in the last 2 years has been attributed to Brexit, which is beyond the scope of this book.

Cybersecurity risks and threats to an organization as identified by the NIST information technology laboratory (Cybersecurity Risks, NIST Information

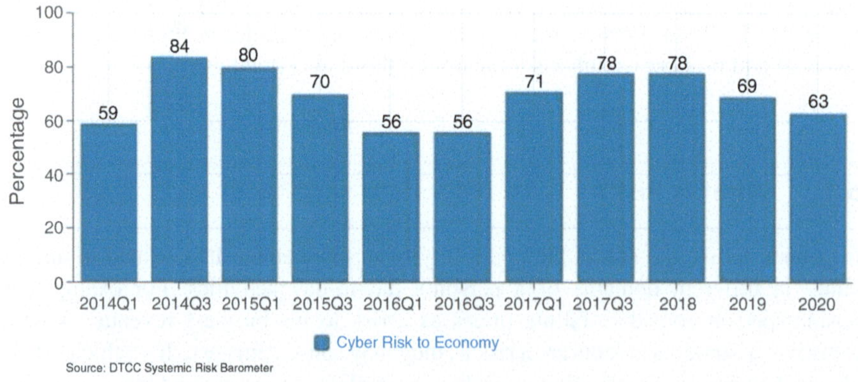

Fig. 6.1 Cyber risk trends in the global economy (2014–2020)

Table 6.1 Cybersecurity risks and threats identified by NIST IT laboratory (Cybersecurity Risks, NIST Information Technology Laboratory 2019)

Sr. no.	Cybersecurity risk	Organization[a]	Security tip number
1	Malicious code	DHS	ST18-004
2	Destructive malware	DHS	ST13-003
3	Hidden threats: Rootkits and botnets	DHS	ST06-001
4	Fake antiviruses	DHS	ST10-001
5	Hidden threats: Corrupted software files	DHS	ST06-006
6	Ransomware	FTC	–
7	Spyware	DHS	ST04-016
8	Denial-of-service attacks	DHS	ST04-015
9	Phishing	FTC	–
10	Business email imposters	FTC	–
11	Network infrastructure devices	DHS	ST18-001
12	Website	DHS	ST18-006
13	Wireless networks	DHS	ST05-003
14	Cell phones and personal digital assistants (PDAs)	DHS	ST06-007

[a]*DHS* Department of Homeland Security, *FTC* Federal Trade Commission

Technology Laboratory 2019) are presented in Table 6.1. NIST also provides a security tip number for every identified cybersecurity risk defining the risk and providing a detailed description of the security measures to protect against those risks.

All these cybersecurity risks are explained below:

- **Malicious code:** Malicious code is an unwanted program that may cause harm to a computer system when executed. It may compromise a computer system or steal data from it. Malicious code can be classified as viruses, worms, malware, or trojan horses.
  - **Virus**: It can destroy files on the infected computer. It can spread through infected removable media, surfing malicious websites, and downloading malicious content.
  - **Worm**: It is a type of virus that self-propagates on the network. Its aim is to exhaust all resources to make the computer system unresponsive.
  - **Malware**: It is malicious software that infects the computer on which it is installed.
  - **Trojan horse**: It acts as a carrier that hides malicious software. It masquerades as legitimate free software that hides malicious software in it.
- **Destructive malware:** Destructive malware is a malicious code designed to destroy data. It hampers the availability of assets and resources in the organization to impact operations.
- **Hidden threats (rootkits, botnets, and corrupt software files):**

- **Rootkit**: Rootkit is malicious software that is installed on the computer without the user's knowledge. It acts as a hidden threat because the user is not aware of any such software installed on his machine. Rootkit allows the attacker to take advantage of any vulnerability found in the target machine so that the attacker can exploit it. Rootkit may not be malicious, but it allows attackers to monitor information on the target computer, modify settings, raise privileges, or perform severe functions without being detected.
- **Botnet**: Botnets are networks of bots. In simple terms, a bot is a robot that automatically performs some functions based on the instructions provided by the controller. Botnets are used in launching DDoS attacks. The attacker infects one computer, gains control, programs it to perform prespecified functions, and uses it to launch other attacks. Like rootkits, botnets are also hidden threats.
- **Corrupted software files**: A corrupt software file contains a malicious code injected by the attacker. The software file may include common file types such as a doc, docx, and pdf. Once the file is infected, the attacker will upload the file to any website. When the user downloads and opens the corrupt file, his computer gets infected.

- **Fake antivirus:** Fake antivirus is a malware designed to steal information by performing unauthorized activities such as modifying system settings. This type of software is difficult to terminate and remove from the system. It generates realistic computer warnings to pretend to be real to the user.
- **Ransomware:** Ransomware is a malware that encrypts files and directories on the machine to make them inaccessible to users. It asks for a handsome amount of ransom to provide the decryption key that is used to unlock the data. Ransoms are often paid for bitcoins. It is observed from past incidents that some users were not able to get the data back even after paying the ransom. Some of them received some files and lost the others after paying the ransom. Therefore, it cannot be confirmed that paying the ransom will be helpful or not.
- **Spyware:** Spyware is malicious software installed on a user's device to steal sensitive information. The data collected by spyware is passed to advertisers, external agencies, or firms. This data is later used to carry out malicious activities.
- **Denial-of-Service attacks:** Denial of Service (DoS) is meant to restrict legitimate users from accessing the services by sending a huge amount of service requests to the service provider. For example, in a DoS attack, an attacker sends a vast number of connection requests to a web server such that it crashes and is unable to fulfill the requests of legitimate clients. In a DoS attack, one attacker machine targets one server machine. In a distributed denial-of-service (DDoS) attack, several attacker machines target one server machine. The attacker machines in a DDoS attack are called zombies or botnets.
- **Phishing:** Phishing is a luring attack in which the target is reached via email, telephone, or text message. The attacker attracts the target to click on a link to redirect him to malicious websites, download malicious software on the target computer, or deduct payment from the target's bank account by fooling him to reveal his username and password for the online banking portal. Phishing attacks

focus on stealing personally identified information, bank account details, credit card data, and other sensitive information.

- **Business email imposters:** The attacker creates a fake email address resembling the official email address of the organization. The fake email address is used to send emails to employees often organization to make them believe that the email is received from the authorized personnel in the organization. The practice of creating such email addresses and sending emails is called spoofing and phishing, respectively. While sending phishing emails, attackers ask for sensitive personal information from the target employees such as their username and password for the computer systems that they are authorized to access. By stealing sensitive information, attackers break into the computer and raise their privileges to perform malicious activities.
- **Network infrastructure devices:** Network infrastructure components are the hardware devices in a network used to send and receive information from the source to the destination device. Some important network devices include routers, switches, firewalls, servers, intrusion detection systems, and storage area networks. These devices are an important target for attackers as most of the network traffic passes through them.
- **Website:** Website security is the protection of public websites from cyberattacks. The most common website attacks include compromising a public website to make it unavailable to the users, stealing information from the web forms filled online by the user, and taking control of the website to redirect users to malicious websites.
- **Wireless networks:** Wireless networks are one of the prime targets of cyberattacks. Some common attacks on wireless networks include evil twins, fake Wi-Fi access points, and man-in-the-middle attacks.
- **Cell phones and personal digital assistants (PDAs):** Attackers are used to lure users to click a malicious link, compromise cell phones and PDAs, steal information, root it, and use it to launch further attacks.

6.3 Cybersecurity Risk Lifecycle

Cybersecurity risk is the probability of exposure from a data breach performed by malicious insiders or external cybercriminals. In other words, risk is the likelihood that a threat will exploit the vulnerability to cause harm to a tangible or intangible asset. It can be mathematically represented as follows:

$$\text{Risk} = \text{Threat} \times \text{Vulnerability}$$

According to this formula, when there is no vulnerability, there is no risk. This is a rare situation because a system without any vulnerability is not possible in real time. However, there is a possibility that vulnerabilities exist in the system, but there is no potential threat to those vulnerabilities because they are unknown to the attacker.

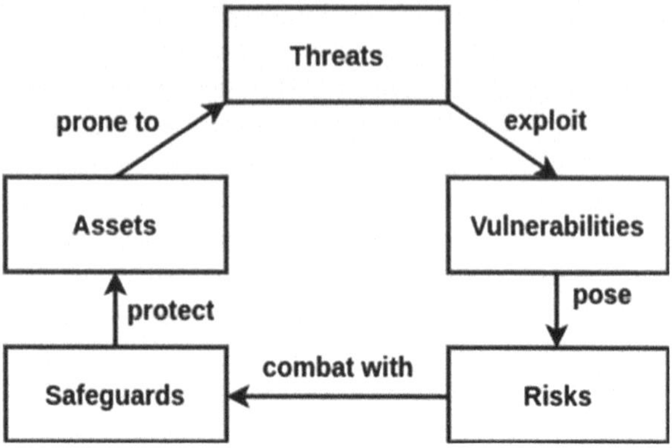

Fig. 6.2 Cyber risk life cycle

Thus, reducing either threat or vulnerability would result directly in a risk reduction. We have already outlined various threats, threat actors, and types of vulnerabilities in the FinTech industry in previous chapters. The entire concept of cybersecurity is based on preventing risks by fixing vulnerabilities and blocking threat actors. Overall, a sample risk life cycle can be presented as shown in Fig. 6.2.

According to this life cycle:

Threats exploit vulnerabilities which pose risks. Risks can be combated with safeguards which protect assets. Finally, assets are prone to threats.

Risk management is a detailed process of identifying factors that could disclose sensitive information and incur losses. The primary objective of risk management is to reduce the risk to an acceptable level. The acceptable level of risk varies for every financial company based on its size, assets, type of data, other factors. It is observed from the recent cyberattacks on FinTech that erroneous risk management plans adopted by FinTech institutions are accountable for the unprecedented upsurge in cyberattacks on financial institutions, especially banks.

FinTech cyber risk management comprises a sequential strategy to assess, analyze, evaluate, mitigate, and monitor cyber risk. Simply put, risk management acts as a tool to implement security tools or safeguards. FinTech risk management taxonomy can be divided into three broad strategies: risk assessment, risk analysis, risk monitor and report, as shown in Fig. 6.3.

The following sections elaborate on the details of risk assessment, risk analysis, and risk monitoring.

6.4 Risk Assessment

The essential component of the risk management model is to identify threats and vulnerabilities, evaluate or assess the risk to determine monetary and nonmonetary assets and compute approximate loss to these assets, and vulnerable systems in the

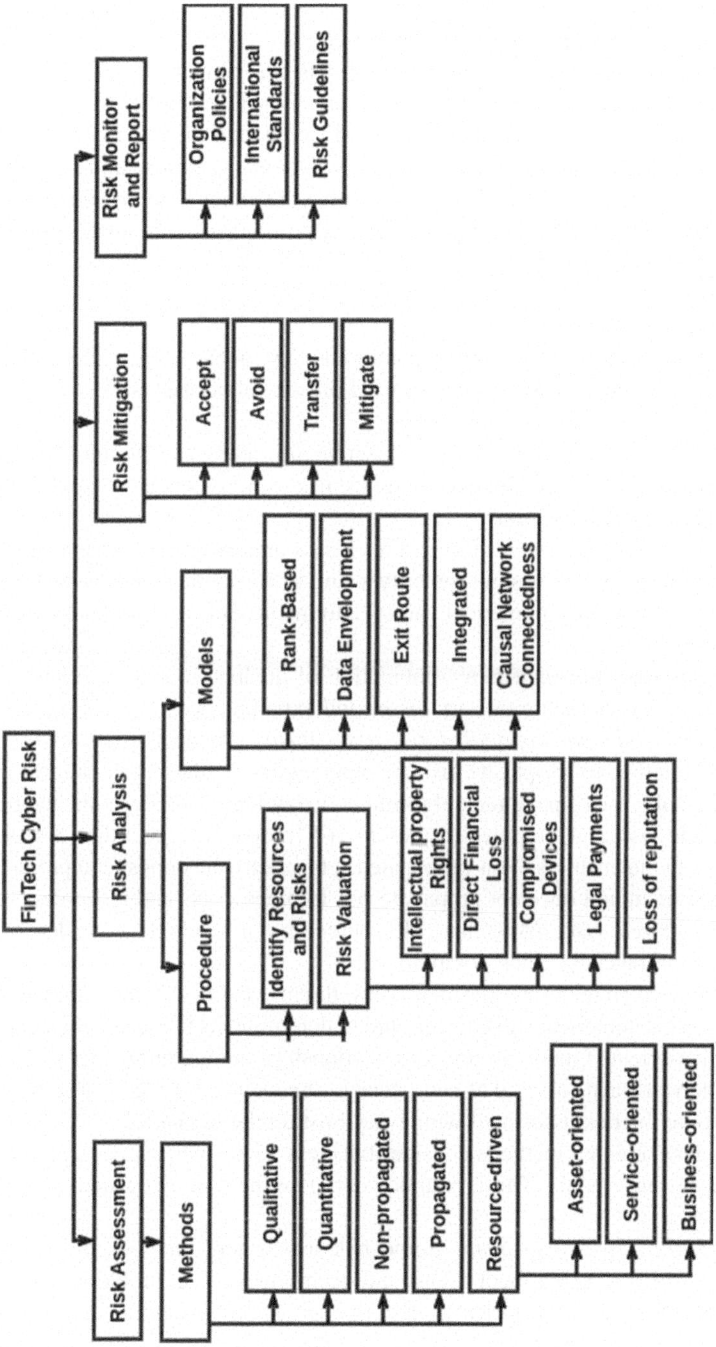

Fig. 6.3 FinTech cyber risk taxonomy

organization. This step uses standard risk assessment methods designed to rate the risk on a scale to determine its importance and prioritizes it based on the probability of occurrence and its impact on critical resources.

Although most of the risk assessment models use similar assessment criteria, taking into consideration various risk factors, threats, vulnerabilities, resources, risk history, and severity of actions taken but they differ in their method to evaluate risk.

Risk assessment is an exercise for upper management to initiate and support risk computation measures. All the decisions, results, outcomes, and documents in the risk assessment process are approved by the upper management and followed by middle-level management.

Risk Assessment Methods

There are two main risk assessment methodologies: quantitative and qualitative. However, hybrid risk assessment is also used on several occasions.

- *Qualitative risk assessment:* It is subjective in nature and assigns intangible values to the losses. Qualitative methods use various levels of appraisement according to expert decisions.
- *Quantitative risk assessment:* It measures losses in numbers and assigns a monetary value to it. It also assigns severity value to losses (low, medium, high). It makes use of matrices, numerical values, and mathematical formulae to compute loss due to risk.
- *Hybrid risk assessment:* It is a combination of qualitative and quantitative risk assessment. It uses both monetary losses and expert advice.
- *Propagated and non-propagated risk assessment:* Propagated risk assessment methods attempt to propagate risk to other assets in the organization. These methods make use of page rank algorithms, fuzzy logic, and dependency graphs to compute risk and graphically present risk propagation to other assets and resources in the business. Non-propagated acts exactly the opposite to propagated risk assessment and does not propagate risk to other assets and resources.
- *Resource-driven risk assessment:* Resource-driven methods consider assets, services, and business when computing risk.
  - Asset-oriented methods consider assets, threats, and associated vulnerabilities to assign a numerical value to risk and to determine its impact on the business.
  - Service-oriented methods consider relationships among numerous services in the network and losses that can occur in the event of a risk. These methods compute the risk associated with every host on the network.
  - Business-oriented methods consider business goals and processes required to achieve those goals. These methods compute the risk associated with every process.
- *Miscellaneous risk assessment:* Some risk assessment methods utilize expert advice with risk assessment tools and techniques. The problem with such methods is the lack of historical data to operate automated tools.

For the FinTech industry, the risk is assessed qualitatively as well as quantitatively. Some financial organizations follow a hybrid approach too. There is an emerging trend in the FinTech industry to use big data and machine learning for assessing credit card risk. Despite its popularity, the reliability of this method over traditional methods, including financial data and scorecard models, is questionable (Bazarbash 2019; Huang et al. 2020).

There is a strong comparison between scorecard-based traditional risk assessment methods and big data-oriented artificially intelligent models. Some financial institutions believe that they can also apply traditional methods to big data with good risk assessment. There are a few research papers that collected financial data from local FinTech lending firms and analyzed the digital footprints left by customers on e-commerce platforms using big data and machine learning (Berg et al. 2020; Agarwal et al. 2019; Frost et al. 2019; Jagtiani and Lemieux 2019).

Machine learning-based lending has several advantages and disadvantages. On the one hand, it brings small borrowers into reality. On the other hand, it bears the risk of financial exclusion, customer privacy, and protection issues.

The primary challenge in FinTech risk assessment is the unavailability of historical data related to cyber threats. Since every financial institution has a market value and reputation among competitors, it does not want to reveal to the world at first that it became a victim of a cyberattack. If some financial institutions accept being a target, they do not share the cyberattack data due to several reasons, including the sensitivity of customer financial data, legal policies, compliance with financial standards, and reputation. For example, only 49% of cyberattacks in the financial sector were reported in the UK in 2017. Moreover, international cyber data sharing also has certain constraints.

6.5 Risk Analysis

Risk analysis is a three-step procedure that (1) identifies critical resources, (2) determines threats that can exploit the vulnerabilities to put the resources at stake, and (3) evaluates risk by assigning a rating to them. This subsection addresses the step-by-step procedure used to analyze risks and puts forward existing risk analysis strategies for FinTech. It also sheds light on risk analysis models used by researchers.

6.5.1 Procedure

Risk analysis follows a three-step procedure explained below:

- *Identify resources:* Risk analysis commences with identifying critical financial resources, both tangible and intangible, that are at stake. For a typical FinTech industry, critical resources include network devices, asset documents, business services, processes and activities, and network and personal information. It is to emphasize here that data stored on a cloud and physical memory are also cataloged when discussing data. The valuation of these resources varies based on the importance of resources.

- *Determine threats and risks:* Risk identification associated potential risks with threats and vulnerabilities. Risk is expressed as a relationship between threats and vulnerabilities. Identified risks are analyzed to determine the monetary and nonmonetary losses that can occur if the risk is triggered. In order to identify the vulnerabilities and threats, previous audit reports, lessons learned documents, anomaly analyses, IT audit records, and test and evaluation systems are referred. Potential threats for a FinTech firm include phishing, denial of service, information theft, and spam attacks. These threats allow the threat actor to gain unauthorized access and exploit the vulnerabilities. This ultimately results in risk.
- *Evaluate risks:* In the previous two steps, the risk analysis procedure outlines critical resources and potential risks. The next step in the analysis part is to evaluate the identified risks to assign a severity rating to them. The severity rate helps to prioritize the risks so that risks with high severity are addressed first. Risk evaluation is also referred to as risk valuation. It makes use of a risk analysis model that computers threat actors, probability of occurrence of threats, and their impact on business processes and activities. The model is expected to evaluate the risk analysis algorithms for financial risk analysis using several financial datasets. Clustering algorithms are used to cluster similar types of risk together. However, it is evident from the research work that there is not a single clustering algorithm that outperforms other clustering algorithms. That means that all the clustering algorithms perform equally well. The risk evaluates the following financial risks:
  - Intellectual Property rights: Intellectual property rights (IPRs) are given to people who create something innovative and useful. IPR gives the creator an exclusive right to creation. It includes copyrights, industrial rights, and patents. Such creations are considered confidential and attributed to the unique designs, processes, services, systems, or activities that are followed by the financial institution. Since IPRs are the private property of the financial institution, it is not intended to share with the competitors. Thus, evaluating the risk of related information theft becomes important.
  - Direct losses: Direct losses due to business or processes are also evaluated. These losses report a direct monetary loss due to physical damage.
  - Compromised devices: Nonfunctioning of compromised devices results in the unavailability of some of the essential services. These services may not count on direct monetary losses, but they influence nonmonetary losses.
  - Legal payments: If the financial institution sues the threat actor, a legal team is hired to follow the case. It involves legal payments that add as a surplus to the risk analysis procedure.
  - Loss of reputation: Finally, all the above factors heighten the loss of reputation among various stakeholders, competitors, government, and users. Loss of reputation is assigned high severity since monetary losses can be compensated but a loss of reputation cannot be.

6.5.2 Strategies

Risk analysis strategies deal with developing stereotypes and risk valuation criteria to analyze the impact of risk on finances. Like risk assessment, risk analysis can be performed quantitatively or qualitatively. Systemic risks are the most severe risks because they break down the entire system rather than affecting individual components. The exposure of financial institutions to systemic risk depends on the size of the institution. The management uses the risk analysis report to make decisions to tackle risks in the future. The most common risk analysis strategies used for risk analysis include questionnaires, operations research, and the Copula function. Discussing these strategies is beyond the scope of this book.

6.5.3 Models

A risk analysis model attempts to analyze cyber threats and provides evaluation tools to assess risks. The outcome of the risk analysis model is used at a managerial level to make strategic decisions about tackling risks. There are several risk analysis models used in research work that are briefed here. Every model has its unique metrics, strategies, and properties to prevent risk.

- *Rank-based Clustering Algorithm (*Kou et al. 2014*):* This is an empirical model based on rank selection. It uses eleven performance measures and three Multiple Criteria Decision Making (MCDM) methods to rank six clustering algorithms for financial risk analysis. The model uses three real-time credit cards and bankruptcy risk datasets to evaluate and rank clustering algorithms. This model validates the fact that none of the clustering algorithms outperforms others under different criteria for evaluating risks.
- *Data Envelopment Analysis Model (*Cooper et al. 2014*):* This model assesses relative risk tolerance. It uses a questionnaire that characterizes risk by four distinct elements: propensity, attitude, capacity, and knowledge. It establishes a relationship between financial risk, its elements, and other variables. The model uses demographic information, socioeconomic, and psychological nature of data to present multidimensionality of risk. The risk score is computed based on a slack-based measure. The model validates the use of questionnaires for assessing risk and concludes that the four characteristics of risk elements bear a weak relationship with each other, implying that these elements can be assessed separately.
- *Exit Route Model (*Amendola et al. 2015*):* It is a competing risk model that estimates the difference among variables to exit the market through bankruptcy, liquidation, and inactivity. Factors influencing financial distress for any exit route are identified. This model investigates the influence and effect of micro-economic indicators and firm-specific factors on multi-States. Financial data from Italian firms is analyzed to validate the results of the model.

- *Integrated Model (*de Gusmão et al. 2018*):* This model integrates fault tree analysis, fuzzy theory, and decision theory to identify vulnerabilities in the cybersecurity system and find the causes of cybersecurity system failure. It is developed for e-commerce websites and enterprise resource planning (ERP) systems. Simply put, the model evaluates the consequences of potential cyberattacks in terms of financial losses and time for restoration. During the five-phase process, the main objective of the model is to evaluate cyberattacks and their consequences.
- *Causal Network* Connectedness *Model (*Gong et al. 2019*):* This model studies the contribution of individual financial firms to compute systemic risk through Systemic Risk index (SRISK), Marginal Expected Shortfall (MES), and Conditional Value at Risk (CoVaR). The model is applied to banks, securities, and insurance companies in Chinese financial markets. It treats the financial system as a network and builds a complex financial network through Granger causality relationships. Then, it measures the connectedness based on Principal Component Analysis (PCA). The model filters out the risk and captures pairwise statistical relations among individual firms.

Although these models are used to analyze systemic risk in the financial sector or cyber risk, they can be used for evaluating and analyzing cyber risks for financial firms, provided cyber threat data is available. Table 6.2 compares all the risk analysis models.

Comparison is based on eight important variables (RA1-RA8) designed to distinguish the capabilities of every approach/model from the rest. Most of the approaches/models provide a proper overview of the risk analysis approach by a specific financial institution and cover domains such as banks, financial firms, the investment sector, e-commerce enterprises, and insurance companies. However, the following major shortcomings are identified:

- All the models are related to financial data in one way or the other and provide an overview of the risk analysis process.
- None of the models provides risk analysis taxonomy, cyber risks that it is considering for analysis, and risk analysis standards that it follows.
- All the models use a distinct approach, target a specific financial domain, and emphasize a particular risk scenario. None of them has proven its potential so that it can be adopted as a unanimous model for all risk scenarios.

6.6 Risk Mitigation

After assessing, analyzing, and evaluating cyber risks, the next step is to mitigate them based on the outcome of risk evaluation measures. There are four ways to address a cyber risk (Harris and Maymi 2018; Landoll 2006; Wheeler 2011):

Table 6.2 Comparison of existing FinTech risk analysis approaches/models

Model	Year	Domain	RA1[a]	RA2[a]	RA3[a]	RA4[a]	RA5[a]	RA6[a]	RA7[a]	RA8[a]
Rank-based	2014	Bank	Yes	Yes	No	No	No	Yes	Yes	No
Data envelopment	2014	Investment	Yes	Yes	No	No	Yes	Yes	Yes	No
Exit route	2015	FinTech firm	Yes	Yes	No	No	Yes	Yes	Yes	No
Integrated	2018	e-commerce	Yes	Yes	No	No	Yes	Yes	Yes	No
Causal network connectedness	2019	Bank	Yes	Yes	No	No	Yes	Yes	Yes	No

[a] *RA:* Risk Analysis, *RA1:* Overview, *RA2:* Methodology, *RA3:* Taxonomy, *RA4:* Cyber risks and threats, *RA5:* Proposed methodology, *RA6:* Parameters to compute risk, *RA7:* Findings, *RA8:* Standards followed

- **Risk acceptance:** It is the strategy adopted by a financial organization to accept risk after understanding its consequences for the business.
- **Risk avoidance:** It is used to avoid altogether the activities posing minor risk to a business.
- **Risk transfer:** It is the two-step policy where some part of the risk is accepted in the first step, and the rest is transferred to another party as the second step.
- **Risk Mitigation:** it is the procedure to control the risk and its consequences to reduce it that is below the threshold value of risk acceptance to business.

Handling risk in the financial sector involves using a combination of all these ways, i.e., some risks are avoided, some are transferred, some are mitigated, and the rest are accepted. Additionally, we outline certain cyber threats and risk mitigation measures for them in Table 6.3.

6.7 Risk Monitoring and Review

Monitoring cybersecurity risks is important to collect cyber data for future risk analyses. There are certain standard risk policies and guidelines for effective risk monitoring and review.

- **Organizational policies:** At the beginners' level, every organization has its own risk monitoring policy, which is designed by the upper management and followed by middle-level management. This policy covers several basic rules and regulations related to cyber risk that the employees must abide by. The depth of rules and safety measures to protect sensitive information depends on several crucial factors such as organization size, budget, the importance of financial data, risk acceptance level, and exposure to vulnerabilities. Organizational policies such as strong passwords, knowledge of social engineering, trained staff, and confidentiality of sensitive financial data are some of the fundamental practices that need to be followed to reduce cyber risk. Some organizations might prefer to avoid or accept the risk, while others may prefer to mitigate it. The analogy of implementing cybersecurity risk monitoring and review policy varies from one organization to another.
- **Risk guidelines:** Apart from organizational policies, FinTech firms also prepare risk guidelines that define the extent to which a risk can be tolerated and what actions are required in case that risk exceeds a certain threshold value.
- **International cybersecurity risk management standards:** To monitor cyber thefts, the financial sector must stringently implement cybersecurity risk management standards released by international organizations such as the National Institute of Standards and Technology (NIST) and the International Organization for Standardization and the International Electrotechnical Commission (ISO/IEC).

Table 6.3 Cyber threats and corresponding risk mitigation measures

Threats	Risk mitigation
Social engineering and phishing	• Educate users • Control of social media interactions • Implement physical security controls
Ransomware	Accept the risk of sensitive data being encrypted and continue taking backups to avoid losing data.
XSS	Deploy content security policy to prevent exploitation of vulnerability.
Brute force	• Use CAPTCHA and restricted access to authentication URLs. • Design a lockout policy to block accounts after a specific number of failed login attempts.
Malware	• Change control process. • Check misconfigurations. • Endpoint security such as antivirus or anti-malware • Host-based security using HIDS and HIPS • Network perimeter security using firewalls, IDS, and IPS by creating access rules • Use of next-generation firewalls (NGFWs) to detect zero-day attacks • Updating the obsolete versions of operating systems and applications • Close unnecessarily opened ports, services, and processes in computer systems. • Compensating controls • Checking data integrity for sensitive data
Cloud-based data breach	• Signing data breach policy with vendor • Data encryption • Identity management
Data breach	• Data storage and backup policy • Access control • Assign limited bandwidth to users • Creating a chain of custody • Use of next-generation firewalls (NGFWs)
Insider threats	• Separation of duties • Mandatory vacation • Dual control • Acceptable use policy (AUP) • Employee exit policy • Succession planning • Manage access control • Limit access to super-user account (Linux) and administrator account (Windows)

6.8 Challenges in FinTech Risk Management

There are several models for managing FinTech systemic and operational risk but there is a scarcity of Fintech cybersecurity risk management models. Despite these collective works for risk identification, assessment, analysis, mitigation, and reporting for FinTech, the following are the open issues and challenges related to FinTech cybersecurity risk management:

- **Unavailability of data:** There are many barriers to obtaining cyber risk data for FinTech cyber risk management. Financial institutions are reluctant to share their cyberattack data owing to reputation loss and reduced market value. Moreover, financial cyber data cannot be shared at an international level in compliance with regulatory standards. There are a couple of research workers who managed to obtain credit card data from local financial institutions, subjected to anonymity. With the lack of real-time cyberattack data from the FinTech industry, it is computationally inefficient to execute a cyber risk management model for FinTech.
- **Emerging technology:** Technological innovation gives birth to new models, services, product delivery platforms, and creative approaches to lure customers. The primary challenge with emerging technology is the cost associated with it and the vulnerabilities in the software and infrastructure used to develop that technology. Most of the startups get themselves into the FinTech business by investing in such technologies, but they are not technically mature to adopt strong cybersecurity controls to safeguard their technology.
- **Market growth:** Customers demand a faster and easier FinTech service. This pushes the financial service providers to respond with quicker technological and product innovation. This, in turn, allows the service providers to increase their market value. However, market growth brings new challenges to the service providers, such as investing in high-quality product development and using third-party cloud services to store data.
- **Partnerships and alliances:** The FinTech industry is growing by collaborating with other financial institutions. This enables them to expand their traditional operations and adopt big data and machine learning technology to process, transform, and analyze the comparatively bigger financial data.
- **Regulatory scrutiny:** FinTech is expanding the business by collaborating with other financial institutions, adopting innovative technology, seeking third-party service providers, and building their market share. Such integration with different parties brings regulatory compliance into the picture. Every financial institution has its own regulations, which may contradict with partner industry's compliance standards.
- **Money laundering:** FinTech firms use cryptocurrency for carrying out financial transactions. Frequent use of illegal currencies results in money laundering and terrorist funding.
- **Critical resources:** Identifying critical resources for finance is crucial to avoid or prevent severe cyber risks. Every resource needs to be prioritized to protect it from potential cyberattacks and measure its impact on financial transactions.
- **Lack of automated risk management model:** Due to the unavailability of cyber data for the financial sector, there is a lack of automated cyber risk management models for FinTech. These models can take cyber threat data as input to apply automated operations and functions to assess, analyze, and monitor cyber risks.
- **Unawareness:** Financial service users and providers are not cyber trained. Therefore, they are unaware of the vulnerabilities and threats that can exploit those vulnerabilities. This makes them susceptible to phishing attacks and social

engineering tactics. It is evident from reported cyberattacks in FinTech that malware is executed accidentally because someone clicked on a malicious link that downloaded the malware on the machine.

6.9 Dealing with Uncertainty in FinTech

Startup companies are fetching massive amounts of funding in the FinTech industry when compared to any other industry. The mentality of financial companies and generational factors have fueled the momentum of the FinTech industry. Artificial intelligence (AI) and blockchain play a pivotal role in enabling FinTech companies to compete and partner with financial giants. Although AI and blockchain have been extensively used in multiple domains for over a decade, they are making significant efforts to reshape the future of Fintech. Apart from the opportunities such as digital wallets, cashless transactions, digital lending, and global payments, there exist some uncertainties in FinTech that need to be addressed.

6.10 Kinds of Uncertainty

FinTech uncertainties can be broadly divided into three categories: (1) dominance of banks over technology, (2) data breach, and (3) cyber risk.

- **The dominance of banks over technology:** Despite growing technologies, there are still many banks that prefer to work in the traditional way. These banks fear technological disruption. Their reluctance to emerging technology and preference for traditional working culture makes the future of FinTech uncertain.
- **Data breach:** Information theft or data breach is one of the important challenges for FinTech. FinTech companies deal with sensitive financial data that includes credit card details and personally identifiable information. Cybercriminals steal information and sell it for monetary gain. Stolen information is also used by hacker groups to send phishing emails, emulate personal identity, illegally transfer money, money laundering, and fund nation-state terrorist activities. Surging data breaches is a cause of concern for financial institutions since it adds to the uncertainty of FinTech security.
- **Cyber risk:** The unrivaled threat of cyber risk is creating havoc in the FinTech industry. Only a handful of cyber incidents are reported from a massive pool of total cyber incidents per year. Many financial institutions believe that concealing cyber incidents helps them not to reduce their market value. However, the reality is something else. A financial institution may be attacked again if the vulnerabilities are not fixed. Implementing a cyber risk management solution is necessary to compute cyber risks in advance and plan some measures to mitigate them at the earliest.

6.11 Reducing Uncertainty

The kinds of uncertainties identified in the previous subsection can be reduced by adopting the following approaches:

- **Expanding the horizon:** FinTech is expanding its approach by involving startup companies and small-to-medium scale businesses that process massive numbers of international transactions such as Airbnb. These are the business vendors that use existing financial platforms to do financial transactions. There is another kind of business that builds financial products from scratch. These companies include WeChat and Alipay. These business vendors provide a ray of hope to reduce uncertainty raised by traditional banks.
- **Active monitoring:** Ransomware attacks are common in banks nowadays, but the impact or devastating outcomes of these attacks can be drastically reduced by taking incremental data backup at regular intervals of time or actively monitoring the assets and resources to detect the threats as soon as they attempt to exploit the vulnerabilities. To instantiate, Finastra, a London-based banking software maker, survived a ransomware attack in the first quarter of 2020 without paying the ransom. Finastra works with over 100 of the largest banks in the world. It took the servers offline once the ransomware attacks were initiated, which helped it save its files from the cloud.
- **Putting blockchain and Fintech together:** Blockchain is acting as the backbone of the FinTech industry. It is the driving force behind the revolutionized financial sector. Establishing trust among people for a secure financial business is the key to the success of blockchain. It has the potential to create transparent, decentralized, immutable, and efficient processes. Blockchain facilitates distributed digital payments, smart contracts, and shared trading to explore the opportunities in the FinTech industry.

6.12 Handling Uncertainty for FinTech Cybersecurity Risk

Researchers believe that systemic risk assessment and analysis models can also be implemented to compute cyber risks for FinTech. This deployment is subject to the availability of cyberattack data. A few researchers produced encouraging results by capturing cyberattack data from small financial firms to assess and analyze the proposed cyber risk models (Cooper et al. 2014; Amendola et al. 2015).

As discussed under challenges faced by FinTech risk management (Sect. 6.7), the unavailability of cyber risk data is one of the key issues in FinTech. Suppose representative cyber risk data is made available by the financial firms. In that case, the researchers will compute a realistic cyber risk score that will help the FinTech industry know the uncertain nature of cyber risks that may threaten their business in the future. We suggest the following measures to handle uncertainty about FinTech cybersecurity risk:

- **Secure digital transactions:** Digital transactions need to be governed by a secure communications protocol standard that ensures the security of credit card transactions over the Internet. One example of a secure communication protocol standard is Secure Electronic Transaction (SET). It was initially supported by Mastercard, Visa, Microsoft, Netscape, and others. It uses a digital certificate that verifies a transaction among merchants by using a combination of digital signatures and digital certificates. In this way, it enforces the privacy and confidentiality of digital data.
- **Protect critical infrastructure:** We have used SaaS, IaaS, and PaaS while discussing cloud-based transactions. One more term, which is related to the security of a service, called SECaaS, is added to cloud-based transactions. It is a business model which the third-party service providers use to integrate security services into the infrastructure. The SECaaS model is inspired by SaaS, which is applied to information security.
- **Know your vulnerabilities:** One basic principle of cybersecurity is knowing the enemies you need to fight with. For an effective FinTech cybersecurity risk management system, it is imperative to list down the vulnerabilities in the system that may be exposed to internal and external threats. Once weaknesses are known, proper measures can be taken to fix them to avoid any risks.
- **Compute risks:** FinTech companies must be aware of the potential cyber risks that can impact their business. Computed risk scores help to prioritize some risks over others. This way, companies can address severe risks with appropriate remedies.
- **Backup data regularly:** One of the protective measures in the cybersecurity arsenal is to back up the data at a regular interval of time. It aids in keeping a copy of the essential data files on an alternative server. In case the primary server is under a distributed denial-of-service attack or ransomware attack, the users can access their data from the alternative server. It also always ensures the availability of data.

6.13 Chapter Summary

This chapter instigates cybersecurity risks in FinTech. It brings forward various cybersecurity risks faced by FinTech and introduces cybersecurity risk trends in FinTech institutions. It provides a comprehensive introduction to risk assessment, analysis, mitigation, monitoring, and review steps. It identifies various challenges to the FinTech risk management process. Various uncertainties in the risk management process are listed toward the end of the chapter. Finally, the chapter proposes solutions to handle the identified uncertainties.

Cybersecurity risks impact almost all the components in the FinTech ecosystem, especially various financial institutions that use innovative technology, FinTech startups that transform traditional financial institutions into contemporary FinTech institutions, and financial customers in the FinTech ecosystem. Technology developers are also related to cybersecurity risk as they need to be aware of potential threats that can exercise vulnerabilities and flaws in the technology that they are developing. Overall, the following questions are answered in this chapter:

- What is a cybersecurity risk, and what are the recent cyber risks trending in FinTech institutions?
- What are risk management and various steps to perform it?
- What are the challenges faced by FinTech risk management?
- What are the uncertainties in FinTech risk management?
- How can these uncertainties be handled?

References

Agarwal, S., Alok, S., Ghosh, P., & Gupta, S. (2019). *Financial inclusion and alternate credit scoring for the millennials: Role of big data and machine learning in Fintech. SSRN scholarly paper* (pp. 1–69). Rochester, NY: Social Science Research Network.

Amendola, A., Restaino, M., & Sensini, L. (2015). An analysis of the determinants of financial distress in Italy: A competing risks approach. *International Review of Economics & Finance, 37*, 33–41.

Bazarbash, M. (2019). *Fintech in financial inclusion: Machine learning applications in assessing credit risk.* IMF Working Paper, WP/19/109, pp. 1–35.

Berg, T., Burg, V., Gombović, A., & Puri, M. (2020). On the rise of FinTechs: Credit scoring using digital footprints. *Review of Financial Studies, 33*(7), 2845–2897.

Cooper, W. W., Kingyens, A. T., & Paradi, J. C. (2014). Two-stage financial risk tolerance assessment using data envelopment analysis. *European Journal of Operational Research, 233* (1), 273–280.

Cybersecurity Risks, NIST Information Technology Laboratory. (2019). https://www.nist.gov/itl/smallbusinesscyber/cybersecurity-basics/cybersecurity-risks.

de Gusmão, A. P. H., Silva, M. M., Poleto, T., Camara e Silva, L., & Costa, A. P. C. S. (2018). Cybersecurity risk analysis model using fault tree analysis and fuzzy decision theory. *International Journal of Information Management, 43*, 248–260.

Frost, J., Gambacorta, L., & Huang, Y. (2019). *Hyun song shin and Pablo Zbinden, BigTech and the changing structure of financial intermediation, BIS working papers 779* (pp. 1–45). Basel, Switzerland: Bank for International Settlements.

Gong, X.-L., Liu, X.-H., Xiong, X., & Zhang, W. (2019). Financial systemic risk measurement based on causal network connectedness analysis. *International Review of Economics & Finance, 64*, 290–307.

Harris, S., & Maymi, F. (2018). *CISSP all-in-one exam guide* (8th ed.). New York: McGraw-Hill.

Huang, Y., Zhang, L., Li, Z., Qiu, H., Sun, T., & Xue, W. (2020). *Fintech credit risk assessment for SMEs: evidence from China.* IMF Working Paper, WP/20/193, pp. 1–43.

Jagtiani, J., & Lemieux, C. (2019). The roles of alternative data and machine learning in fintech lending: Evidence from the LendingClub consumer platform. *Financial Management, 48*, 1009–1029.

Kou, G., Peng, Y., & Wang, G. (2014). Evaluation of clustering algorithms for financial risk analysis using MCDM methods. *Information Sciences, 275*, 1–12.

Landoll, D. (2006). *The security risk assessment handbook: A complete guide for performing security risk assessments* (2nd ed.). Boca Raton: Auerbach Publications.

Wheeler, E. (2011). *Security risk management: Building an information security risk management program from the ground up.* Waltham: Syngress.

Secure Financial Market Infrastructures (S/FMI)

7

Financial market infrastructure (FMI) serves as the backbone of financial markets. It allows financial transactions to take place between people, financial institutions, and businesses in a cheaper and more efficient manner. It is the key component between financial institutions that exchange payments, securities, and derivatives. It allows customers and financial firms to purchase goods and services safely. It strengthens financial stability and economic growth by recording, clearing, and settling monetary and other financial transactions.

Simple examples of FMI include depositing salary into an employee's account, taking cash from an ATM machine, and paying for online purchases. It is estimated that payments worth 360 billion pounds take place every day in the UK through FMI (Financial Market Infrastructures 2019). FMIs also play some other essential functions, such as transferring shares between traders and the stock market, helping banks borrow money from other banks and financial institutions in the market, and lending and borrowing loans to buy houses and invest in the business. FMIs played a pivotal role in the financial crisis of 2007–2009. They acted as a stabilizing force behind settling uncertainty in monetary transactions.

Focusing on FMIs, cyber threats have emerged as a persistent systemic risk. Its persistence makes it difficult to detect and eradicate completely. It is equally difficult to measure the breadth of damage caused by cyberattacks (Cyber Resilience for Financial Market Infrastructures, Financial Inclusion Global Initiative, The World Bank 2019). The primary motivation behind these attacks is to make money, disrupt services to cause financial losses, and steal sensitive data.

This chapter introduces the concept of financial market infrastructures and several types of FMIs. It identifies various vulnerabilities of the systemically important payment systems and security issues in central counterparties. It presents available security services and mechanisms to secure FMIs. Finally, it presents a mapping of each FMI component with security objectives.

G. Kaur et al., *Understanding Cybersecurity Management in FinTech*, Future of Business and Finance, https://doi.org/10.1007/978-3-030-79915-1_7

7.1 What Is FMI?

Financial market infrastructure is defined as a multilateral system designed to record, clear, or settle payment systems among participating financial institutions. Apart from handling payment systems, it also includes settlements, securities, derivatives, or other financial transactions (Principles for Financial Market Infrastructures 2011). The participating financial institutions are referred to as buyers and sellers. FMIs establish common rules and procedures for participating entities that consider a specialized risk management framework to deal with risks. It ensures financial stability and economic growth by effectively managing risks that may incur in the financial system (Maskay 2014). Financial stability and market functioning rely on the continuity of services provided by FMI (Oversight Framework for Financial Market Infrastructures (FMIs) and Retail Payment Systems (RPSs) 2020). A complete structure of FMI along with essential components is presented in Fig. 7.1.

7.1.1 Payment Systems

A payment system is a set of rules and procedures used to transfer funds between participating entities. It operates based on an agreement between the entities and the operator. It enables lending and repayment of money, payments for goods and services offered, salaries, and benefits for the general public (Oversight Framework for Financial Market Infrastructures (FMIs) and Retail Payment Systems (RPSs) 2020). It is generally categorized as either a foreign exchange transaction or a retail payment system. Foreign exchange (FX) transactions are the most liquid sector of payment systems in the financial market. It primarily deals in international trade and investments through exchange rates of currencies and transfer of funds. It generates the largest number of payments every day. It is estimated that the daily turnover of the foreign exchange market is 5.3 trillion dollars.

On the other hand, a retail payment system handles large volumes of low-value funds transfer in the form of cash, checks, credits, debits, and debit card transactions. It primarily deals with payments and transfers within the country. It is operated by a private or public sector Real-Time Gross Settlement (RTGS) or Deferred Net Settlement (DNS) mechanism.

The types of payment transactions covered by payment systems include domestic card payments, credit transfers (internet and mobile payments), direct debits, and inter-bank transactions (International Monetary Fund 2016). Domestic card payments are used to make payments within the country. It uses the credit or debit card issued by the bank and the merchant's registered account. Credit transfers work like a direct cash transfer between a payee and a payer. It is also called e-transfer or electronic transfer that makes use of Internet services and mobile payments. Credit transfers can be used to pay electricity and water bills, purchase and sell goods and services, and shop online. It provides a fast mode of payment where the payee does not need to wait for the payment.

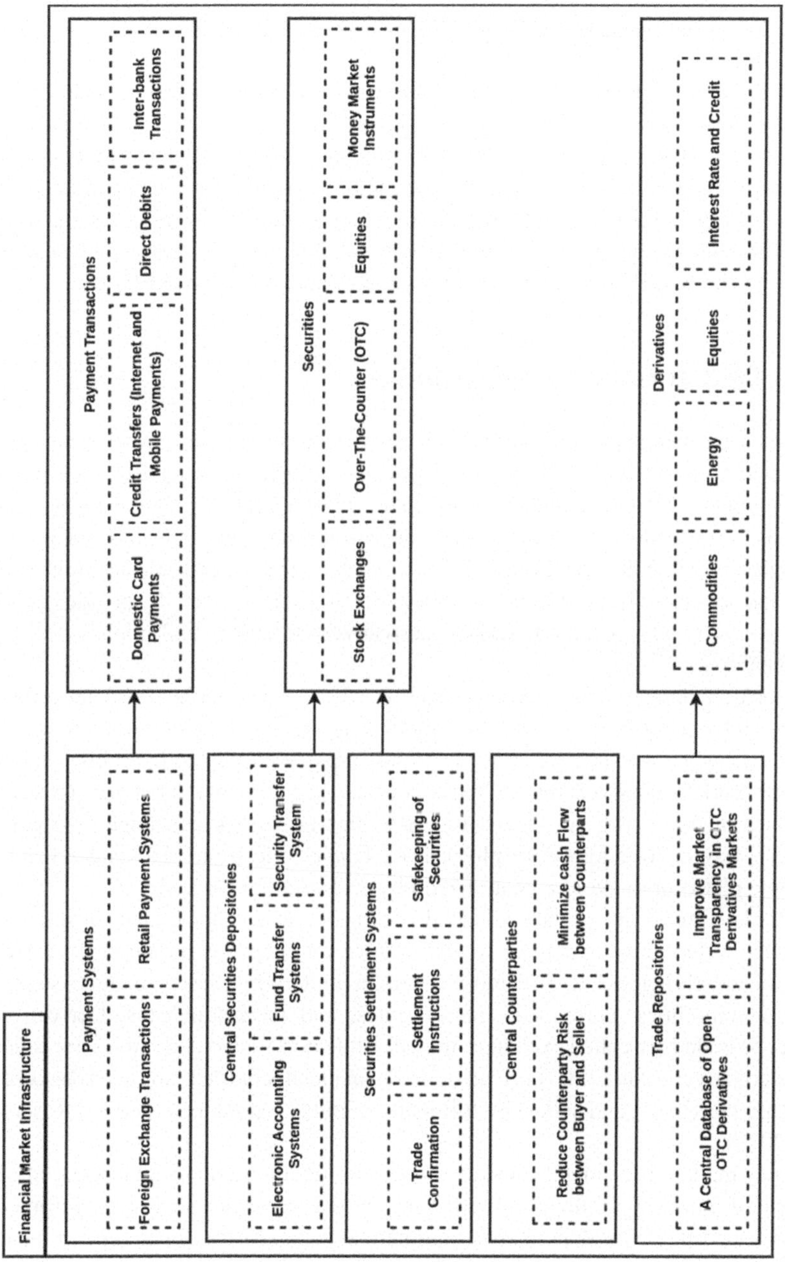

Fig. 7.1 Essential components of FMI

In contrast, direct debits or debit transfers begin with the delivery of the payment. In a debit transfer, the bank notifies if the payment is not successful. Thus, it works on the principle of "no news is good news." Despite the popularity of credit transfers, debit transfers are used predominantly by many countries (International Monetary Fund 1998).

Inter-bank transactions provide great liquidity to financial markets. It describes monetary transactions between banks. For example, national banks seeking a loan from the central bank or central bank seeking a loan from the world bank are classified as inter-bank transactions. It also includes payment transactions between two banks for transferring an amount from one user account registered with one bank to the other user account registered with another bank. Inter-bank transactions can be carried out through RTGS or National Electronic Fund Transfer (NEFT).

7.1.2 Central Securities Depositories

A central securities depository holds a security account for fund transfer either in a certificated or uncertificated form. It plays a key role in ensuring the integrity of security issues. It may maintain a record of legal ownership for security. The functions performed by a central security depository may vary depending upon the jurisdiction in which it is operating. It is responsible for the electronic accounting of assets and services, fund transfer, and security transfer system. It includes stock exchanges, Over-The-Counter (OTC) derivatives, equities, and money market instruments.

A stock exchange is a centralized location where government and corporations can buy and sell equities. Equities are stocks that are sometimes used interchangeably. It acts as an investment hub for two counterparties involved in an investment. The New York Stock Exchange (NYSE) and Nasdaq are the two most popular stock exchanges in the world. All the trading activities in a stock exchange take place through a broker. In addition to physical exchanges, electronic exchanges use an electronic platform to avoid a centralized physical location for trade.

OTC derivatives are private financial contracts that are not traded on an asset exchange. A derivative is a security with a price that depends on the or is derived from an underlying asset. The most common underlying assets include stocks, bonds, commodities, currencies, interest rates, and market indexes. Derivatives that can be traded are called exchange-traded, while non-traded derivatives are called OTC derivatives. An OTC derivative is a financial contract arranged between counterparties (buyer and seller) by following minimal regulations (Federal Reserve Bank 2020).

Money market instruments allocate short-term funding to financial institutions. It is a type of mutual fund that is invested in low-risk securities such as government securities, certificates of deposit, and commercial paper. Money market instruments maintain a stable net asset value for a share. The value of a share may increase or decrease depending on the business of a firm in the market (Federal Reserve Bank 2020).

7.1.3 Securities Settlement Systems

Security settlement systems are a critical component of financial market infrastructures. It enables securities for a settlement between the trading parties. It acts as an intermediator between borrowers and lenders to secure the flow of funds and maintain their security portfolios (BIS 2001). It allows the transfer of payment either free of cost or against payment. When the transfer is made against a payment, delivery of the security is taken care of, if and only if payment is made. It also ensures the safekeeping of securities by providing additional security clearing and settlement instructions.

With the soaring cross-border trades and settlements, the integration of global markets is also increased. Like central securities depositories, it also includes stock exchanges, Over-The-Counter (OTC) derivatives, equities, and money market instruments. Any lapse in the security settlement system may result in a systemic risk to securities markets. It may further cause liquidity or credit losses for the participating entities (BIS 2001).

7.1.4 Central Counterparties

A central counterparty acts as an intermediator by acting buyer to the seller and vice versa. It interposes itself between counterparties to financial contracts traded in the financial market (BIS 2004). It is also called clearinghouses. CCPs place themselves between buyer and seller to reduce the complexity of trade. Once the buyer and seller finish a transaction, a post-trading system ensures that all trade agreements are effectively enforced by matching all buy and sell orders in the market (clearing), transferring securities under each contract (settlement), and safekeeping securities (custody) (Stamegna 2017). Before CCPs were used in trade, all the participating entities (buyers and sellers) used to interact with each other directly to create a complex web of connections among themselves, as shown in Fig. 7.2(a). This netting is also called a bilateral arrangement. After CCPs came into the picture, it acts as an intermediator between the buyers and sellers to reduce complexity, as shown in Fig. 7.2(b).

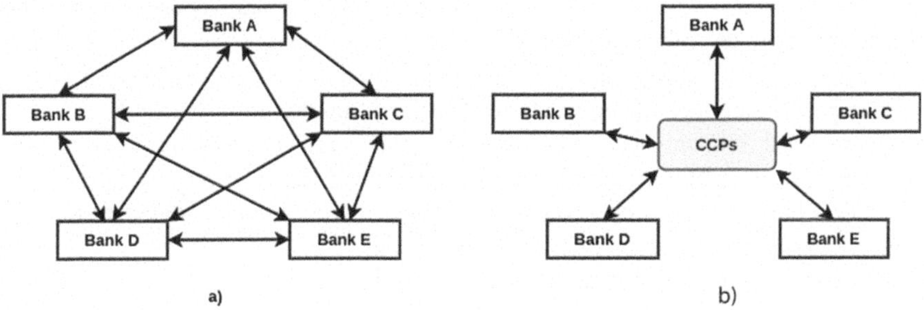

Fig. 7.2 CCPs reduces the complexity of trade. (**a**) Before CCPs. (**b**) After CCPs

It is used by derivatives exchanges, security exchanges, and trading systems. It can reduce risks between buyers and sellers by binding on them through legal procedures and imposing effective risk control measures. Due to this, it is feasible to reduce systemic risk as well. The effectiveness of risk controls is critical to minimize cash flow between counterparts and achieve risk-reduction benefits. Central counterparties' failure to control risk can disrupt not only the financial market but also the other settlement systems. It also tends to enhance the liquidity of the financial market by supporting anonymous trading in some cases (BIS 2004).

CCPs maintain a regulatory contract between the counterparties involved in the business. It is a central node between the trading parties and is exposed to credit risk that a counterparty defaults on outstanding contracts. The credit risk is managed by taking collateral or "margin" from the counterparties (Rehlon and Nixon 2013). Obviously, CCPs are central nodes in the financial markets, and their significance is expected to increase as OTC derivatives are made mandatory by G20 leaders for trade between counterparties.

CCPs offer two key risk-reducing benefits including a reduced web of connections between counterparties and managing defaults in case a counterparty fails. They have a tremendous potential to reduce systemic risk and reinforce financial stability by addressing the deficiencies associated with bilateral arrangements (Chande et al. 2010).

7.1.5 Trade Repositories

A trade repository maintains a central database of transactions and data. It is a new component of FMI and is gaining importance in the OTC derivatives market. By centralizing the transactions and dissemination and storage of collected data, it enhances the transparency of information to relevant authorities and the public. An important function performed by trade repositories is to provide information that supports risk reduction, operational efficiency, and cost savings for the participating entities and the market (Principles for Financial Market Infrastructures 2011). Trade repositories store commodities, energy, equities, interest rate, and credit. Since several stakeholders use the data stored by trade repositories, it is critical to maintaining accuracy, reliability, and data availability. Trade repositories can be characterized by the following benefits:

- The centralization of data provides a transparent market infrastructure.
- Timely and reliable access to data stored in trade repositories significantly improves the ability to identify risks posed to the financial system.
- Trade repositories provide a common platform for various stakeholders to support the consistency of data formats and representations.
- Centralized and reliable data increases its usefulness.

7.2 Vulnerability of the Systemically Important Payment Systems (SIPS)

Payment systems are critical to the efficient and effective functioning of FMIs. They transfer funds between participating entities and are referred to as the systemically important payment systems (SIPSs). SIPSs are a major channel through which financial shocks can be transmitted across domestic and international financial markets. Safe and efficient payment systems are a key requirement for maintaining financial stability and improving the economic growth of financial markets.

Big financial systems have the potential to let down small businesses in a financial crisis. There can be several reasons, including big FinTech firms, services offered by them, the complexity of their business, their global reach, and the degree of their financial connections with other financial institutions.

There are several vulnerabilities in SIPSs that negatively impact the global financial business. The following vulnerabilities are identified in the systemically important payment systems:

- **Size of FinTech institution:** larger firms make more impact on the global financial system because their failure distresses the other financial institutions, stakeholders, payment systems, and participating entities. The fundamental vulnerability here is that the financial risks that erupted from the failure of big FinTech industries can easily propagate to small financial institutions, stakeholders, creditors, and shareholders.
- **Systemic risk:** Risk of systemic failure or systemic risk can completely turmoil the financial system (Chouinard and Ens 2013).
- **Dissimilarities I business models:** There are dissimilarities in the business models followed by all FinTech institutions. These differences must be considered for assessing the importance of payment systems. Similarly, the system must have a well-founded legal basis to work under all jurisdictions (Bank for International Settlements 2001).
- **Interconnectedness between different FinTech institutions:** Small financial institutions depend on big FinTech firms for their business. This interconnectedness provides a channel to transmit shocks from big to small FinTech institutions (Chouinard and Ens 2013). It also raises the possibility of common exposures among these institutions.
- **Cross-jurisdictional activity:** More cross-border trade activities indicate more risk toward systemic failure. It also has more probability for a global failure.
- **Complexity of business:** Complex businesses are not easy to unwind in case of a systemic risk.
- **Substitution:** Big financial institutions pose more risk for a global failure than small ones. The vulnerability occurs when there is no substitute for the big financial institutions in case of a risk that leads to global distress or failure.

Based on the discussion on vulnerabilities that lead to the breakdown of the financial system, there is a need to safeguard the financial system against the failure of such institutions. Adopting some remedial policies is the second step to recovering the financial system after the collapse. Finally, identifying the systemically important payment systems is a key step to end "too big to fail" and another financial crisis. Regulators take different approaches to assess financial institutions that can help them to develop more effective policies and frameworks (Chouinard and Ens 2013).

7.3 Cybersecurity Issues of Central Counterparties (CCPs)

Besides financial risks, CCPs are prone to cyberattacks. According to Herjavec Group (Hackerpocalypse: A Cybercrime Revelation, Herjavec Group, Q3 2016), the global annual cost of cybercrime is estimated to increase to around USD6 trillion by 2021. Juniper Research (Juniper Research 2015) and the World Economic Forum (World Economic Forum 2016) estimated the impact of a single global cyber-attack around USD121 billion. Beyond the financial crisis, cyberattacks can disrupt services, financial markets, and a broad spectrum of loss of confidence (Boer and Vazquez 2017). As reported by Carnegie Endowment for international peace (Timeline of Cyber Incidents Involving Financial Institutions 2021), data breach, malware, and distributed denial of service (DDoS) are the most common cyberattacks that resulted in significant financial losses for various financial institutions. Nonetheless, the list of individual security risks is never-ending.

Cyberattacks are becoming more sophisticated with time. The perpetrators may be hacker groups, criminal gangs, or state-sponsored actors. Their motive is to induce financial instability, destabilize jurisdictions, steal data, demand money, disrupt network communications, and harass financial institutions. Evidently, payment systems, including banks, stock exchanges, and other financial firms, are the primary targets of cyberattacks. Even the major FinTech institutions suffer menacing cyberattacks over the years. These statistics reveal that cyberattacks are one of the biggest challenges that FinTech has been facing in the past couple of years. Advanced persistent threats intend to steal sensitive and valuable data from financial industries (Tounsi and Rais 2018).

Money laundering or cyber frauds are quite common cyber risks to CCPs. Cryptocurrency is frequently used in cross-border financial transactions owing to its ease of use. It does not need to be exchanged. The risk associated with cryptocurrency transactions is that any regulatory compliance or authority does not govern them. This makes it vulnerable to cyber risks as attackers can launder it through legitimate financial institutions, especially in FMI.

Based on the types of cyberattacks witnessed by CCPs, the following cybersecurity issues impact the financial transactions in CCPs: confidentiality, integrity, and availability (Bouveret 2018). Confidentiality issues arise when confidential information of a counterparty is leaked to third parties in the case of data breaches. Integrity issues arise when information is misused in a cyber fraud or financial fraud. Financial frauds are quite common in CCPs that result from custody and investment risks. Finally, availability issues are linked to business disruptions which is one of the objectives of cyberattacks. Business disruptions prevent financial firms from operating, resulting in financial losses and frauds.

Different cybersecurity issues have different impacts on financial businesses. Data breaches take a long time to materialize. The same is the case with reputation and litigation losses. More commonly, it is apparent that the risk of loss of confidence is one of the highest for the financial sector.

Despite having risk management procedures, CCPs are exposed to significant cybersecurity issues that can lead to diverse financial risks. Some key risks associated with CCPs are summarized below (Rehlon and Nixon 2013):

- **Failure of central node (CCP):** Since CCPs are placed in the central part of the financial network, they themselves become crucial. The situation deteriorates when the CCPs fail as a clearinghouse. Considering that a CCPs manages thousands of counterparties, its failure can be a contagion. In the worst-case scenario, the financial markets may need to be shut down temporarily to resolve the situation.
- **Shock amplification through CCP:** Failure of CCPs can propagate financial stress among other counterparties connected to it. The impact of shock propagation can be limited by using risk management policies for the financial system.
- **Central clearing:** To manage risks, CCPs need to impose strict regulations on their counterparties. This includes creditworthiness, liquidity, and operational reliability of counterparties. This makes it essential to clear trade among counterparties who fall under the restrictions for adequate technical and financial resources.
- **Counterparty risk:** The risk occurs when a buyer is not able to pay the price, or a seller is unable to deliver the securities. In other words, insufficient funds are one of the reasons that cause counterparty risk. It is treated as a liquidity risk.
- **Custody and investment risks:** Custody risks are associated with safekeeping securities. It consists of inadequate record-keeping, negligence, fraud, cyberattacks, and loss of assets held by the custodian.
- **Legal risks:** CCPs interact with different counterparties that may belong to different jurisdictions and law bodies. This introduces legal risks to cross-border settlements.

According to the Bank of England's new consultation rules, a CCP needs to report any incident to the Bank if that incident affects the security of its information technology systems and has a significant impact on the continuity of services (Bank of England 2018). Furthermore, an appropriate risk management model is also required. The main factors that affect CCP risk management are the trade-off between margins and default funds. If these two factors are balanced individually, most of the custody and investment, legal, and credit risks in CCPs would be settled (Haene and Sturm 2009).

7.4 Securities Settlement Facilities (SSFs)

Securities Settlement Facilities (SSFs) are clearing and settlement facilities that are governed by 19 standards, collectively known as SSF standards. These standards are provided by the "Financial Stability Standards." This section provides an overview of all these standards (Assessment of ASX Clearing and Settlement Facilities 2020; Financial Stability Standards for Securities Settlement Facilities, Bank of Australia 2012).

Standard 1: Legal Basis
"A securities settlement facility should have a well-founded, clear, transparent and enforceable legal basis for each material aspect of its activities in all relevant jurisdictions."

A security settlement facility has several inbuilt risks that arise from its functions. However, it should be a legal entity that is separate from other entities that may expose it to risks. Legal basis provides a high degree of certainty in different jurisdictions for performing cross-border transactions. SSF should have clear contracts, procedures, and rules for relevant jurisdictions. These contracts are consistent and understandable. Since SSFs work in multiple jurisdictions, they are prone to various financial risks, which are mitigated by using an effective risk management process.

Standard 2: Governance
"A securities settlement facility should have governance arrangements that are clear and transparent, promote the safety of the securities settlement facility, and support the stability of the broader financial system, other relevant public interest considerations and the objectives of relevant Stakeholders."

A security settlement facility should have clear and transparent objectives that place a high priority on the safety of securities. It explicitly supports the financial stability of the system. The governance arrangements should be documented to provide a clear and direct line of accountability and responsibility. This documentation is made available to participating entities, banks, owners, and the public whenever required. Since the board of directors governs the procedures and rules, the documentation should clearly specify its functioning, including the redressal of conflicts. The management should have appropriate experience, skills, and integrity to render their duties. It should also include compensation arrangements to promote effective risk management. Finally, the security settlement facility's operations, functions, risk management processes, internal and external control mechanisms, and accounts should be audited on a periodic basis.

Standard 3: Framework for the Comprehensive Management of Risks
"A securities settlement facility should have a sound risk management framework for comprehensively managing legal, credit, liquidity, operational and other risks."

As mentioned in Standard 2, security settlement facilities should have risk management processes to identify, analyze, measure, monitor, and mitigate risks.

The risk management process should be reviewed periodically. SSF should ensure that financial obligations imposed on participants are proportionate to the scale and activities performed by the participants. SSF should provide incentives to participants to manage risks and review and address material risks such as liquidity risks. It should also prepare appropriate plans to recover the risks.

Standard 4: Credit Risk

"A securities settlement facility should effectively measure, monitor and manage its credit exposures to participants and those arising from its settlement processes. A securities settlement facility should maintain sufficient financial resources to cover its credit exposure to each participant fully with a high degree of confidence."

Credit risks arise from the settlement processes. SSFs should establish a robust framework to manage current and future exposures to credit risks. SSFs should identify the sources of credit risks and propose mitigation measures to control these risks. If required, additional risk controls should be proposed. SSFs should establish explicit rules and procedures that address credit losses and replenish any financial resources during financial stress.

Standard 5: Collateral

"A securities settlement facility that requires collateral to manage its or its participants' credit exposures should accept collateral with low credit, liquidity and market risks. A securities settlement facility should also set and enforce appropriately conservative haircuts and concentration limits."

SSFs limit the assets to those with low credit, liquidity, and market risks. It should consider the broad effect of policies on the market. It should establish prudent valuation practices to reduce the adverse pricing effects of risks. A securities settlement facility should use a collateral management system that is well designed and operationally flexible.

Standard 6: Liquidity Risk

"A securities settlement facility should effectively measure, monitor and manage its liquidity risk. A securities settlement facility should maintain sufficient liquid resources in all relevant currencies to effect same-day and, where appropriate, intraday and multiday settlement of payment obligations with a high degree of confidence under a wide range of potential stress scenarios that should include, but not be limited to, the default of the participant and its affiliates that would generate the largest aggregate liquidity obligation for the securities settlement facility in extreme but plausible market Conditions."

SSFs should have a robust framework to manage their liquidity risks from participants, banks, settlement agents, custodians, and other entities. It should have effective operational and analytical tools to identify, measure, and monitor funding flows. SSFs should maintain sufficient liquid resources in the form of assets. It should have a sufficient degree of confidence to understand liquidity risks. This is achieved by associating with central bank accounts, payment services, or securities services.

Standard 7: Settlement Finality

"A securities settlement facility should provide clear and certain final settlement, at a minimum by the end of the value date. Where necessary or preferable, a securities settlement facility should provide final settlement intraday or in real time."

SSF rules should define the last point of settlement by providing a complete settlement statement. It should consider adopting real-time gross settlement (RTGS) or multiple batch processing during the settlement day. Finally, it should provide a point after which unsettled payments may not be revoked by a participant.

Standard 8: Money Settlements

"A securities settlement facility should conduct its money settlements in central bank money where practical and available. If central bank money is not used, a securities settlement facility should minimize and strictly control the credit and liquidity risk arising from the use of commercial bank Money."

Money settlements are conducted to avoid credit and liquidity risks. If central bank money is not used, SSF should conduct money settlements with little or no credit or liquidity risk. The objective is to reduce credit and liquidity risk by signing legal documents with any commercial bank money settlement agents.

Standard 9: Central Securities Depositories

"A securities settlement facility operating a central securities depository should have appropriate rules and procedures to help ensure the integrity of securities issues and minimize and manage the risks associated with the safekeeping and transfer of securities. A securities settlement facility operating a central securities depository should maintain securities in an immobilized or dematerialized form for their transfer by book entry."

SSFs should follow strict rules and procedures to provide robust accounting practices. These practices help safeguard the rights of securities and prevent unauthorized creation and deletion of securities. SSFs should prohibit overdrafts and debits in security accounts and protect assets against custody risks. It may require additional tools to address these risks.

Standard 10: Exchange-of-Value Settlement Systems

"If a securities settlement facility settles transactions that comprise the settlement of two linked obligations (for example, securities or foreign exchange transactions), it should eliminate principal risk by conditioning the final settlement of one obligation upon the final settlement of the other."

SSFs act as an exchange-of-value settlement system that should eliminate principal risk by ensuring the final settlement. It should link the final settlement of one obligation to the final settlement of the other through an appropriate delivery versus payment (DvP), delivery versus delivery (DvD), or payment versus payment (PvP) settlement mechanism.

Standard 11: Participant Default Rules and Procedures
"A securities settlement facility should have effective and clearly defined rules and procedures to manage a participant default. These rules and procedures should be designed to ensure that the securities settlement facility can take timely action to contain losses and liquidity pressures and continue to meet its obligations."

As mentioned in earlier standards, SSFs should have rules and procedures to meet obligations in the event of a participant default and replenishment of resources. Rules and procedures should not only be created but implemented. It should be made available to all participating entities and the public. The most important thing is that stakeholders should also be involved in testing and reviewing the rules and procedures.

Standard 12: General Business Risk
"A securities settlement facility should identify, monitor and manage its general business risk and hold, or demonstrate that it has legally certain access to, sufficient liquid net assets funded by equity to cover potential general business losses so that it can continue operations and services as a going concern if those losses materialize. Further, liquid net assets should at all times be sufficient to ensure a recovery or orderly wind-down of critical operations and services."

SSFs should have a robust risk management system to identify, monitor, and mitigate general business risks. General business risks may include financial losses, credit risk, liquidity risk, negative cash flows, poor execution of business strategy, and excessive operating expenses. Assets of high-quality and liquid resources should be made available to address general business risks. SSFs should maintain a viable plan to raise additional equity. This plan should be approved by the board of directors and updated regularly.

Standard 13: Custody and Investment Risks
"A securities settlement facility should safeguard its own and its participants' assets and minimize the risk of loss on and delay in access to these assets. A securities settlement facility's investments should be in instruments with minimal credit, market and liquidity risks."

SSFs should hold their own and participant's assets at supervised and regulated entities to have robust accounting practices, safekeeping procedures, and internal controls. They should also evaluate their exposure to custody risks by considering their relationship with each other.

Standard 14: Operational Risk
"A securities settlement facility should identify the plausible sources of operational risk, both internal and external, and mitigate their impact using appropriate systems, policies, procedures and controls. Systems should be designed to ensure a high degree of security and operational reliability and should have adequate, scalable capacity. Business continuity management should aim for timely recovery of operations and fulfilment of the securities settlement facility's obligations, including in the event of a wide-scale or major disruption."

SSFs should serve several key objectives to tackle operational risks. First, it should have a robust risk management framework to identify, monitor, and mitigate operational risks. The framework should have appropriate systems, policies, procedures, and controls to achieve its objectives. Second, the board of directors should clearly define the roles and responsibilities of addressing operational risks. These policies should be tested and reviewed regularly. In the case of cross-border transactions, managing operational risks may require it to provide adequate operational support to participants during the market hours of each relevant jurisdiction. Third, SSFs should arrange for Business Continuity Programs (BCPs) to enable the securities settlement facility to complete settlement by the end of the day of the disruption, even in case of extreme circumstances. These plans should be tested regularly. Fourth, contingency testing should be made compulsory to deal with operational stress. Finally, outsourcing and other dependencies are an inseparable part of SSFs. It should ensure that operations meet the resilience, security, and operational performance requirements of these SSF Standards for multiple jurisdictions.

Standard 15: Access and Participation Requirements

"A securities settlement facility should have objective, risk-based and publicly disclosed criteria for participation, which permit fair and open access."

SSFs should ensure secure and open access to their services. The participation requirements for these services should be tailored to and commensurate with the security settlement facility's specific risks. SSFs should also monitor compliance with their participation requirements on an ongoing basis and it should be disclosed publicly.

Standard 16: Tiered Participation Arrangements

"A securities settlement facility should identify, monitor and manage the material risks to the securities settlement facility arising from tiered participation arrangements."

SSFs should ensure that their rules, procedures, and agreements allow them to gather basic information about indirect participation in order to identify, monitor, and mitigate risks. Material interdependencies between direct and indirect participation should be identified as they might affect SSF. It should regularly review risks arising from tiered participation arrangements.

Standard 17: FMI Links

"A securities settlement facility that establishes a link with one or more FMIs should identify, monitor and manage link-related risks."

SSFs should identify, monitor, and mitigate all potential sources of risks arising from the link arrangement. Link arrangements should comply with the SSF standards, which means it should also be well-founded, legal, consult central banks, and manage risks.

Standard 18: Disclosure of Rules, Key Policies and Procedures, and Market Data
"A securities settlement facility should have clear and comprehensive rules, policies and procedures and should provide sufficient information and data to enable participants to have an accurate understanding of the risks they incur by participating in the securities settlement facility. All relevant rules and key policies and procedures should be publicly disclosed."

All the rules, procedures, and policies should be clearly disclosed to participants. It includes clear descriptions of the system's design and operations and rights and obligations of SSFs. It should complete regularly and disclose publicly responses to the CPSS-IOSCO Disclosure Framework for Financial Market Infrastructures.

Standard 19: Regulatory Reporting
"A securities settlement facility should inform the Reserve Bank in a timely manner of any events or changes to its operations or circumstances that may materially impact its management of risks or ability to continue operations. A securities settlement facility should also regularly provide information to the Reserve Bank regarding its financial position and risk controls on a timely basis."

SSFs should immediately report to the Reserve Bank in case of a security incident such as data breach and risks. It should provide regular audit reports, management accounts, risk management reports, periodic activity, and any other information as specified by the Reserve Bank from time-to-time basis.

7.5 Available Security Mechanisms

In order to secure financial market infrastructures, certain security mechanisms and standards are required. This section puts forward X.800 mechanism and NIST standard as available security solutions to secure FMIs.

7.5.1 X.800 Security Services

X.800 is a security architecture for open and interconnected systems. It was published by the International Telecommunication Union (ITU) in 1991. It defines a security service as a service provided by a protocol layer of communicating systems, which ensures the security of systems or data being transferred (Security Services 2019). It is defined in the RFC 2828 as a processing or communication service provided by a system to protect a service (RFC 2828 2000). X.800 security services provide two types of security mechanisms: specific and pervasive. Figure 7.3 presents several types of X.800 security services.

7.5.1.1 Specific Security Mechanisms

Specific security mechanisms are specific to a particular protocol layer to provide a security service to that protocol layer. There are eight specific security mechanisms.

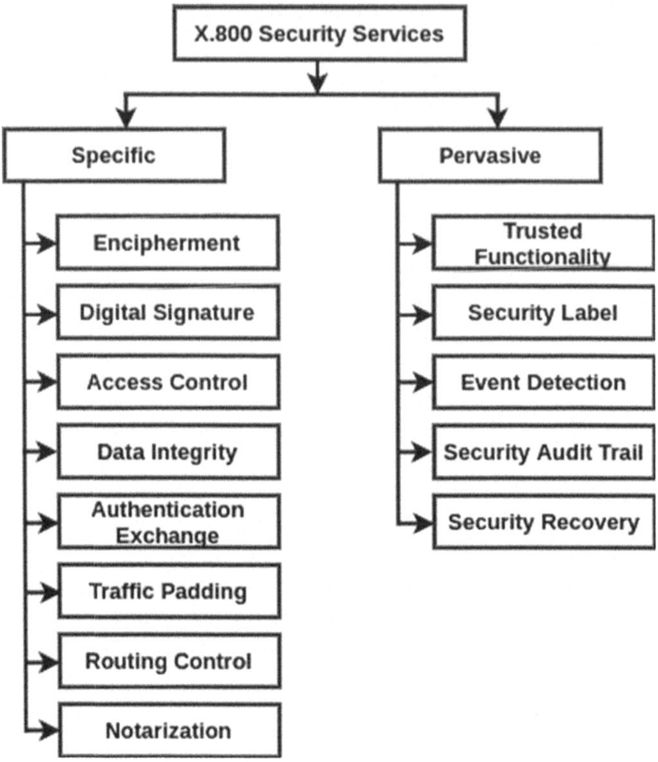

Fig. 7.3 Types of X.800 Security Services

Encipherment: It uses mathematical algorithms to transform data into a form that is not readily interpreted by any unauthorized entity. It makes use of a pair of cipher keys to encrypt the data on the sender side and decrypt it on the receiver side. Encipherment algorithms can be symmetric or asymmetric. Symmetric algorithms share a common key between the sender and receiver. Sender uses the encryption key to encrypt the data before transferring it to receiver who uses the same key (called a decryption key) to decrypt it at his end as shown in Fig. 7.4.

In asymmetric algorithms, different keys are used for encryption and decryption as shown in Fig. 7.5. Every user has his own key pairs that include a private and a public key. A private key is known to the user only while the public key is shared with everybody else. When the sender wants to send data, he encrypts it with the receiver's public key (encryption key). Receiver gets the encrypted data and uses his private key (decryption key) to decrypt data.

If an unauthorized person attempts to steal the data in communication, he would not be able to decrypt the data as he does not possess the private key of the actual receiver. This way encipherment ensures the confidentiality of data.

Digital signature: Digital signatures are used to prevent forgery attempts. A user digitally signs the document and encrypts it before sending it to the receiver. Since

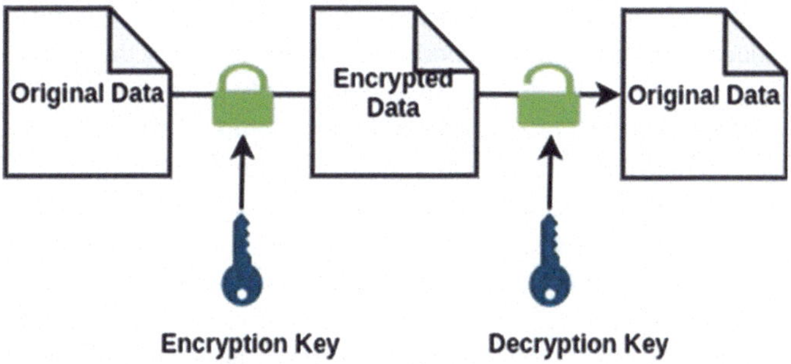

Fig. 7.4 Symmetric encryption

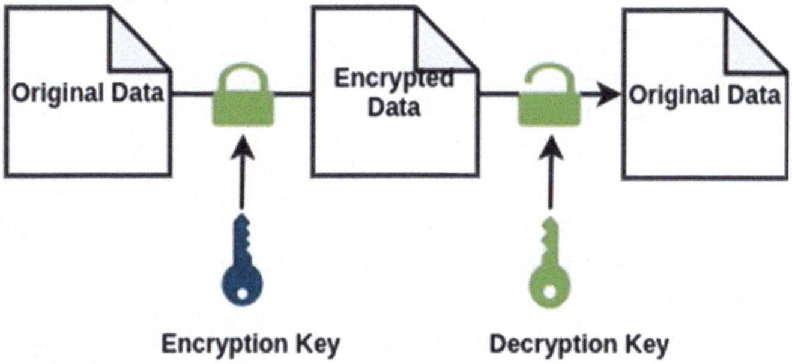

Fig. 7.5 Asymmetric Encryption

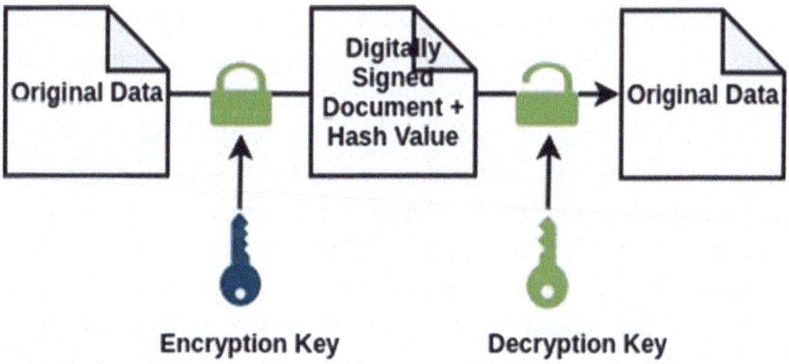

Fig. 7.6 Digital Signatures

the receiver verifies that the document is signed by the authorized sender, he accepts it. It ensures the integrity of data. Figure 7.6 shows the concept of digital signatures.

The sender signs the document with his private key by using a hash algorithm that provides a hash value to sign the document. A hash value is sent along with the digitally signed document. The receiver gets the signed document and hash value. It computes the hash value again at its end to verify that the received hash value is valid. Then he only uses the sender's public key to decrypt the signed document.

Access control: It prevents unauthorized access to a resource. It controls who can access a resource and under what conditions. It also ensures that those accessing resources are authorized to do so. In other words, it assures access rights to resources. Access control consists of two main components: authentication and authorization. Authentication is a technique used to verify the identity of personnel. It is used to verify that a person is what he claims to be. Authentication itself is not sufficient to protect data. An additional layer in the form of authorization is also required. Authorization determines whether a user should be allowed to access the data that he is requesting.

Data integrity: It is the overall accuracy, completeness, and consistency of data. It assures that data received are exactly as sent by the authorized sender. It ensures that data is not modified, lost, tampered, deleted, or added during transfer. Data integrity mechanisms are used to protect the integrity of either a single unit of data or fields within these units.

Authentication exchange: It is a mechanism intended to ensure an entity's identity through information exchange. Authentication exchange can be characterized as strong or weak. Strong authentication exchange uses cryptographic techniques to protect messages that are exchanged between two parties. On the other hand, weak authentication exchange does not use cryptographic techniques. In general, weak authentication exchange mechanisms are vulnerable to attacks (Security Mechanisms 2002).

Traffic padding: Traffic padding mechanisms are used to protect against traffic analysis attacks. To do so, random data bits are inserted into traffic to fill the gaps in the data stream. Insertion of random bits frustrates the traffic analysis attacks. Traffic padding refers to the generation of spurious data or data units. The aim is to conceal data being transmitted so that any interceptor is unable to interpret the data. Consequently, traffic padding mechanisms can only be effective if they are protected by some confidentiality service (Security Mechanisms 2002).

Routing control: Routing control mechanisms control the data routes for data transmission. This is used to divert the data to a different route for detecting a passive attack. The alternative paths are predetermined. Similarly, data-carrying certain security labels are also routed through special routes (Security Mechanisms 2002).

Notarization: The notarization mechanism makes use of a trusted third party to assure certain properties of data such as integrity, time, origin, or destination. This assurance is provided by a trusted third party in a testified manner (Security Mechanisms 2002).

7.5.1.2 Pervasive Security Mechanisms

Pervasive security mechanisms are not specific to any layer to provide a security service. They are directly related to the level of security required. There are five pervasive security mechanisms.

Trusted functionality: It is used to either extend the scope or establish the effectiveness of other security mechanisms. Any functionality that provides access to security mechanisms is treated as trusted functionality.

Security label: Security labels indicate sensitivity levels associated with system resources. Security labels are transmitted with data. It may be additional data associated with transferred data or may be implicit.

Event detection: It is used to detect apparent violations of security.

Security audit trail: Security audit refers to data collected and potentially used to perform a security audit. Auditors review and examine system records to test the adequacy of activities performed in the system controls. It verifies compliance with standards, operational policy, and procedures. Audit trails are used to detect data breaches in security and recommend any indicated changes in policy, control, and procedures.

Security recovery: It takes requests from different mechanisms and takes recovery actions by applying a pre-defined set of rules.

7.5.2 NIST

NIST Special Publication (SP) 800-95 (a guide to secure web services) and NIST 800-12 (a guide to information security) are the two standards that provide security guidelines for an organization. These standards can be adopted by the financial market infrastructure to secure their services.

NIST 800-95

NIST 800-95 provides background to web services and their relationships to security. It provides practical guidance on current and emerging standards applicable to web services. Since FMIs use web services to impart services to customers, it is necessary to discuss the security aspects of Service-Oriented Architecture (SOA) followed by web services. There are various aspects of web services such as messaging, discovery, portals, roles, and coordination as presented in Fig. 7.7. These aspects are supported by a credit check service and an interest rate service.

Messaging services are used to send messages across the network in the form of requests and responses. On receiving a request, the web service takes appropriate action and responds back. For example, in processing a loan application by the client, the loan service uses a credit check service to define an interest rate service. Discovery services are used to bind to or communicate with the newly added services to the existing system. In the loan example, the loan services need to

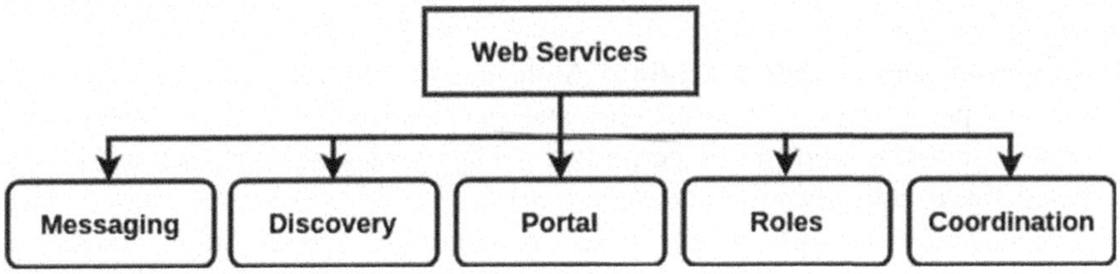

Fig. 7.7 Various aspects of web services

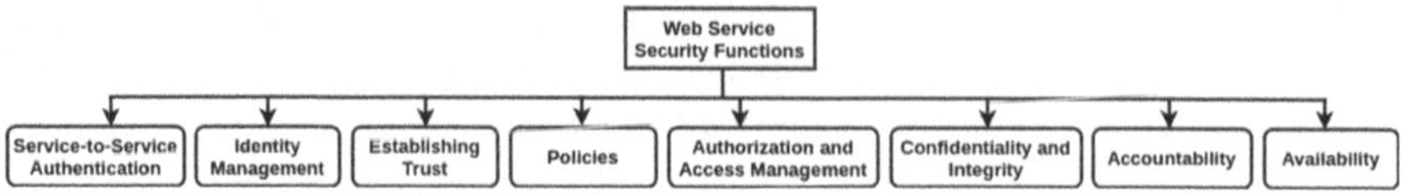

Fig. 7.8 Web service security functions

discover a rating service before defining an interest rate and using it. The rating service provides information about bank's rates (Singhal et al. 2007).

Portal service provides a web interface to a human-readable interface to provide functionality. It is an interactive graphical user interface that takes inputs from a user, processes the requests in the background, and returns results on the interface. A bank's web portal provides its users with the opportunity to use online banking services by logging into their bank account and performing activities related to sending or receiving money, to name a few.

A web service performs multiple roles, such as acting as a requester of web services, provider of web services, and an intermediator. When multiple providers, requesters, and intermediators are involved, coordination is required among different components to provide web services.

Elements of security: After understanding the web services, it is important to list the elements of security of web services. A web service security service relies on the following elements:

- **Identification and authentication:** Identification and authentication verify the identity of a user, process, or device.
- **Authorization:** It defines the permission to use a computer or resource granted by the system owner.
- **Integrity:** It ensures that data is not altered in an unauthorized manner.
- **Non-repudiation:** It ensures that the sender of the data cannot deny sending the data.
- **Confidentiality:** It protects information access and disclosure.
- **Privacy:** It is maintained by complying with Federal law and organizational policy.

Web Service Security Functions: NIST 800-95 also defines the threats and risks faced by web services (Singhal et al. 2007). Following web service security functions, standards, and technologies are used to improve web service security as shown in Fig. 7.8:

- **Service-to-Service authentication:** Authentication limits access to resources, identify participants in transactions, and personalize information. Service-to-service authentication can be performed using various methods such as HTTP-based token authentication and Secure Socket Layer (SSL) certificates. Token authentication supports tokens based on multiple authentication standards, including usernames, X.509 certificates, and Kerberos tickets (Singhal et al. 2007).

- **Identity management:** Identity management consists of identity-related events, information, and documents by which an identity can be verified. An identity management system is responsible for the verification of the identities of entities, registering them, and issuing certificates. These certificates are referred to as digital identifiers of an entity. Registering a human entity requires one to fulfill several security guidelines. For example, users who wish to access e-commerce websites are required to provide a valid email address and credit card number. On obtaining the digital identifier, it can be used to relate to other information available in the organization. Furthermore, different organizations have different policies to deal with authentication issues.
- **Establishing trust:** Establishing trust between remote web services is useful to deploy web services on a large scale. Trust relationships can be direct or pairwise. Direct trust relationships are easy to maintain, while pairwise trust relationships are the tightest form of relationships. Every authorized entity is required to share its information with other entities. In order to share information, every entity needs to have a copy of certificates or public keys of other entities. This makes the system unscalable.
- **Policies:** Policies describe how to communicate with other entities in the system. It drafts rules for communication, messaging, message formats, and other related information. Policies also define assertions to specify confidentiality, integrity, and information about security tokens.
- **Authorization and access management:** The objective of authorization and access control is to allow only authorized users to access the resources. There are several types of access control mechanisms, such as role-based, attribute-based, and policy-based. A role-based access control mechanism associates a set of privileges with a particular role. It simplifies access control by providing a role-based hierarchy. For example, developers, administrators, and guests are assigned different roles and privileges to manage their tasks and control their access to the system. Attribute-based access control uses subject, resource, and environmental attributes. These attributes identify the characteristics of the subject, resource (web service), and environment (operational, technical, or situational), respectively. Policy-based access control is an extension of attribute-based access control. It brings a policy-based environment to focus on mandatory access controls. Policies define rules to perform functions.
- **Confidentiality and integrity:** Confidentiality and integrity of service-to-service interchanges ensure that data is confidential and not tampered with while in transit. It uses end-to-end security protocols to transfer data in a secure manner that cannot be disclosed to unauthorized personnel on the fly.
- **Accountability:** Accountability is concerned with the responsibility of an authorized individual to perform a certain set of activities. Financial services often require extensive auditing. Lack of auditing standards for web services serves as a hindrance to effectively implementing accountability across the service-oriented architecture.
- **Availability:** Availability ensures that web service continues to operate correctly. It also assures reliability and quality of service.

NIST 800-12

NIST 800-12 standard provides detailed insights about information security. It focuses on protecting information and systems from unauthorized access, use, disclosure, disruption, modification, or destruction in order to provide confidentiality, integrity, and availability (Nieles et al. 2017). It is important to protect an organization's information assets and its reputation. In cyber warfare, publicized security events can have catastrophic consequences on the profitability and reputation of the organization. Therefore, it becomes extremely important to protect critical information.

Information security policy is defined in NIST SP 800-95 standard as "*statements, rules or assertions that specify the correct or expected behavior of an entity*." That means information security policy specifies correct access control rules to protect confidentiality, integrity, and availability of information. It defines rules, regulations, procedures, and guidelines to describe how an organization manages, protects, and distributes information. Managerial decisions vary significantly for every organization depending upon the policies designed to do so.

There are three types of information security policies: program policy, issue-specific policy, and system-specific policy. A program policy is used to create an organization's information security program. It sets the direction of asset security and its implementation. Every program policy has a purpose, scope, set of responsibilities, and compliance that provides a clear vision of the output desired after successful implementation of the policy. The issue-specific policy is designed to address areas of specific concern in the organization. For example, it may target the proper usage of systems by the employees. It is written in a clear manner so that every employee can understand it. Unlike program policies, issue-specific policies must be reviewed regularly. Some common examples of issue-specific policies include internet usage, email privacy, bring your own device (BYOD), and social media policy.

System-specific policies are confined to a particular system. Unlike program and issue-specific policies, system-specific policies are not broad and do not cover the entire organization. These are like issue-specific policies because they relate to specific technologies or systems.

7.6 Security of Various Components in FMI

It is evident that FMI components have vulnerabilities, and they are exposed to cybersecurity issues as well. This section emphasizes identifying the type of security objectives for each component of FMI. To begin with, there are several financial risks faced by FMI. Each of these risks is summarized below. After that, every FMI component is mapped with a financial risk to understand the security exposures.

7.6.1 Financial Risks

The following are the financial risks faced by FMI:

- **Systemic risk:** Systemic risks are the results of interdependencies among participating banks and the inability of banks to meet their obligations and perform as expected. This may have an adverse effect on FMIs. Systemic risk can lead to reversed transactions or deliveries, delayed settlements, and disruption of services in financial systems. Furthermore, if one participating entity depends on other entities for payments, clearance, and settlements, it will spread the disruptions more quickly to reach the broader economy. Systemic risks are prominent in payment systems of FMI. Interdependencies can be grouped into three broad categories: system-based, institution-based, and environmental dependencies (Bank for International Settlements 2008). In system-based dependencies, FMIs are directly linked. They can be vertical (interdependence between different essential components of FMI such as between a payment system and trade repository) and horizontal (interdependence within the same component such as within two payment systems). In institution-based interdependencies, FMIs are indirectly linked by a financial institution. Finally, environmental dependencies include broad factors such as physical infrastructure and network providers. Systemic risks target payment systems the most.
- **Custody and investment risk:** FMIs face a lot of custody risks, including losses due to assets held in custody, financial fraud, poor administration, inadequate record-keeping, and negligence. Investment risks comprise losses due to investing their own resources in market, credit, or liquidity risks. These risks are also responsible for the safety and reliability of FMI's risk management systems. Custody and investment risks target central securities depositories, central counterparties, securities settlement systems, and trade repositories of FMI.
- **Liquidity risk**: Liquidity risk is related to the possession of insufficient funds to complete a transaction by the participating entities. Other types of liquidity risk can be sellers not receiving funds and buyers not receiving the product on time. Failure of settlement banks is also treated as a liquidity risk for FMI. Liquidity risks have the potential to cause systemic risk. They are mostly found in central counterparties and securities settlement systems of FMI.
- **Credit risk:** Credit risks may occur due to several reasons such as unsettled transactions between entities, the inability of a participating entity to meet financial obligations within a stipulated time, and failure of settlement banks themselves. FMIs may face replacement cost risk due to unsettled transactions with an entity. As a result, FMIs need to replace the original transaction at the current market price. Credit risks are prevalent in central counterparties and securities settlement systems of FMI (Financial Market Infrastructure Risk 2007).
- **Legal risk:** Financial transactions between different countries are liable to legal terms and regulations. Legal risk arises if an application is unlawful, involves other law bodies, and delays in recovering financial assets. Different bodies of

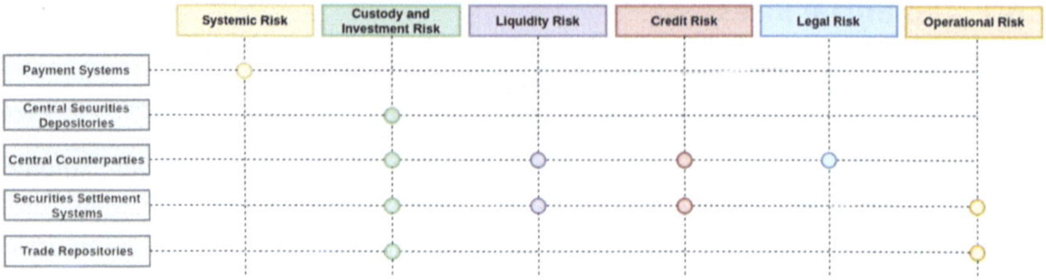

Fig. 7.9 FMI components exposed to different types of financial risks

law are not only applicable to international transactions but to different jurisdictions also. Legal risks affect the central counterparties of FMI the most.

- **Operational risk:** As evident from the name itself, operational risks are caused by irresponsible data and finance handling habits. Some common causes of operational risks include erroneous human transactions, data losses, information leakage, and deficiency in the information system. The erroneous operations may lead to internal and external threats to data security, failure of management systems that relies on information, fraudulent transactions, and incomplete settlements. Operational risks affect the securities settlement systems and trade repositories of FMI.
- **General business risk:** General business risks are related to operational and administration activities performed by FMI. These risks include financial losses due to increased debts and falling growth, resulting in an imbalanced revenue and cost curve. Severe financial losses may result in reputation loss, losses in other operations, poor execution strategy, and other business factors. Failure to manage business risks can lead to operational and legal risks. General business risks can occur in any essential component of FMI. Figure 7.9 demonstrates the type of financial risk against each FMI component.

7.6.2 Security Objective of each FMI Component

Every financial risk category is prone to confidentiality, integrity, availability, accountability, and authenticity issues. This section puts forward security issues faced by FMI by mapping financial risks faced by FMI with the security objectives to identify data security issues in FMI.

Systemic Risk

- *Interdependency among participating entities:* Systemic risk brings down the entire enterprise. When participating entities are dependent on each other for completing transactions, it poses an accountability issue in case the transaction is not completed due to any reason.

Custody and Investment Risk

- *Loss of assets held by the custodian:* From the data security point of view, assets in FMI include data and information related to clients, participating entities, buyers, sellers, monetary transactions, and third-party entities involved. The loss of any of these assets can cause confidentiality, authenticity, and data availability.
- *Fraud:* Financial fraud in FMI refers to illegitimate monetary transactions that can cause harm to the business. The participating entities (buyers and sellers) may not possess legitimate sources to prove their identity. This type of risk can be mapped with authenticity and integrity issues.
- *Poor Administration:* Management is responsible for administering financial settlements and exchanges between entities. It is held responsible for poor administration, which can be mapped with accountability issues.
- *Inadequate Record-keeping*: Inadequate record-keeping may result in incomplete information or data classification. Data classification is the process of labeling data based on its sensitivity. Data may be classified as public, confidential, private, and restricted. Inadequate record-keeping poses confidentiality and integrity issues to data security.
- *Negligence:* Negligence is somehow related to data handling, data classification, and record-keeping. Therefore, it can be mapped with authenticity and integrity issues.
- *Investing your own resources in the market:* Investing your own resources in the market is highly vulnerable and poses an accountability issue as the owner is solely responsible for any financial losses.
- *Credit or Liquidity Risk:* Credit or liquidity risks explained below pose all security issues.

Liquidity Risk

- *Insufficient Funds:* Insufficient funds may result in incomplete transactions, which pose an availability issue.
- *Seller does not receive funds:* Any type of unavailability of data or funds in a settlement or transaction is treated as an availability issue. Further, there are issues with its confidentiality as the originality of the funds may not be certain. It means that funds can be tampered with in transit.
- *Buyer does not receive the product:* Product is an OTC derivative contract that is exchanged between the participating entities. Like a seller not receiving funds, any type of unavailability of data or funds in a settlement or transaction is treated as an availability issue.
- *Failure of Settlement Banks:* Failure of settlement banks is a high-level liquidity risk. It can result in disruption of services for an unspecified time. A person from the management is also held responsible for this failure. Therefore, this risk can be mapped with availability and accountability issues.

Credit Risk

- *Replacement Cost Risk:* Replacement cost risk occurs in case of failure of a transaction, and the entity responsible returns the cost of the failed transaction. This type of risk can be mapped with authenticity and confidentiality issues.
- *Unsettled Transactions:* It is the root cause of replacement cost risk and can be mapped with confidentiality and integrity issues.
- *Failure of Settlement Banks:* Failure of settlement banks is a high-level credit risk. It can result in disruption of services for an unspecified time. This type of risk can be mapped with availability and accountability issues.

Legal Risk

- *Different Law Bodies:* FMI business with participating entities that belong to two different jurisdictions or legal regulations can be mapped with accountability issues because law bodies are to be held accountable for financial transactions.
- *Cross-border Transactions:* International financial business transactions pose a risk to confidentiality and integrity of information in addition to accountability issues in the CIAAA principle.
- *Delay in recovery of financial assets:* Any type of unavailability issue is treated as an availability issue. Moreover, delays in recovery may cause authenticity issues also.

Operational Risk

- *Data Loss:* Data loss indicates incorrect data, which can be attributed to an integrity issue.
- *Leakage:* Just like data loss, information leakage is also attributed to an integrity issue.
- *Deficiency in Information System:* Information systems are responsible for handling data, entities, and transfer of transactions by using a central repository. Deficiency in information systems may result in an integrity issue.
- *Insufficient Capacity:* This type of risk can be mapped with availability and integrity issues as insufficient capacity may lead to loss of data.
- *Internal and External Threats:* Cyber threats have the potential to exploit vulnerabilities in the software systems, especially central repositories used to store sensitive data. Internal and external threats cause harm to confidentiality, integrity, and availability of data.
- *Management Failure:* Management is responsible for the overall administration, such as taking decisions, handling settlement issues, transferring money, and other miscellaneous information. Management failure can be mapped with accountability issues.
- *Human Errors:* Humans are prone to errors and can be held responsible for the type of data or assets they are managing. It can be mapped with accountability issues.
- *Fraud:* Financial fraud in FMI refers to illegitimate monetary transactions that can cause harm to the business. The participating entities (buyers and sellers) may

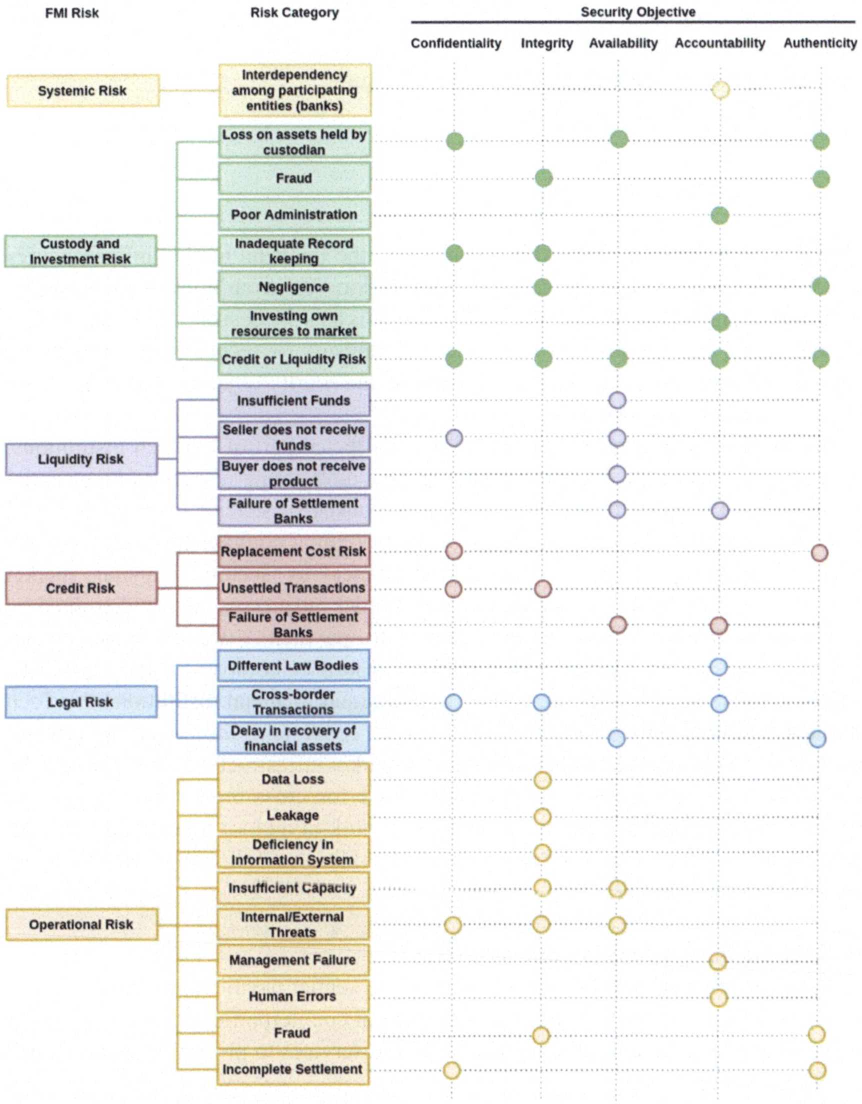

Fig. 7.10 Security objectives of each FMI component

not possess legitimate sources to prove their identity. This type of risk can be mapped with authenticity and integrity issues.

- *Incomplete Settlement:* Incomplete settlements can be mapped with authenticity and confidentiality issues.

Figure 7.10 presents an overview of the mapping of different categories of financial risks with security objectives to summarize security issues in FMI.

Finally, a combined analysis of Figs. 7.9 and 7.10 provides a comprehensive mapping of FMI components with security objectives. This mapping helps to secure financial market infrastructures from security issues.

7.7 Chapter Summary

This chapter provides a detailed introduction to the financial market infrastructures and their essential components. It identifies various vulnerabilities of the systemically important payment systems and security issues in central counterparties. It presents available security services and mechanisms to secure FMIs. Finally, it presents a mapping of each FMI component with security objectives to help secure financial market infrastructures.

Financial market infrastructure is the worst affected part of FinTech institutions. It witnesses most of the cyberattacks that have a devastating impact on its essential components. Financial market infrastructures consist of several types of financial risks that may lead to cybersecurity risks in its essential components, especially the payment systems. It is of utmost importance to secure financial market infrastructures so that the national and cross-border businesses are not disrupted.

Financial market infrastructures deal with payments, wealth management, crowdfunding, capital markets, stock markets, insurance companies, and capitalists. All these financial activities are related to traditional financial institutions, FinTech startups, and financial customers of the FinTech ecosystem. Moreover, the government is also a closely related part of financial market infrastructures as it governs the standards, rules, guidelines, and practices used for cross-border transactions. In simple words, financial market infrastructures work in a close relationship with all components of the FinTech ecosystem. Overall, the following questions are answered in this chapter:

- What are financial market infrastructures?
- What are the vulnerabilities in systemically essential payment systems?
- What are cybersecurity issues faced by central counterparties?
- What are the available security standards and services to protect financial market infrastructures?
- What are security issues faced by various components of FMI?

References

Assessment of ASX Clearing and Settlement Facilities. (2020). https://www.rba.gov.au/payments-and-infrastructure/financial-market-infrastructure/clearing-and-settlement-facilities/assessments/asx/

Bank of Australia. (2012). *Financial Stability Standards for Securities Settlement Facilities,*

Bank of England. (2018). *Consultation on a new rule for Central Counterparties relating to incident reporting* (pp. 1–5). London

BIS: Bank for International Settlements. (2001). *Recommendations for securities settlement systems* (pp. 1–55). https://www.bis.org/cpmi/publ/d46.pdf.
BIS: Bank for International Settlements. (2004). *Recommendations for central counterparties, consultative report* (pp. 1–55). https://www.bis.org/cpmi/publ/d61.pdf.
BIS: Bank for International Settlements. (2008). *The interdependencies of payment and settlement systems*, Basel pp. 1–83
Boer, M., & Vazquez, J. (2017). Cyber security & financial stability: How cyber-attacks could materially impact the global financial system, *Institute of International Finance*, pp. 1–9.
Bouveret, A. (2018). *Cyber risk for the financial sector: A framework for quantitative assessment.* IMF Working Paper, WP/18/143, pp. 1–29.
CARNEGE. (2021). Timeline of Cyber Incidents Involving Financial Institutions. https://carnegieendowment.org/specialprojects/protectingfinancialstability/timeline.
Chande, N., Labelle, N., & Tuer, E. (2010). *Central counterparties and systemic risk* (pp. 1–8). Ottawa: Bank of Canada.
Chouinard, É., & Ens, E. (2013). Assessing the systemic importance of financial institutions, Bank of Canada. *Financial System Review*, 37–44.
Cyber Resilience for Financial Market Infrastructures, Financial Inclusion Global Initiative, The World Bank. (2019). https://pubdocs.worldbank.org/en/189821576699037673/FIGI-ECB-OperationalCyber-FinalWeb-12-13.pdf.
Federal Reserve Bank. (2020). *Financial market infrastructure & reform.* New York: Federal Reserve Bank. https://www.newyorkfed.org/financial-services-and-infrastructure/financial-market-infrastructure-and-reform.
Financial Market Infrastructure Risk. (2007). *Current Report of the financial market infrastructure risk task force, New York*, pp. 1–19.
Financial Market Infrastructures. (2019). *What happens when you pay?* https://www.bankofengland.co.uk/knowledgebank/financial-market-infrastructures-what-happens-when-you-pay
Haene, P., & Sturm, A. (2009). *Optimal central counterparty risk management.* Bern: Swiss National Bank.
Herjavec Group, Q3. (2016). *Hackerpocalypse: A Cybercrime Revelation*, https://www.herjavecgroup.com/hackerpocalypse-cybercrime-report/.
International Monetary Fund. (1998). *Payment systems, monetary policy, and the role of the central bank* (pp. 1–273) Washington, DC: International Monetary Fund. https://asean.elibrary.imf.org/doc/IMF071/05174-9781557756268/05174-9781557756268/Other formats/Source_PDF/05174-9781455246670.pdf.
International Monetary Fund. (2016). *Supervision and systemic risk management of financial market infrastructures – technical note* (pp. 1–37). Washington, DC: International Monetary Fund.
Juniper Research. (2015). *The future of cybercrime & security: financial and corporate threats & mitigation.* Hampshire: Juniper Research. https://www-cdn.webroot.com/5415/0396/2242/The-Future-of-Cybercrime-and-Security-Juniper.pdf
Maskay, N. M. (2014). *Analytical framework in assessing systemic financial market infrastructure: Interdependence of financial market infrastructure and the need for a broader risk perspective* (pp. 1–370). The Southeast Asian Central Banks (SEACEN), Research and Training Centre, Malaysia.
Nieles, M., Dempsey, K., & Pillitteri, V. Y. (2017). *An introduction to information security*, NIST special publication 800-12, revision 1, pp. 1–101. https://nvlpubs.nist.gov/nistpubs/SpecialPublications/NIST.SP.800-12r1.pdf.
Principles for Financial Market Infrastructures. (2011). *Consultative report, bank for international settlements* (pp. 1–148).
Rehlon, A., & Nixon, D. (2013). Central counterparties: what are they, why do they matter and how does the bank supervise them? *Bank of England Quarterly Bulletin 2013 Q2, 53*(2), 147–156.

Reserve Bank of India. (2020). *Oversight Framework for Financial Market Infrastructures (FMIs) and Retail Payment Systems (RPSs). version 2.0* (pp. 1–77).

RFC 2828. (2000). https://tools.ietf.org/html/rfc2828

Security Mechanisms. (2002). https://flylib.com/books/en/4.178.1.22/1/

Security Services. (2019). http://www.idc-online.com/technical_references/pdfs/data_communications/Security_Services.pdf

Singhal, A., Winograd, T., & Scarfone, K. (2007). *Guide to secure web services, recommendations of the National Institute of Standards and Technology*, NIST Special Publication 800-95, pp. 1–128.

Stamegna, C. (2017). *Recovery and resolution of central counterparties (CCPs)* (pp. 1–13). Brussels: European Parliamentary Research Service.

Tounsi, W., & Rais, H. (2018). *A survey on technical threat intelligence in the age of sophisticated cyber-attacks*. Computers & Security, *72*, 212–233.

World Economic Forum. (2016). *Global risks report 2016*. Cologne: World Economic Forum.

Cybersecurity Policy and Strategy Management in FinTech

8

Cyberattacks are on the rise with every passing day so is the cost associated with the damage caused by them. To protect the financial institutions from the menace of these cyberattacks, a cybersecurity policy and strategy sets the standards to monitor cyber activities on the premises, design prevention and detection measures, and take appropriate actions to curb these activities. Several terms are associated with a cybersecurity policy that is understood differently by the stakeholders. However, having a common understanding of these terms and their relation to each other is essential.

Cybersecurity follows a "layered security" approach which provides "Defense in Depth." It is the practice of combining multiple security controls to monitor, detect, and thwart cyberattacks. Relying on a single security control for providing a complete security solution is never recommended by cyber professionals because every security control has its limitations and boundaries.

The fundamental requirements to prepare a cybersecurity policy and strategy are to know the assets, people, business objectives, potential threats, disaster recovery plan, business continuity plan, and security awareness program. If a FinTech institution has vague information about its assets and potential threats to exploit those assets, cybersecurity policy is of no use. Cybersecurity policy needs to be aligned with business objectives so that business continuity is not disturbed even during a security incident. Employees and users need to be cyber educated so that they know what to do and what not to do with their working hours. Every individual in the institution must be aware of his duties and responsibilities, especially if he controls sensitive information.

This chapter provides a comprehensive introduction to various cybersecurity policies and strategies used to protect FinTech institutions from belligerent cyberattacks. It commences with important policies and strategies that form the foundational basis of cyber defense. Several necessary measures that reflect the preparedness and prevention against cyberattacks are presented toward the end of the chapter. Figure 8.1 provides an overview of cybersecurity policies discussed in this chapter.

G. Kaur et al., *Understanding Cybersecurity Management in FinTech*, Future of Business and Finance, https://doi.org/10.1007/978-3-030-79915-1_8

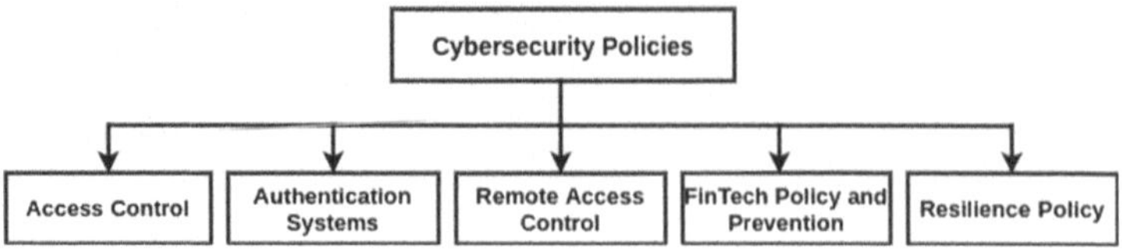

Fig. 8.1 Cybersecurity policies

8.1 Access Control

Controlling access to the assets is one of the main controls provided by the central theme of security. Access control prevents unauthorized personnel from accessing a piece of information. It not only controls unauthorized access but also provides a relationship between different entities. Access is the transfer of information from an object to a subject. An object can be a computer, laptop, or mobile phone, while the subject can be any user. Access control has a strong relationship with the CIA triad. It helps ensure that only authorized personnel can access objects (confidentiality), prevents data tampering by unauthorized means (integrity), and makes data available to authorized personnel (availability) (Chapple et al. 2018).

Access control performs multiple functions. It identifies and authenticates users to access resources. Alternatively, it ensures that access is authorized. It grants and restricts access based on a user's identity. Finally, it also monitors and records all attempts to access a resource. There are four types of access controls, commonly known as deterrent, recovery, directive, and compensating access controls.

- **Deterrent access control:** It attempts to discourage security policy violations. Deterrent controls continuously depend on the discretion of individuals to not take unwanted action. Some examples include policies, security awareness training, locks, fences, security badges, guards, mantraps, and security cameras.
- **Recovery access control:** It attempts to repair or restore resources, functions, and capabilities after a policy violation. To do so, a backup is generally maintained, which is retrieved after a policy violation takes place. Some examples include backups and restores, antivirus software, databases, and system imaging.
- **Directive access control:** It attempts to direct, confine, and control the actions of users to encourage them to comply with security standards. Some examples include notifications, signboards, monitoring, supervision, and procedures.
- **Compensating access control:** It provides an alternative way to use a primary control. For example, if an organization uses smart cards to access employees to premises, it takes some time for new employees to receive their smart cards. In this case, a hardware token can be issued to new employees so that they can be granted access to the premises temporarily until they receive their smart card.

Overall, access controls can be classified into three categories: preventive, detective, and corrective. Preventive access controls attempt to stop or prevent unauthorized activity. For example, they are using fences and locks to secure a physical location. Deterrent access controls are sometimes classified as preventive controls. Detective access controls attempt to detect or identify unwanted or unauthorized activity. These controls come into action after the activity has occurred. Some examples include CCTV or security cameras. Corrective access controls modify the environment to return systems to their normal status after a policy violation. Recovery access controls are classified as corrective controls.

8.2 Authentication Systems

Authentication is the process of testing or validating the claimed identity of a user. It requires the user to provide additional information to prove his identity. The most common form of authentication used is passwords. An authentication system takes the username and password from the user and matches it with a database to find out whether the identity can be validated or not. The user's capability and the system to maintain the secrecy of the authentication factors reflect the security of the authentication system.

Authentication systems are security measures used to secure data and systems by requiring additional information beyond username and password. By providing this additional information, users ensure that they are who they say they are. The additional information allows authentication systems to be called multiple-factor authentication (MFA). MFA makes the system less vulnerable to security issues such as weak passwords. MFA pairs a password with an external verification such as a PIN or token number received on a mobile device that the user approves before signing into the service. Some important authentication methods include challenge questions, unique identifying items such as physical devices or external applications, biometric identifiers such as retina scan, fingerprints, or facial recognition, and location-based authentication.

Authentication systems are ideal for businesses that process sensitive information, such as FinTech institutions. Since banks process credit card data and user account information, a secure user account is needed, which is protected by authentication systems, especially MFA.

Authentication systems provide multiple advantages such as enabling multiple-factor authentication, securing systems against password theft, offering offline authentication services, securing single sign-on, and managing users. Current authentication systems offer a wide range of authentication methods than passwords alone. Following are the common types of authentication methods used nowadays (5 Authentication Methods that Can Prevent the Next Breach 2019):

- **Password-based authentication:** Passwords are the most common method of authentication. A strong password is a combination of lowercase and uppercase characters, numbers, and special symbols. There are various rules associated with the creation of a strong password, including minimum length, frequency of change of password, and use of characters. Weak passwords are prone to hacking attempts. Moreover, passwords can be stolen easily. It is a fact that users use the same password for managing multiple accounts. For example, using the same password for a bank account and personal email address. If this password is stolen, both accounts are at risk of being compromised.

- **Multifactor authentication:** It requires more than one method to authenticate the user, for example, a combination of password and CAPTCHA. It adds a layer of security to access the user account. Sometimes, challenge questions are answered by the user before logging into the account. The answers to these questions are provided by the user and stored in the system at the time of registration.
- **Biometric authentication:** Biological features such as retina, fingerprints, and voice and face recognition are unique for every individual. They cannot be stolen or hacked. Thus, they are more secure than password-based authentication and multifactor authentication. However, biometric features can be used in combination with passwords to illustrate multifactor authentication. Biometric features can be easily compared to database entries to find a match.
- **Certificate-based authentication:** Digital certificates can be used to identify a user, system, or device. A digital certificate is an electronic certificate that contains the digital identity of the user. It contains a public key issued by the certification authority. The corresponding private key of the public-private key pair is kept safely with the user. A combination of the public and private keys is used to prove the identity of the user.
- **Token-based authentication:** It uses an encrypted string of random characters called a token to authenticate users. The credentials are entered only once, and the token is used over and again by the user.

8.3 Remote Access Control

The remote access policy defines the standards for connecting to a computer from any host computer outside the organization. The policy is designed to minimize the potential exposure to FinTech institutions from damage resulting from the unauthorized use of their resources. Damages include loss of integrity, confidentiality, intellectual property, and critical internal systems of the institution (Information Security Policy, Jana Small Finance Bank 2008).

The scope of this policy for a financial institution applies to all contractors, vendors, employees, and agents associated with the institution. The policy considers that any user accessing the services from a remote location is given the same privilege as any other user accessing the services onsite (Information Security Policies 2012). Secure remote access must be strictly controlled by using an authentication system such as password, multifactor, biometric, digital certificate, or token. There are certain requirements for establishing remote access to a computer that ensure that the system uses standard hardware configurations and up-to-date antivirus solutions to protect against cyber threats as there may exist software vulnerabilities that can be exploited by the adversaries (Remote Access Policy Template 2019). Any exception to the requirements mentioned in the remote access policy must be approved by the management.

8.4 Policy and Strategy

Cybersecurity policy and strategy are designed to tackle growing cyberattacks on financial institutions. It responds to the menacing consequences of sophisticated cyber threats. Technology is used in every sector of society, including banks, hospitals, education, commerce, business, and government. The increasing use of technology brings the fear of cyber espionage. This fear motivates policymakers to be prepared for the upcoming threats.

A cybersecurity policy aims to protect fundamental principles like privacy and civil liberties. It also provides regulations to protect sensitive information and handle complex transactions securely (Ciglic 2018). The policy and strategy need to be balanced to enhance cybersecurity among increasing cyber risks and changing cyber threat landscape as discussed in Chap. 4. cybersecurity policy does not address all national and international security aspects, but it provides a practical guide to the specific areas of cybersecurity regulation.

A cybersecurity policy framework describes important cybersecurity concepts such as protection of interconnected systems and data, identification of critical infrastructures such as systems and assets, setting minimum security guidelines for protecting information systems, referring to international standards for information security such as NIST and ISO/IEC, protecting sensitive information from unauthorized access, and designing and implementing security controls to avoid, detect, counterfeit, or minimize cyber risks. Figure 8.2 presents the major works covered by a cybersecurity policy.

A cybersecurity strategy accomplishes three main tasks: (1) establishing and empowering a cybersecurity agency, (2) developing and updating cybercrime laws, and (3) developing and updating critical infrastructure protection laws. A cybersecurity strategy can be designed at the national and international levels, but the tasks remain the same. A national cybersecurity strategy outlines the vision and mission statements of a country to protect its critical infrastructure and develop cybercrime laws to defend against cyber threats, whereas an international cybersecurity strategy focuses on the international standards to achieve the same.

A cybersecurity strategy provides clearly defined principles to understand threats, vulnerabilities, and their potential consequences. It prioritizes cyber threats to handle the severe ones first. A cybersecurity strategy follows a practical approach like a cybersecurity policy. It emphasizes delivering an outcome-based practice that protects civil liberties and privacy of people (Ciglic 2018).

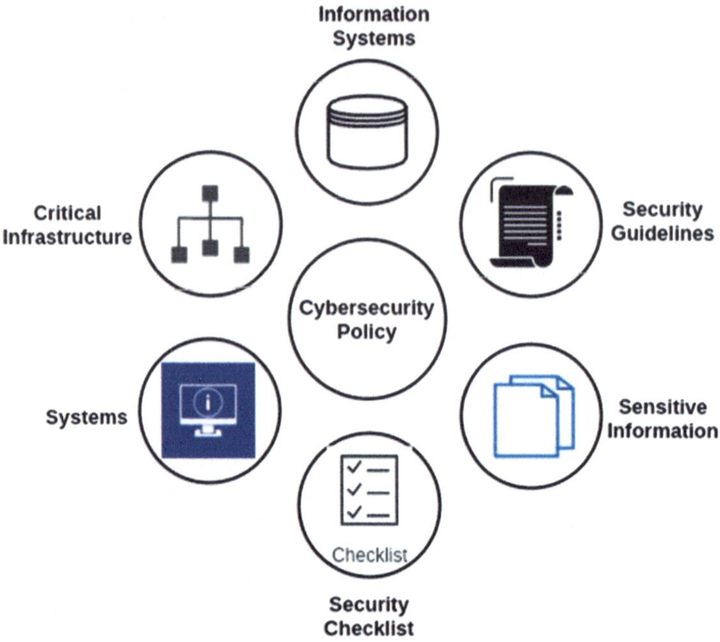

Fig. 8.2 Major works covered by a cybersecurity policy

8.5 Prevention and Preparedness

Cybersecurity exercises play an important role to test the preparedness of financial institutions and prevent cyber threats. These exercises help the banking institutions to think about hypothetical cyber situations and design their responses to protect against cyber threats. Such exercises also warn the management and policymakers about the possible repercussions of the core bank functions, identify gaps in current response policy, and practice communication in a real-time cyberattack situation (Maurer and Nelson 2020).

These exercises are also called tabletop exercises and penetration testing. The range of activities in these exercises varies depending on the infrastructure, activities, critical information, and risk appetite policy of the FinTech institution. Leading financial institutions follow these exercises as a routine to strengthen their policies to protect against cyber threats. Every exercise has a different objective. Some major exercises include (Maurer and Nelson 2020):

- **Quantum Dawn:** This exercise was first hosted in 2011 by SIFMA. Each exercise simulates a different set of recent cyber incidents. To substantiate, the exercise simulated ransomware in 2019 after the outbreak of WannaCry ransomware that impacted 150 countries across the globe. The post-exercise lessons learned to provide a clear vision to the participants. Starting with a small group of US financial institutions, this exercise hosts 180 financial institutions across the globe now.

- **Cyberattack Against Payment Systems (CAPS):** It is a series of tabletop exercises hosted by FS-ISAC with its member institutions. The exercise helps prepare the participants for cyberattacks against their systems and processes.
- **Exercise Cyber Star:** It is a periodic exercise to test the cyber preparedness and response capabilities of stakeholders in the finance and banking sectors. It is hosted among Singapore's 11 critical infrastructures.
- **Exercise Raffles:** This exercise aims to test the business continuity and crisis management of financial institutions. It covers banking and payment service disruptions, trading disorders, data theft, and the spreading of rumors and falsehoods on social media.
- **Waking Shark:** It simulated cyberattacks detected in the United Kingdom. T This exercise participants include financial market infrastructure providers, financial authorities, government agencies, major financial institutions, and the UK treasury.
- **Hamilton Series:** This series consists of exercises led by the US treasury to improve the cyber response capabilities of the USA. It includes participants from the private as well as the public sector.
- **G7 cybersecurity exercise:** This is a cross-border cybersecurity exercise in which participants from 24 financial institutions from the G7 countries come together to assess their situation on cyberattacks in the financial sector.

8.6 FinTech Policy and Prevention

Digital data is growing exponentially with the digitization of financial services, and so does the risk of data breaches. Thus, the need to safeguard digital data from unauthorized access is also increasing. Cybersecurity policies provide documented guidance to strengthen the cyber risk management of financial institutions. Significant financial services such as payment systems, monetary transactions, and sensitive customer data are the core elements that need protection.

The cybersecurity policy addresses cybersecurity principles for regulators, policymakers, supervisory committees, and service providers. These principles guide these players to cooperate with international counterparties, understand customer needs, provide secure delivery of services, manage internal risks, and document lessons learned from cyber incidents (Digital Financial Services (DFS) 2019). In addition, these policies promote cyber-hygiene, educate users, and limit cybersecurity incidents (Bouyon and Krause 2018). This section sheds light on effective cybersecurity policies to prevent cyber threats in FinTech institutions.

8.6.1 Establishing and Using Firewall

A Firewall is a system designed to protect against unauthorized access to or from a private network. Firewalls manage, control, and filter network traffic. It is typically deployed between a private institutional network and the internet link. It becomes too difficult to prevent malicious traffic from entering the network without the use of firewalls. Firewalls filter traffic based on a set of rules. These rules distinguish legitimate network traffic from malicious or unauthorized traffic.

Firewalls can be implemented as hardware, software, or both. Hardware firewalls are devices installed physically in the institution to prevent any unauthorized activities from outside the network. It provides broad protection for the entire network. Many operating systems have a default application firewall (software form of a firewall) that prevents unauthorized access to the computer system. It intends to be an application-specific firewall to prevent application-specific attacks. Both firewalls are important and relevant in different situations (Chapple et al. 2018).

Firewalls can be classified as stateful and stateless firewalls. A stateful firewall filters the entire state of the network connection. It monitors all data packets under the connection. If a suspicious packet is received from any malicious host (as identified in the rules), it is dropped. On the other hand, stateless firewalls do not focus on the entire network connection but individual packets only. Stateless firewalls use clues from source and destination hosts to allow or deny any packet. There is a third category of firewalls called next-generation firewalls, also known as next-gen firewalls. It is a multifunction device composed of several security features capable of detecting zero-day cyberattacks.

Firewalls are only one point in security solutions. Totally relying on firewalls is not a good idea as they follow a rule-based prevention policy. Firewalls let any malicious traffic enter the network if a corresponding rule to prevent it is not found. They also act as a single point of failure. If the organization entirely depends on firewalls as a security control, its failure will let the entire organization fail to prevent cyberattacks. Further, they are mostly unable to block or filter malicious code or viruses. It is accomplished by antivirus software.

8.6.2 Installing and Using Antivirus

Antivirus software scans all applications, files, and devices to identify any known malicious activity. It offers little or no protection against unknown or zero-day malware. Every operating system comes equipped with antivirus software. Popular antivirus software includes Microsoft Security Essentials, McAfee AntiVirus, Avast Antivirus, Trend Micro Antivirus, ESET NOD32 Antivirus, Sophos Antivirus, and Symantec Norton AntiVirus. However, there are many other antivirus products on the market.

Antivirus software uses a signature-based detection method to identify potentially known viruses on a system. Thereby, every antivirus software maintains a large database of virus signatures that is used to detect a malicious application or file on the system after scanning. If a virus is found on the system, the antivirus software takes one of the following actions:

- If the virus can be eradicated, it disinfects the affected files and restores them in the system.
- If the antivirus does not know how to disinfect the files, it may quarantine the files until the administrator inspects them manually.
- If there is no quarantine policy, the infected files are deleted to preserve the integrity of the system.

Modern antivirus software products can detect and remove various viruses and malicious codes such as worms, Trojans, rootkits, spyware, logic bombs, and many other forms of malware. Alternatively, modern antivirus solutions are rarely limited to viruses. Moreover, the vendors regularly add new signatures to the antivirus database to detect newly recognized viruses. Therefore, it becomes mandatory to apply patches and update antivirus software.

8.6.3 Removing Unnecessary Software

Unnecessary software may be installed intentionally by the user, or they may get installed with legitimate software. Unnecessary software includes applications and software that the user does not use anymore. Whatever be the case, it is essential to uninstall unnecessary software from the computer or mobile phone due to several important reasons, including memory space taken by them and malicious activities that illegitimate software can perform.

To instantiate an example, Trojan-Banker is a malware category that targets banking institutions. It is designed to access confidential information processed during online banking transactions. It may come embedded with genuine software that the user installed on his machine without knowing that it contains a Trojan. Trojan-Banker is legitimate software until it is installed on a computer system. Once installed, it may gain unauthorized access to steal user's files and systems. In more severe cases, it may transfer a handsome amount of money from a user's account.

There are some software and applications that are installed without the user's permission. Such software is downloaded with other legitimate applications. Potentially Unwanted Applications (PUAs) come bundled with genuine applications that are available free of cost. They are sometimes called potentially unwanted programs (PUPs). PUA automatically gets installed when the application to which it is bundled is installed. It can take the form of adware, spyware, or hijackers. When PUA behaves like popping up an advertisement, it is referred to as adware. PUAs slow down the device by consuming memory. They can also lead to other PUPs and spyware programs that aim to steal sensitive data from the target device and send it to the attacker. Thus, it is necessary to remove all unnecessary software from the electronic device.

8.6.4 Disabling Nonessential Services

Some popular operating systems preload the applications and software from installed software programs and place the icon in the system tray. This is done to reduce the load time of the application and provide easy access to the programs. Although it appears helpful, it takes a lot of memory space unnecessarily. Disabling nonessential services allows the operating system to load the required applications at a much faster rate.

Some services run in the background and consume system memory. Such services slow down the device. Therefore, it is essential to identify all nonessential services running in the background and disable them from providing space to essential services. This is also known as hardening the operating system by allowing only essential services.

8.6.5 Securing Web Browsers

A web browser is one of the most heavily used programs on computers and mobile phones. It is also the most popular target of attackers. Attackers generally snoop on web traffic to exploit it to access the device. Nowadays, web browsers are used not only to access websites, but also support interactive web content in the form of videos, web forms, games, and images. This interaction makes them vulnerable to many web-based cyberattacks.

The foremost action to secure web browsers is to keep them updated. All major web browser vendors regularly release patches that fix some existing vulnerabilities. It is of utmost importance for the users to apply the patches as soon as they are available. There are certain hardening steps that make it difficult for the attackers to target web browsers, such as disabling cookies, blocking pop-up notifications and windows, scanning and blocking files using antivirus, and blocking pop-up plugins to install and execute automatically (Securing Web Browsers 2019).

8.6.6 Applying Updates and Patches

Updates and patches fix a known or identified a vulnerability in software, application, or operating system. The vendors regularly release them. Software updates offer a lot of benefits:

- They repair a security loophole, remove a computer bug, and fix vulnerability.
- Updates help patch the security flaws that attackers love to exploit. Hackers can take advantage of the unfixed vulnerabilities by writing an exploit code.
- Patches also protect documents and information.

8.6.7 Requiring a Strong Password

Password is the easiest method of authentication but is prone to data theft. Attackers find it very easy to steal credentials. Strong passwords make it harder for the attacker to crack them. Therefore, it is always recommended to create a strong password for any authentication system. The following are the characteristics of a strong password:

- Minimum password length
- A mixture of both uppercase and lowercase letters
- A mixture of numbers and letters
- Inclusion of at least one special character

Some common tips to secure the passwords include:

- Change the passwords regularly.
- Do not use the same passwords for multiple accounts.
- Never write it down.
- Never tell anyone.
- Avoid typing a password on an untrusted computer or mobile phone.
- Never save it on a web browser.
- If there is a little suspicion that the password has become known to somebody, change it immediately.

8.6.8 Visitors and BYOD

Bring your own device (BYOD) is a policy that allows employees to bring their personal computers and mobiles to their workplace and connect to the organizational network. The policy motivates employees and improves job satisfaction. If the policy is open-ended, it allows any device to connect to the organizational network. Not all visitor or employee devices are secure. They may have unpatched vulnerabilities which can be exploited by the attackers. Moreover, the malicious applications and software on one device may be transferred to another device connected to the organizational network. As a result, it poses a security risk to the organization. Users need to understand the benefits and consequences of the BYOD policy before signing off.

8.7 Resilience Policy

Cyber risks and their consequences for financial stability are growing. However, cyberattacks such as distributed denial of service, data breaches, ransomware, and cyber fraud are not new for FinTech institutions. Their frequency and impact have grown faster than other firms. This growth highlights the inevitability of cyberattacks and the impossibility of completely protecting the integrity of critical resources.

Attackers have diverse motives, sophisticated technology, advanced toolkits, and a variable level of expertise behind cyberattacks. These considerations make the attacker landscape complex and unpredictable. On the other hand, cybersecurity policy is based on the "predict and protect" principle. Combining these two statements, it is evident that cybersecurity policy is lacking behind the attackers. It hinders the capability to prevent or stop cyberattacks. The seriousness of the situation can be judged from the fact that FinTech is one of the most popular and targeted institutions among attackers due to the plethora of money associated with it.

Increasing dependency on digitization is also the cause of concern. Digital technologies bring the fear of technical failures, human errors, and natural disasters. Digital assets are more attractive to attack vectors who attempt to infiltrate and steal valuable information. The unprecedented upsurge in attacker activities and constant attacks pose unique challenges to cybersecurity professionals (Dupont 2019). A detailed discussion of cyberattacks witnessed by FinTech institutions is provided in Chap. 4.

The current situation of protecting FinTech institutions against cyberattacks can be improved by following a resilience policy. Cyber-resilience policy provides the capacity to withstand, recover from, and adapt to external shocks caused by cyber risks. It prepares organizations to face adverse events and continue business in those conditions. The basic principles of a cyber-resilience policy include simple regulations, internationally harmonized, principles-based, and risk-based. It maximizes resilience while minimizing risks (Maurer and Nelson 2020).

The main characteristics of a cyber-resilience policy for FinTech institutions are (Workshop 6 2018):

- **Cyber-hygiene:** Cyber-hygiene is the basic characteristic of a cyber-resilience policy. It ensures that users are cyber educated. There are always software flaws and unpatched vulnerabilities that pose severe damage to the institution after attackers exercise them. The main concern of a cyber-resilience policy is to get rid of these flaws and unhandled vulnerabilities. Regular updates and installation of patches are the basic steps needed to cover these flaws. Further, as a regular exercise, vulnerabilities in the computer systems and networks must be identified and fixed. These basic steps help to prevent many cyberattacks and reduce the chances of cyber risks. Cyber-hygiene provides a basic level of security, awareness, and familiarity with IT tools and cyber practices among people.
- **Time of cyber incidents:** Threats can be internal or external. Advanced persistent threats may remain hidden for a long time without getting noticed. This means that institutions may succumb to a false sense of security that makes them more vulnerable. The crux of the statement is that it is the time of cyber incidents that matter. Financial institutions may become a victim of cyberattacks that they did not expect. Therefore, they need to be prepared for all types of cyberattacks.
- **Operational and business impact:** Cyberattacks impact information systems and have a high impact on operations and business. The most severe cyberattacks

may cause systemic risk, letting the entire infrastructure down. This raises concern over business objectives that must consider cyber-resilience policy while designing, planning, and implementing business strategies and policies.

8.8 Chapter Summary

Cybersecurity is not an IT problem, but it is an enterprise-wide security problem that requires an interdisciplinary approach and a comprehensive security policy and strategy to address cyber issues. An effective cybersecurity policy and strategy ensures healthy cybersecurity practices in the organization. This chapter provides a comprehensive introduction to various cybersecurity policies and strategies used to protect FinTech institutions from threatening cyberattacks. It prevents several cyberattacks by following fundamental cyber practices and educating users, employees, and people in the organization. These policies provide an extensive overview of a wide range of cyber practices, from selecting a password to predicting a cyberattack.

Government (financial regulators and legislators) designs cybersecurity policies for carrying out financial activities. The FinTech ecosystem cannot be secured by implementing cybersecurity policies. Overall, the following questions are answered in this chapter:

- What is the need for a cybersecurity policy in a financial institution?
- What are the major areas covered by a cybersecurity policy?
- How does a cybersecurity policy prepare a financial institution to prevent cyberattacks?
- What cybersecurity practices can be followed to protect against cyberattacks?
- How important is the cyber-resilience policy in predicting and protecting against cyberattacks?

References

5 Authentication Methods that Can Prevent the Next Breach. (2019). https://www.idrnd.ai/5-authentication-methods-that-can-prevent-the-next-breach/

Bouyon, S., & Krause, S. (2018). Cybersecurity in finance: Getting the policy mix right! *Report of a CEPS-ECRI Task Force*, pp. 1–52.

Chapple, M., Stewart, J. M., & Gibson, D. (2018). *Certified information systems security professional, official study guide* (8th ed.). Hoboken: Sybex, A Wiley Brand.

Ciglic, K. (2018). *Cybersecurity policy framework: A practical guide to the development of national cybersecurity policy, Microsoft.*

Digital Financial Services (DFS). (2019). *Cybersecurity for financial inclusion: Framework & risk guide*, Guideline Note No.37, Digital Financial Services (DFS) Working Group, pp. 1–24.

Dupont, B. (2019). *The cyber-resilience of financial institutions: significance and applicability.* Journal of Cybersecurity, Volume 5, Issue 1, pp. 1–7.

Information Security Policies. (2012). *Sample Information Security Policies* (pp. 1–90). Austin: Abound Resources.

Jana Small Finance Bank. (2008). Information Security Policy, pp. 1–20. https://www.janabank.com/images/policies/info-security-policy.pdf
Maurer, T., & Nelson, A. (2020). *International strategy to better protect the financial system against cyber threats*. Washington DC: Carnegie Endowment for International Peace.
Remote Access Policy Template. (2019). *Version 1.0, national cybersecurity society*, pp. 1–3.
Securing Web Browsers. (2019). https://www.f-secure.com/v-descs/articles/securing-web-browsers.shtml
Workshop 6. (2018). *Cyber-security and operational resilience, international conference of banking supervisors*.

Designing Cybersecure Framework for FinTech

9

A cybersecurity framework serves as a set of guidelines, standards, and practices to manage cyber risks arising from voluminous and sophisticated cyber threats. A cybersecurity framework prioritizes a repeatable, flexible, and cost-effective approach to prevent cyber threats and improve the organization's cyber resilience. It is important to understand the significance of a cybersecurity framework for financial institutions.

The risk of cyber threats has increased unprecedently over the years. It is pertinent to realize that cybersecurity provides several benefits to a financial institution, including business growth, higher return on investment, reduced risks, and aligning business objectives with information technology. It also increases the resilience of financial institution from cyberattacks.

The next important question after understanding the importance of a cybersecurity framework is to decide which cybersecurity framework. There are many cybersecurity frameworks, but the one that fits the business needs of a particular organization is the best cybersecurity framework for that financial institution. Nevertheless, a financial institution can design its own cybersecurity framework depending on the customized requirements.

This chapter lays the foundation for designing a comprehensive cybersecurity solution for the financial sector. It provides technical insight into five main requirements for designing a cybersecurity framework for FinTech. It presents available standard frameworks for financial institutions that can be referred for identifying cybersecurity vulnerabilities and threats, protecting institutional assets and critical information systems, detecting internal and external cyber threats, responding to cybersecurity incidents, and recovering information systems after the occurrence of a cybersecurity incident.

G. Kaur et al., *Understanding Cybersecurity Management in FinTech*, Future of Business and Finance, https://doi.org/10.1007/978-3-030-79915-1_9

9.1 General Cybersecurity Framework

A cybersecurity framework provides computer security guidance for assessing and improving the ability of private sector organizations to prevent, detect, and respond to cyberattacks. It aids organizations to balance the rapidly growing cyber threat landscape against the need to fulfill business objectives. A cybersecurity framework performs twofold functions. It addresses risks and supports business. According to statistics made available by NIST (Cybersecurity Framework 2020), none of the organizations in the USA was using a cybersecurity framework in 2012. The numbers werc increased to 30% in 2015 and are expected to be 50% in 2020.

A cybersecurity framework evaluates assets, identifies threats, and trains people to prevent cyberattacks. It guides organizations to protect their essential information systems and assets from internal and external threats. For a financial institution, adversaries may exercise several threats to launch cyberattacks that may have devastating outcomes. Extensive details of cyber threats, vulnerabilities, and risks are presented in Chap. 4, 5, and 6.

This section sheds light on prominent requirements that need to be met for designing a cybersecure framework for FinTech. The following subsections dig deeper into these requirements.

9.1.1 Determining Scope of Information Technology

The first and foremost requirement for designing a cybersecurity framework for FinTech is to determine the scope of information technology. It considers all information resources that are processed in the financial institution. For example, in a bank, a sample set of information resources consists of customer information, payments, money transfers, online banking, mobile banking, and credit card details. A cybersecurity framework needs to assure the security of data at rest and in transition. That means it needs to secure customer's personal information such as credit card details and bank account information representing data at rest. It must secure payments, monetary transactions, and money transfers which represent data in transition.

Information technology plays a stupendous role in every financial institution. It manages data, information systems, asset inventory, customer relationships, payments, central repositories, and many more. In the process of designing a cybersecurity framework, the role of information technology cannot be ignored at all. In fact, information technology is placed at the core of the framework. In a financial sector, information technology manages digital data, supports online banking and online payment systems, maintains central databases to store customer information, handles security settlement documents, and establishes relationships among participating entities. The mentioned activities are a representative subset of a whole bunch of many other activities discussed in detail in Chap. 7.

9.1.2 Determining the Value of Information and Assets

The second requirement for designing a cybersecurity framework for FinTech is to determine the value of information and assets. Every asset is valuable. It adds value (whether small or large) to the overall assets of the organization. Assets can be tangible and intangible. The financial institution prepares a list of assets that add financial value to the business. Some common assets for a financial institution include cash flow, customer deposits, user accounts, insurance, trademarks, copyrights, and patents. The next step is to make a balance sheet that provides complete cash flow details, which means computing total expenditure and income. After preparing the balance sheet, the assets are added to find a total amount of assets.

9.1.3 Defining the Cybersecurity Threat Level

The third requirement for designing a cybersecurity framework for FinTech is to define the cybersecurity threat level. Cybersecurity threats represent malicious acts that damage, steal, or disrupt data. Financial institutions face several cyber threats that originate from different threat sources. A comprehensive cybersecurity framework for FinTech identifies potential threats that financial institutions face and prioritizes them for mitigation. It includes essential countermeasures to defend against cyber threats. It also collects threat intelligence information to identify, analyze, and predict future cyber threats.

9.1.4 Personnel Screening and the Insider Threat

The fourth requirement for designing a cybersecurity framework for FinTech is to understand insider threats. Financial institutions are generally prepared for external threats, but they ignore internal threats. Insiders or employees who cause financial or reputational damage to a financial institution are known as insider threats. An insider threat originated within the target organization. Insider threat does not need to be a current employee. A former employee, business partner, consultant, or board member can be an insider threat.

A cybersecurity framework prepares an insider threat defense plan that monitors user activities such as emails and files on data sources. It identifies and discovers the location of sensitive information files. It also controls who can access what information and with what privileges. In order to maintain privileges, it must follow a least privileged access control to resources. Finally, it applies security analytics to alert any abnormal behavior.

9.1.5 Cybersecurity Awareness and Training

The fifth requirement for designing a cybersecurity framework for FinTech is to plan cybersecurity awareness and training programs for people in the organization. This program makes users aware of suspicious emails and phishing attacks. It educates users not to reveal personally identifiable information such as date of birth and social insurance number to irrelevant forms. It imparts knowledge related to clicking malicious links in emails or visiting suspicious websites. More details on cybersecurity awareness are provided in Chap. 5.

Several cyberattacks, such as adware, ransomware, and denial of service, pose serious security threats to financial institutions. These threats target users by offering them free gifts, vouchers, and vacation offers. These fake offers intend to click on fake advertisements that redirect to malicious websites. In severe cases, these malware samples demand ransom to release critical user information.

Cybersecurity awareness programs allow people to know how to respond to cryptic cyberattacks such as phishing and social engineering. These programs make people aware of what are vulnerable situations and how to respond to those situations to stay protected.

9.2 Available Standard Frameworks

Based on the importance of a cybersecurity framework, this section presents available standard cybersecurity frameworks.

9.2.1 NIST CSF

NIST Cybersecurity Framework (CSF) is a crucial framework for private sector organizations in the United States that provides five core functions: (1) identify, (2) protect, (3) detect, (4) respond, and (5) recover. Figure 9.1 presents a glimpse of NIST CSF. It is a cyclic framework in which the first step is repeated after the last step and so on.

These functions act as the backbone of the framework. They represent the five primary pillars of a successful cybersecurity framework. They aid organizations in convincing their management of cybersecurity risk at a high level and enabling risk management decisions (The Five Functions, NIST Cybersecurity Framework 2020). The following subsections discuss these functions in detail.

9.2.1.1 Identify

This is the first function of the CSF and assists in developing cybersecurity understanding of the management. It identifies cybersecurity risk to systems, assets, data, and capabilities. Following is the list of activities performed by this function (NIST Cybersecurity Framework Core Explained 2020):

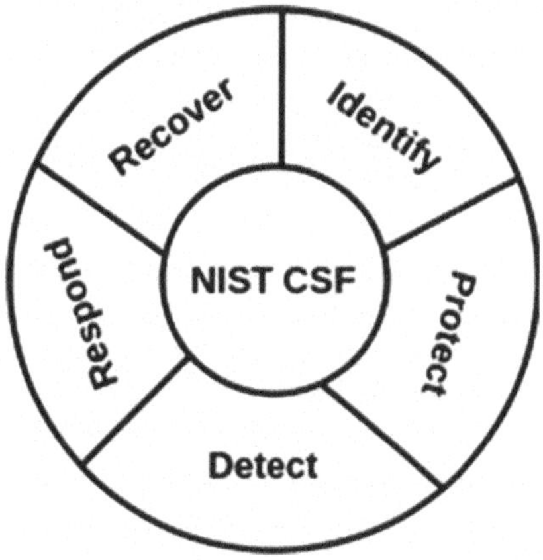

Fig. 9.1 Core functions of NIST CSF

- **Asset Management:** It identifies hardware and software assets within the organization and establishes an asset management program.
- **Vulnerability Management:** It identifies vulnerabilities in assets, external and internal threats to the organization, and risk response activities.
- **Governance:** It identifies cybersecurity policies and establishes an information security governance program.
- **Risk Management:** It identifies a risk management strategy and setting up risk appetite limits for the organization.
- **Supply Chain Management:** It identifies a supply chain management strategy to support risk decisions associated with managing supply chain risks.
- **Business Environment:** It identifies the business environment in the organization to support the supply chain and critical infrastructure sector.

The functions identified in this step lay the foundation for the rest of the steps in the cybersecurity framework. Overall, this step identifies what the organization has, the risks, and how the cybersecurity framework aligns with the business goals.

9.2.1.2 Protect

This is the second function in the NIST CSF which outlines the safeguards used to ensure the secure delivery of services. It limits the impact of a cybersecurity incident. Following activities are performed by protecting function (How to comply in 2020 with the 5 functions of the NIST Cybersecurity Framework 2020):

- **Identity Management and Access Control:** It protects identity management and access control within the organization. Identity management authenticates the identity of the users who attempt to access resources. Access control covers physical and remote access to resources. Identity management and access control are explained under the cybersecurity policies section in Chap. 8.

- **User Awareness and Training:** It empowers employees by imparting training and making them aware of the cybersecurity issues and practices in the organization.
- **Data Security:** It establishes data security protection consistent with the organization's risk policy to protect confidentiality, integrity, and availability of information.
- **Information Protection:** It implements information protection processes and procedures to maintain and manage assets and resources.
- **Organizational Resources:** It protects organizational resources through maintenance activities.

This step protects sensitive information, enables cybersecurity risk management decisions, addresses threats, and improves activities.

9.2.1.3 Detect

The detect function of the framework develops and implements appropriate activities to recognize a cybersecurity event. Following activities are performed by detect function (The Five Functions, NIST Cybersecurity Framework 2020):

- **Anomalies and Events:** It ensures that abnormalities and security events are detected on time, and their potential impact is analyzed to take appropriate action.
- **Monitoring:** It monitors security events and information systems to detect any malicious activity.
- **Detection:** It places and tests procedures and processes to detect security events with high accuracy. These processes are maintained to provide awareness of anomalous events.

9.2.1.4 Respond

The response function includes activities to act regarding the detection of a cybersecurity event. Following activities are performed by respond function (NIST Cybersecurity Framework Core Explained 2020):

- **Response Planning:** It plans procedures to follow during and after a security incident.
- **Analysis:** It analyzes planned procedures to support recovery activities such as forensic analysis. It also determines the impact of a security incident.
- **Mitigation:** Mitigation activities prevent the expansion of an event and attempt to resolve it.
- **Improvements:** A lessons learned document is prepared that identifies the gaps in currently planned procedures and processes. These gaps are analyzed to find improvements in current response activities.

9.2.1.5 Recover

The recover function is the last function in the NIST CSF. It identifies actions to maintain plans for cyber resilience policy and restore the impacted processes after a security event. In simple words, the recovery function attempts to reduce the impact of a security event by reinstating everyday operations. Following activities are performed by recover function (The Five Functions, NIST Cybersecurity Framework 2020):

- **Recovery Planning:** It ensures recovery planning procedures and processes to restore systems and/or assets affected by a cybersecurity incident.
- **Communication:** Internal and external communications are coordinated during and after the security incident to ensure proper recovery.
- **Improvement:** A lessons learned document is prepared that identifies the gaps in currently planned procedures and processes. These gaps are analyzed to find improvements in current recovery activities.

9.2.2 FFIEC

The Federal Financial Institutions Examination Council (FFIEC) was built on NIST CSF and developed the Cybersecurity Assessment Tool (Digital Financial Services (DFS) 2019). The tool helps financial institutions identify their risks and determine their cybersecurity preparedness. The tool was published in 2017 in response to the increasing number and sophistication of cyberattacks against financial institutions. It provides a repeatable measure of the cybersecurity readiness of an institution over time. The approach is highly admired and adopted by financial institutions, especially banks.

The assessment is completed in two parts. In the first part, an inherent risk profile is created that identifies an institution's inherent risk relevant to cyber threats. The second part measures the cybersecurity maturity of the institution. Maturity determines the cybersecurity preparedness of the institution (Cybersecurity Assessment Tool, FFIEC 2017). The assessment is completed periodically so that the institution can perform effective risk management. Figure 9.2 presents the functions performed by the assessment tool.

9.2.2.1 Inherent Risk Profile

Inherent risk profile identifies activities, services, and products under the following categories (Cybersecurity Assessment Tool, FFIEC 2017):

- **Technology and Connection Types:** Certain technologies, services, and products may pose more inherent risks depending on their complexity and nature. This category includes several Internet Service Providers (ISPs) and third-party connections. Third-party connections also include outsourced services, several insecure connections, cloud services, and personal devices.
- **Delivery Channels:** This category presents whether products and services are delivered through online and mobile channels. Like technology and connection types, delivery channels also pose inherent risks depending on the nature of services and products.

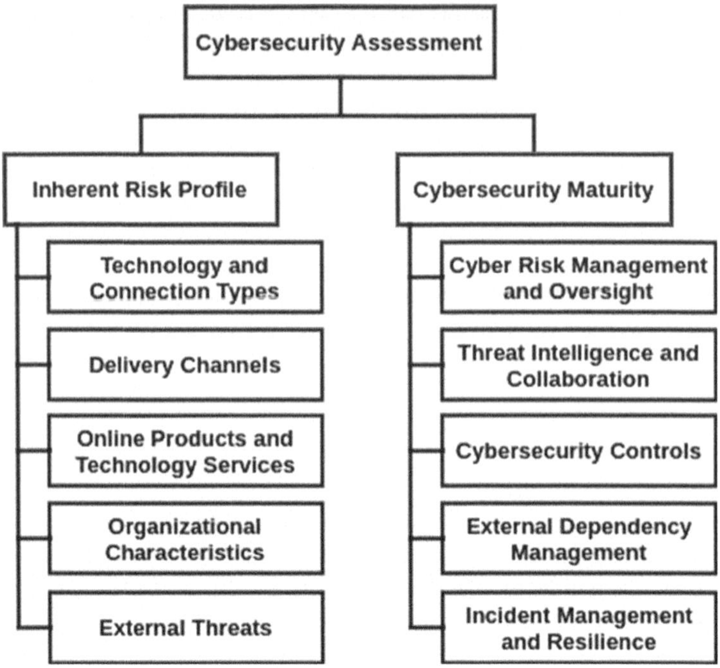

Fig. 9.2 FFIEC's cybersecurity assessment process

- **Online Products and Technology Services:** This category includes payment services, such as debit and credit cards, Interac-e transfers, retail wire transfers, automated clearinghouses, and correspondent banking. It also considers whether the institution provides technology services to other organizations.
- **Organizational Characteristics:** This category considers organizational characteristics such as mergers and acquisitions, number of direct employees and cybersecurity contractors, changes in security staffing, the number of users with privileged access, changes in information technology (IT) environment, locations of business presence, and locations of operations and data centers.
- **External Threats:** The volume, sophistication, and type of cyber threats impact the inherent risk exposure to the organization.

9.2.2.2 Cybersecurity Maturity

After determining the inherent risk profile of the institution, the next step is to compute the maturity level within the following domains:

- **Cyber Risk Management and Oversight:** It addresses the board of directors' oversight and management's development and implementation plan to prepare cybersecurity policies. It also establishes accountability and an effective cybersecurity program for the enterprise.

- **Threat Intelligence and Collaboration:** Threat intelligence refers to acquiring and analyzing information to identify, analyze, and predict cyber threats. It includes processes to effectively discover, analyze, and understand cyber threats and share threat information with internal and external parties. More details on threat intelligence are provided in Chap. 4.
- **Cybersecurity Controls:** Cybersecurity controls are the practices and processes used to protect assets, resources, and information by strengthening the security posture of the organization. It is achieved through continuous monitoring and protection.
- **External Dependency Management:** It involves establishing and maintaining a comprehensive program to observe and manage external dependencies that access organizational resources. It also includes third-party vendors.
- **Incident Management and Resilience:** Cyber incident management includes establishing, identifying, and analyzing cyber incidents. It prioritizes cyber incidents to mitigate severe incidents before others. Cyber resilience tests the preparedness of the organization to handle future cyberattacks.

9.2.3 CPMI-IOSCO

The Committee on Payments and Market Infrastructures (CPMI) at the Bank for International Settlements (BIS), in collaboration with the Board of the International Organization of Securities Commissions (IOSCO), developed the document for "Guidance on cyber resilience for financial market infrastructures" (Cyber Guidance) in June 2016. The guidance applies to financial market infrastructures, which are defined as the critically important institutions responsible for clearing settlements systems and keeping a record of settlements and monetary transactions (Digital Financial Services (DFS) 2019).

The guidance is based on cybersecurity principles to identify the dynamic nature of cyber threats. It emphasizes that cybersecurity is not just information technology, but it is more than that. The framework suggests that an organization needs a principle-based framework and an IT cybersecurity framework to protect financial institutions against cyberattacks.

9.2.4 ECB-CROE

The European Central Bank (ECB) published their "Cyber Resilience Oversight Expectations for financial market infrastructures" (CROE) in 2018. The ECB considered a range of international guidance frameworks, including NIST CST, FFIEC, and CPMI-IOSCO. The primary objective of this standard is to comply with CPMI-IOSCO to assess the framework.

The ECB-CROE is an important document because it provides a bridge for the requirements set out in CPMI-IOSCO and NIST. However, it is not designed to be a cybersecurity framework. Its main goal is to be used as a tool to supervise by the authorities. It acts as an assessment tool that provides oversight to organizations to assess their cybersecurity situation (Digital Financial Services (DFS) 2019).

9.2.5 FSSCC Cybersecurity Profile

The USA's Financial Services Sector Coordinating Council (FSSCC) was established in 2002 by financial sector representatives in the USA. It collaborates with the US government agencies to protect critical infrastructure in the financial sector from cyberattacks. This framework is heavily based on the NIST CSF framework and CPMI-IOSCO Guidance.

9.2.6 Center for Internet Security (CIS): CIS 20 Controls

Working on the CPMI-IOSCO's recommendations that an organization needs a principles-based framework and an IT cybersecurity framework; several stakeholders highlight the value of the "CIS 20" as an example of an IT cybersecurity framework. The Center for Internet Security (CIS) is a nonprofit entity based in the USA. It follows a bottom-up approach to cybersecurity. It does not work on standards established by the top management, which are just followed by the lower management. It presents 20 cybersecurity controls and guidelines that address most financial institutions' cybersecurity needs (Digital Financial Services (DFS) 2019).

9.3 Chapter Summary

This chapter provides the essential details to design a comprehensive cybersecurity framework for a financial institution. It lays stress on basic requirements that form the foundation of a cybersecurity framework to protect the FinTech ecosystem. After working out the required information, the chapter presents available cybersecurity frameworks for financial institutions. These frameworks guide identifying vulnerabilities, assets, and threats to a financial institution, protecting the critical infrastructure, detecting a cybersecurity incident, responding to a cybersecurity incident, and recovering from a cybersecurity incident. Overall, the following questions are addressed in this chapter:

- What is the importance of a cybersecurity framework?
- What are the main requirements for designing a cybersecurity framework?
- What are the available standard cybersecurity frameworks for financial institutions?

References

CyberSaint. (2020). *NIST Cybersecurity Framework Core Explained.* https://www.cybersaint.io/blog/nist-cybersecurity-framework-core-explained

Digital Financial Services (DFS). (2019). *Cybersecurity for financial inclusion: Framework & risk guide*, Guideline Note No.37, Digital Financial Services (DFS) Working Group, pp. 1–24.

FFIEC: Federal Financial Institutions Examination Council. (2017). *Cybersecurity Assessment Tool.* https://www.ffiec.gov/pdf/cybersecurity/FFIEC_CAT_May_2017.pdf

Forescout Technologies. (2020). *How to comply in 2020 with the 5 functions of the NIST Cybersecurity Framework.* https://www.forescout.com/company/blog/how-to-comply-with-the-5-functions-of-the-nist-cybersecurity-framework/

NIST: National Institute of Standards and Technology. (2020). *Cybersecurity Framework.* https://www.nist.gov/cyberframework

NIST: National Institute of Standards and Technology. (2020). *The Five Functions, NIST Cybersecurity Framework.* https://www.nist.gov/cyberframework/online-learning/five-functions

Conclusion

10

The financial industry has grown tremendously with the evolution of the Internet over the last couple of decades. It has captured the market by supporting a wide range of applications including artificial intelligence, blockchain technology, digital identity, cashless wallets, e-commerce, banking, robotics, social media, and big data analytics. The FinTech revolution not only interacts with big financial giants, but also lures startup companies. FinTech has transformed business processes and models ever since its first use. It has established itself with emerging technologies that form its core functionality.

FinTech is a blend of traditional and contemporary financial institutions. It comprises traditional banks and modern digital payment methods that form the foundation of electronic money transactions. The rising popularity of FinTech comes with the growing cyberattacks that threaten financial stability. These cyberattacks are becoming a big point of concern for financial institutions. Digital world has opened the doors for new opportunities for the financial sector. However, it also brings the danger of cyberattacks that target financial market infrastructure.

The primary motive of cyberattacks on FinTech is to breach sensitive data, disrupt essential services, lower down financial stability, and engage in politically inclined activities. There are several prominent cyber incidents that exemplify those cyberattacks that have transformed the physical war into cyberwar among the rival countries. However, when we focus on the financial sector, these cyberattacks result in catastrophic ramifications. These attacks not only steal information but misuse it to perform severe cyberattacks such as distributed denial of service, ransomware, phishing, and malware, to name a few.

Since the FinTech industry increasingly relies upon electronic data and emerging technologies, it has become extremely concerned with the security of data. This brings cybersecurity risk management into picture that attempts to identify vulnerabilities in the system, find threats that can exploit the vulnerabilities, analyze risks in case vulnerabilities are exploited, and propose some risk mitigation techniques to reduce the negative effect of risks on the financial sector.

G. Kaur et al., *Understanding Cybersecurity Management in FinTech*, Future of Business and Finance, https://doi.org/10.1007/978-3-030-79915-1_10

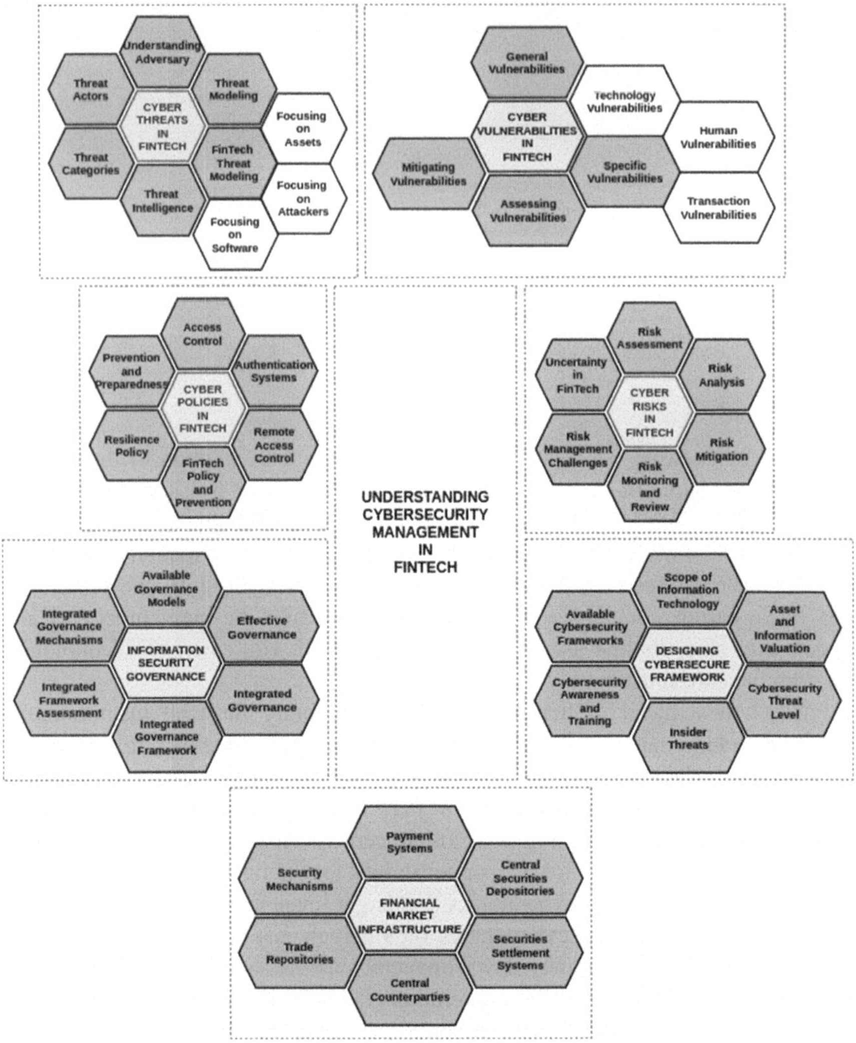

Fig. 10.1 Overview of various cybersecurity management issues discussed in this book

As Fig. 10.1 shows, this book emphasizes presenting major cyberattacks on FinTech institutions and using that data to identify potential cyber threats and vulnerabilities that can be exploited by these threats. Based on these vulnerabilities and cyber threats, we stress the need for a cyber risk management model that identifies, assesses, analyzes, evaluates, and mitigates cyber risks in the FinTech industry. We also compared existing risk analysis models and proposed some cyber risk mitigation measures based on the identified cyber threats.

The primary challenges and open issues with the FinTech cyber risk management framework are put forward. Additionally, three types of uncertainties in the FinTech industry are presented and certain measures to reduce them are also proposed. FinTech cybersecurity risk management is extremely important, keeping in mind the digitalization of business that relies on digital transactions.

To manage cybersecurity threats, vulnerabilities, and risks, cybersecurity policies are prepared by the accountable personnel in the financial institutions. Various cybersecurity policies address critical issues, such as who can access what resources and with what privileges. These policies allow a FinTech institution to be prepared for identifying cyber threats, analyze cyber risks, and mitigate them to protect information systems and sensitive user information. Furthermore, a cyber-resilience policy paves the way for restricting unauthorized personnel to access and misuse organizational resources.

In addition to cybersecurity policies, information security is ensured by following guidelines, procedures, and best cybersecurity practices designed by the top management and the board of directors. These governance strategies are implemented by the lower management individuals at the bottom of the organizational structure. Lower management represents a technical workforce that performs day-to-day operations in a financial institution. Information security governance is integrated with different prominent components including government, customers, stakeholders, media, and management. All these components play their part in designing, deploying, implementing, and documenting information security governance standards.

The next imperative concept that the book stresses is financial market infrastructure which is worst affected by cyberattacks. Before understanding the cybersecurity vulnerabilities and security issues in financial market infrastructures, it is important to understand the essential components of financial market infrastructure. These components include payment systems, central securities depositories, securities settlement systems, central counterparties, and trade repositories. These components are involved in performing monetary transactions, purchasing and selling shares from the stock market, and maintaining a central database of settlements (contracts) between the participating entities.

Since financial market infrastructures are involved in national and international financial transactions between various participating entities that may belong to different jurisdictions, there are many financial risks that may lead to cybersecurity risks in different essential components. The chapter on financial market infrastructures maps cybersecurity objectives with the financial risks identified in essential components of financial market infrastructures. The identified cybersecurity objectives can be used to do detailed research on security issues that can arise out of financial risks in financial markets.

Finally, based on the cybersecurity management concepts discussed throughout the book, the last chapter introduces primary requirements to design a comprehensive cybersecurity framework for FinTech. To do so, every financial institution needs to identify the scope of information technology, find the value of information and assets, determine cybersecurity threat levels, understand insider threats, and conduct cybersecurity awareness programs. There are standard cybersecurity frameworks such as NIST CSF that form the fundamentals of a comprehensive cybersecurity framework. These frameworks can be referenced to design a new cybersecurity framework for financial institutions.

The manufacturer's authorised representative in the EU is Springer Nature Customer Service Centre GmbH, Europaplatz 3, 69115 Heidelberg, Germany. If you have any concerns regarding our products, please contact ProductSafety@springernature.com

Printed and bound by CPI Group (UK) Ltd, Croydon, CR0 4YY
30/09/2026
02225699-0002